A

Morning

After War

PETER LANG
New York • Washington, D.C./Baltimore • Bern
Frankfurt am Main • Berlin • Brussels • Vienna • Oxford

K. J. Gilchrist

A
Morning
After War

C. S. LEWIS AND WWI

PETER LANG
New York • Washington, D.C./Baltimore • Bern
Frankfurt am Main • Berlin • Brussels • Vienna • Oxford

Library of Congress Cataloging-in-Publication Data

Gilchrist, K. J.
A morning after war : C.S. Lewis and WWI / K.J. Gilchrist.
p. cm.
Includes index.
1. Lewis, C. S. (Clive Staples), 1898-1963—Knowledge—History. 2. Literature and history—Great Britain—History—20th century. 3. World War, 1914-1918—Great Britain—Literature and the war. 4. War and literature—Great Britain—History—20th century. 5. War in literature. I. Title.
PR6023.E926Z663 2005   823'.912—dc22   2004026011
ISBN 0-8204-7612-9 paperback
ISBN 0-8204-7859-8 hardcover

Bibliographic information published by **Die Deutsche Bibliothek.**
Die Deutsche Bibliothek lists this publication in the "Deutsche
Nationalbibliografie"; detailed bibliographic data is available
on the Internet at http://dnb.ddb.de/.

Cover image by K. J. Gilchrist: detail from *A Morning After War*
(oil on canvas, 2004) © K. J. Gilchrist

Cover design by Lisa Barfield

The paper in this book meets the guidelines for permanence and durability
of the Committee on Production Guidelines for Book Longevity
of the Council of Library Resources.

© K. J. Gilchrist 2005
Peter Lang Publishing, Inc., New York
275 Seventh Avenue, 28th Floor, New York, NY 10001
www.peterlangusa.com

Printed in the United States of America

For those whose spring
ended before summer
and those who remembered through their winter

And from there we sailed on,
glad to escape our death
yet sick at heart for the comrades we had lost.
—Homer, *The Odyssey*

Contents

Illustrations

MAPS

Acknowledgments

WHEN I WAS READING WORKS FROM WWI during a period in 1986, I was also communicating with Sheldon Vanauken, a friend of C. S. Lewis, about the disillusion felt by veterans of WWI and about Lewis. Vanauken suggested that "In the light of [our phone conversation . . .] I could not but wonder if in your speaking of 'the numbing of feeling, loss of interest, feeling old & worn . . . the *Wasteland*' with respect to the WWI generation was, also, in your mind, you." He was somewhat humorously and yet seriously referring to circumstances I was then in the midst of, but also to my deepening intrigue regarding that immense and dark abyss, The Great War. This was not long after I had finished an M.A. thesis on C. S. Lewis's anti-Modernism, through which I became interested not only in Lewis's preference for anything decidedly *not* Modern, but more. How was it, I wondered, could Lewis and others such as J. R. R. Tolkien, Siegfried Sassoon, Owen Barfield, Georges Bernanos, T. S. Eliot, or even Evelyn Waugh—the last too young to fight in the war—go through the disillusion of the war and post-war years, and then turn to Christianity in some form or other? This seemed very strange when others like Ernest Hemingway, Virginia Woolf, Samuel Beckett, or Vera Brittain who had gone through the war years, came to *very* different views thereafter. I wanted to understand the disillusion that The Great War created—to understand both social and individual reactions to the war, but also to understand individuals' very different reactions to it, positive or otherwise. It meant first understanding the war itself.

Those who encouraged me on this path I wish to thank. Among these are Dr. John Willingham, who in the summer of 1984 at Magdalene College, Cambridge, suggested that I write my thesis on Lewis, and who has since both contributed to and supported my studies of the war. I wish also to thank Marjory Lamp Mead for her expertise and for many kindnesses. As the book was prepared in part by assistance from the Clyde S. Kilby Research Grant for 2003 from the Marion E. Wade Center at Wheaton College, I owe many thanks to the staff at the Wade Center for the grant, their friendly help, and for access to materials. My notes have important marginalia deriving from the technical assistance which came from very kind and helpful staff at the Imperial War Museum. Alan Wakefield, Curator at the Imperial War Museum's Photo Archives, provided invaluable assistance in finding photographs and establishing research dates. Special thanks are owed to the P. B. Marazzi family of St. Margaret's Hotel, London, for their kind hospitality over a number of years. Thanks go to Jean Cadron, who not only provided unexpected and valuable information, but who also acted as an accidental tour guide near Riez and Bernenchon. Thanks go to both Robert Elfvin and Vince Carter for criticisms of the text, and to Vince for sharing his experiences of war. Head Porter at University College, Oxford, Dusty Miller, and the student who occupied C. S. Lewis's former rooms are owed many thanks for their good humor and for access to those rooms in September of 2003. The staff at Peter Lang, especially Phyllis Korper, have been very good to me in many ways, and I thank them. With deep gratitude I thank my wife Joni not only for surviving some unusual heat in France, not only for superbly navigating the streets of Lille and other mazes, not only for indulging me hours wandering fields with trench maps, not only for reading and editing, but also for brightening life when the topic of war hovered darkly.

Imperial War Museum Photo Archives. The photo of A. G. Sutton's grave courtesy of Liz Tait. Otto Dix's "Verwundeter" ("Wounded Man"), Fall 1916, was provided by the Los Angeles County Museum of Art and copyright © Artists Rights Society. The photo of Oxford University O.T.C. Cadets, excerpts from Warren Lewis, and excerpts from the Dunbar interview are courtesy of and copyright © the Marion E. Wade Center. The maps of Monchy Defenses and Fampoux Trenches are used by permission of The National Archives (Public Records Office) and the Ordnance Survey. Images from military files are used by permission of The National Archives (Public Records Office) Image Library. Exerpts from military files and battalion diaries are courtesy of The National Archives (Public Records Office). Sheet 36aS.E. is used by permission of the Ordnance Survey. Excerpts from Linda McGreevy, *Bitter Witness*. New York: Peter Lang Publishing, copyright © 2001 are reprinted by permission of the publisher. Excerpts from Mrs. Penelope Hatfield are copyright © and reproduced courtesy of Mrs. Penelope Hatfield. Excerpts from Martin Somerville's obituary are used by permission, Eton College Archives. Quotations from "The Aftermath of Victimization: Rebuilding Shattered Assumptions" are copyright © 1985 and used by permission of Ronnie Janoff-Bulman. "Siegfried Meeting Fear © Courtesy of the Arthur Rackham Estate/The Bridgeman Art Library; the Arthur Rackman picture is reproduced with the kind permissoin of his family."

Every effort has been made to contact copyright owners of material used in this book. If in any instance attempts have not been successful, I offer my apologies to those concerned.

Abbreviations

SOURCES OFTEN USED ARE ABBREVIATED WITHIN TEXTUAL citations by the following means:

AMR—*All My Road Before Me: The Diary of C. S. Lewis.* New York: Harcourt, 1991.

CL—*C. S. Lewis, Collected Letters, Volume 1: Family Letters 1905–1931.* London: HarperCollins, 2000.

CWG—Commonwealth War Graves Commission. http://www.cwgc. org/cwgcinternet/search.aspx

D—*Dymer. Narrative Poems.* New York: Harcourt, 1969.

LP—"Lewis Papers: Memoriors of the Lewis Family, 1850–1930" The Wade Collection. Wheaton, Illinois: Wheaton College.

SBJ—*Surprised by Joy.* New York: Harcourt, 1955.

SIB—*Spirits in Bondage.* New York: Harcourt, 1984.

WD—"War Diary" (for 1st Somerset Light Infantry). Kew: Public Records Office: WO95/1499.

WO—War Office records from the Public Records Office, followed by references

Introduction

C. S. LEWIS ONCE EXPLAINED THAT COMMUNICATION requires a listener not only to hear a message and understand what has been said, but also requires the listener to understand what has *not* been said. Understanding what has not been said has been much of the difficulty in understanding Lewis's service in the First World War. In work independent from one another, both Don King and I have shown that Lewis obscured facts about his war service and its lingering effects. This book traces the events of C. S. Lewis's service in the Great War, explores his wartime relationships, and examines the lingering trauma he suffered as a result of his experiences as revealed in his early poetry. But beneath these things, this work presents an understanding of what Lewis did not say about his war.

Ernest Hemingway encountered work by people who attempted to discover what was unsaid in his own narratives:

> Lately I had read with distaste various books written about myself by people who knew all about my inner life, aims and motives. Reading them was like reading an account of a battle where you had fought written by someone who had not only not been present, but in some cases, had not even been born when the battle had taken place. All these people who wrote of my life both inner and outer wrote with an absolute assurance that I had never felt. (Hemingway 8)

Hemingway was not alone in such distaste. C. S. Lewis's brother, Warren Hamilton Lewis, also anticipated with dismay those who would write of some yet-undiscovered fact regarding his famous brother—those who would undoubtedly write, to use T. S. Eliot's phrase, "assured of certain certainties." Tracing Lewis's war from the present means, obviously, that many lines are faint if not erased by time or by the human hand. In one instance, with assistance from Warren and by the natural reticence of his father Albert, Lewis was able to obscure some facts of his war experiences. Other facts Lewis obscured with seeming self-deprecation.

For many veterans of combat, the reasons for suppression revolve around one fixed point: trauma and the renewal of trauma through remembering. As Great War veteran and painter Otto Dix observed, when we peer into the abyss of war, it peers also into us. That is both a reason why veterans do not speak about their war experiences and why many scholars of war have not wished to look too deeply into the actualities of their subject.

One brief example will serve well here. I once interviewed a WWI veteran about his time in France. Among other things, he told me about hearing on the tail of a continual and shattering bombardment the sudden and odd silence of the Armistice on 11 November 1918, silence broken solely by a bird chirping and a solitary French soldier running down a road shouting "La guerre est fini!" The soldier I interviewed, Emmet Johns, could not speak with any more "absolute assurance" on his experience than could Hemingway on points of his own experiences. And it was not just that Johns was 103 years old at the time of the interview; he was lucid, describing events in great detail. When I asked him to discuss what is a common view of those days and of those who fought in France—the disillusion of his generation after the war—he gave what I thought then was a surprisingly dismissive answer: "Oh, I don't know. You'll know more about all that." Of course, I didn't know. I had never heard the question discussed by someone who was actually in France in 1918.

One thing was readily apparent from Mr. Johns's answer. Quite apart from the extended pondering of other better-known members of the Great War generation, writers like Vera Brittain, Siegfried Sassoon, Erich Remarque, or Ernst Junger—who decades beyond the war's end continued to unravel the tangle of significances war held for them—Mr. Johns apparently had not performed such a task during his long life. He commented solely on events. Determining their significances he left to others. I do not find Mr. Johns's answer surprising today. I wonder if it was diversionary, approaching an area of his experience not to be revisited in the way I asked, an answer made to deflect.

There may often be good reasons for reticence about one's war experiences; nonetheless it creates difficulties for those who attempt to piece together a soldier's story. Stephane Audoin-Rouzeau and Annette Becker have defined the difficulty. Historiography concerning the war has neglected these crucial aspects of events: the actualities, the violence of the war, are those points, and due to these aspects, "On the whole, the reality of war is kept at bay," yet "avoiding these issues is an error" (16). The effect of this error is profound. In neglecting the realities of war for an individual like Lewis, "an essential vector of historical understanding is overlooked and we deny ourselves access to many phenomena of memory-building and recollection, and to the profusion and variety of literary and artistic creation that has accompanied warfare. The history of combat violence is therefore a necessary history" (17). Thus, we often neglect the topic of war for the simple reason T. S. Eliot articulated: "Humankind cannot bear very much reality."

Given the difficulties Lewis's reticence creates for biographers, I must here say something of my methods of probing his service. Understanding what has *not* been said by a soldier requires a deep context to be built around his war experiences. In relating a single experience, veterans themselves often take extraordinary time in building a detailed context in relating an event. As if describing a dream which on its face value can sound absurd and unmoving to a listener who has not experienced it, they are careful to build the context and the *feeling* of their experiences, which is the soul of any experience—be it a pleasant dream or a nightmare. Building such a deep context assures that both the facts of an event and its corresponding feelings are communicated in a holistic articulation. Building a context of fact and feeling is essential in tracing Lewis's war service and attempting to understand it.

Much has been said concerning the attempts of scholars to reach the "truth" of war experiences. John Keegan's work, *The Face of Battle* is the definitive work in the area. Keegan, a long-time educator at Sandhurst, understands Hemingway's dismay with those who write too assuredly of events and people removed from them in time and place. Despite his many years of experience involving research into war, his talks with veterans, and his teaching and writing about war, Keegan approaches his subject with caution that Hemingway would have appreciated: "I have never been in a battle. And I grow increasingly convinced that I have very little idea of what a battle can be like." (13).

Keegan's appraisal is critical to studies such as this. Those who write about soldiers in war align themselves along a spectrum. At one end are those who merely catalogue individual soldiers' experiences, erect a textual museum as it were, with only the barest facts established for either interpretation or contexts. At the other end are those who examine larger, historical contexts—maps, battle plans, and the like—and disregard individual soldiers' accounts of events. Between these two points is an interplay of the two bodies of material: the larger historical views and the personal remembrances of soldiers, each informing the other. A. J. P. Taylor, whose cynical work *The First World War* long served as a standard, "is skeptical about oral history, which he warns, can degenerate into 'old men drooling over their youth.'" (Holmes 10). If we have regard for the tales of soldiers, Keegan writes, in an attempt to discover the facts of battle and its effects on a person, we should do so "in light of what all, and not merely some, of the participants felt about their predicament" and only then will we "have taken the first and most important step in understanding battle 'as it actually was.'" (34).

The difficulty is that the vast collection of soldiers' accounts (diaries, memoirs, letters, fictions, and even dramas—I think of the veteran R. C. Sherriff and his play *Journey's End*) are solely from veterans who would (and we must assume that some *could not*) talk about their war experiences. These historical and personal accounts that remain for us to examine must be used to create contexts for those soldiers who do not speak. Even then, such evidence must be considered as expressing only general tendencies and experiences.

Diaries and memoirs, as well as fiction and drama loosely or tightly based on personal experiences, proliferated in the decades immediately after the war. In more recent years, renewed attention to the period has produced numerous studies of the war and its long shadow. Such studies are useful in noting many individual soldiers' reactions and in building contexts of central tendencies in soldiers collectively. The catch is what David Thompson and Geoffrey Warner say in their history of England:

> The thought and culture of the first five post-war years inevitably reflected the violence of war and the equal violence of reaction against war. English culture had been as profoundly shattered by the experience as had Britain's economy or her international position. It seems likely that public life at all levels suffered a deterioration of standards and a decline of taste. But such tendencies are difficult to prove or assess, and there was a propensity . . . to see pre-war conditions in rosier hue than they had ever merited. (85)

It is likewise difficult to prove or assess the impact of the war on an individual, especially when he or she gives little indication in letters, diaries, and/or autobiography, if happily such have survived.

I approached my study, then, by examining a variety of documents, personal and historical, combining contexts large and small. However, as Keegan remarks of the documents available to us, "too often they are not" used "in the right way" (32); he cites the example of Jac Weller, whose studies, deeply informed on various levels, yet bear a significant impediment for readers. Of one study Keegan says that by its choice of focus, automatically [it] distorts perspective and too often dissolves into sycophancy or hero-worship, culminating in the odd case in a bizarre sort of identification by the author with his subject—an outcome common and understandable enough in literary or artistic biography but tasteless and even mildly alarming when the Ego is a man of blood and iron, his Alter someone of scholarly meekness and suburban physique. (26)

I do not know why it should be "understandable" in literary and artistic biography. Indeed, it is inappropriate there also, and such work ultimately refracts the vision for readers who seek an accurate view of their subject.

I believe that such "hero-worship, culminating in the odd case in a bizarre sort of identification by the author with his subject" has been, beyond Lewis's own reticence, the other chief impediment to our understanding Lewis in war. *Distinction* is something that has been applied too easily to Lewis by many. Yet it becomes clear that his war experiences distinguish him solely in one respect, one not noted by those who have previously studied Lewis. As Sassoon is reported to have said, "A man who endured the war at its worst was everlastingly differentiated from everyone—except his fellow soldiers." As such, C. S. Lewis is, as Paul Fussell noted of him, "a representative young man from the period" (40).

It is difficult to see Lewis the soldier. "Jack" Lewis as a 2nd lieutenant is an image seemingly incongruous to the icons various people have tenderly constructed of this man as the scholar, the Christian apologist, the children's book writer. For example, George Sayer's biography *Jack: A Life of C. S. Lewis*, provides a poem-by-poem analysis of Lewis's first book of poems, *Spirits in Bondage*. Whereas it contains poems written in France and while Lewis was in hospital after being wounded, it remains centrally a book of war poetry, a record of the trauma of Lewis's war. Yet only one dismissive mention of the war exists in Sayer's analysis of the book. Sayer writes that

The theme of "Victory" is the triumph of the human spirit and its renewal out of the ashes of destroyed ideals. It opens with a fine lament for the dead heroes and heroines of romantic myth and poetry. (146)

Sayer's analysis examines only the philosophical, the literary, and the theological. Lewis was, in writing these poems, a young soldier who was being treated to visions of agony and death on a daily basis, and was intent on killing men in the trenches opposite his own. Sayer simply asks (and I give his answer in full):

Why did he write almost nothing about the war? I can offer only two suggestions: One is that he felt it too strongly, so strongly that he could not bear to recall it. The other

is that he was preoccupied with his life as an undergraduate and with his dependence
on a father who was jealous and suspicious of his relationship with Mrs. Moore. (150)

It is a combination of both feeling the war strongly and other preoccupations,
but Sayer's explanation is an avoidance of the reality and violence of Lewis's
war, something Audoin-Rouzeau and Becker have shown is a tendency in
regards to WWI. A view similar to Sayer's was asserted by Walter Hooper in
Spirits in Bondage: "unlike so many who wrote 'war poems,' Jack did not consider war—with its bullets, corpses and barbed-wire—a fit subject for poetry.
So, while he did write about the violence and ferocity of war, what he wrote
is not gruesome. This in itself makes those poems whose subject is war so pecu-
liarly his own" (*SIB* xxxvi). As I have written elsewhere, silence on the gruesome elements of war is not a suitable means of judging war's effects on a
person; silence can be misleading (Gilchrist 62). But more: war poetry is not
simply that which discusses bayonets and barbed wire. Rather, war writing
(poetry or prose) presents the events (here bayonets, shells, bullets, and barbed
wire) that causes trauma as well as the after-effects of that trauma. And such
effects lie not merely with "veterans" proper. Vera Brittain, serving as a VAD
in WWI, a war that consumed all of her close male friends including her
brother and fiancé, did not talk so much about the "bullets, corpses and
barbed-wire" but focused on the disorienting estrangement of her generation
from the generations either side of her own, the dissolution of her own values
and expectations for the rest of life. Studies today note that soldiers who suffer post-traumatic stress disorder (PTSD) have an experience or experiences that
have left behind just this kind of disorienting trauma, a trauma that has at its
center a shift in personal paradigm. So great was Vera Brittain's trauma that she
suffered hallucinations. This as a nurse—she did not fight in the trenches. What
of the combat soldier's trauma? Larger contexts than have been so far constructed in studying Lewis need to be considered in order to understand his experiences and his response to them. Building those contexts means looking
deeply into the abyss of war, and that means to take one's breath in pain to both
tell and to read such a tale.

    While I do, indeed, look not only into Lewis's letters, diary, autobiogra-
phy, and earliest poetry for part of the context of his war experience, Lewis
readers should not be confused, as some have been, by his argument in *The
Personal Heresy*: the assumption that if we read an author's work we may
interpret his or her life by that work. It is not irony that Lewis began his argu-
ments in the book with a recollection of his war experience, that he had seen
a collection of poems during the war containing the work of veteran poets. The
blurb on the cover promised the reader that the poems would communicate

intimate things which the soldiers never told their family, lovers, or comrades (*Heresy* b).

What Lewis debated in the exchange between himself and E. M. W. Tillyard in the book were the immediate effects of poetry upon readers, as distinct from assumptions to which their later pondering of the texts may lead them. Lewis concedes that a poet's work has something of the writer in it (*Heresy* 3), but to create a perception of a poet through a poem is not the aim of poetry. Such a perception is what readers conjecture only after experiencing the work immediately and in its own right (5). Simply stated, if we look for details of the poet's life in the poetry, we shall arrive at a skewed perception of the poet (4), and—straight to Lewis's point—we do not read the poem if we read thus.

I am not interested in discovering solely through his poetry some intimate thing about Lewis he had never told anyone else, nor am I interested in teasing out the literary issues he and Tillyard debated. Rather, I am interested in the image of Lewis that appears through a collection of contexts. And in part we can find the soldier Jack Lewis within his literary contexts, even as Warren Lewis observed of his brother. In his memoir of Jack, Warren referred to the long and difficult relationship Jack had with Mrs. Moore: "I dwell on this rather unhappy business with some regret, but it was one of the central and determining circumstances in Jack's life. He hinted at it, darkly, in *Surprised by Joy*, and it is reflected with painful clarity in various passages in his books" (13). If various passages of Lewis's books reveal much about that relationship, it may be said that his early poetry reflects the war experience—that before it is myth, before it is Romance, it is war poetry centrally. The war is more than simply hinted at darkly in those works.

When working with chapters of this book treating PTSD, I concentrated upon soldiers who suffered acutely in the war or who had, at least, given voice to their traumatic experiences as much as memory allowed. I came upon Linda F. McGreevy's work on Otto Dix. In her book, *Bitter Witness*, she asserts eloquently considerations central to the use of a veteran's memories in building contexts:

> Autobiography may well be the hallmark of memory. This amalgam of objective conscious recollection is invariably essential to art's authenticity. The sharing of autobiographical memories, by which an individual testifies to both personal and collective events, is the linchpin around which the work and its reception revolves. Yet memory has a peculiarly dualistic nature, being both individualized or private, and collectively objective or public. Memory is also essentially non-linear, colored by emotional perceptions that occur randomly during and after the events recalled. Such memories can thus be conflicted, particularly when and if the initial experience is traumatic and remains unresolved, whether privately or publicly. (1)

In examining C. S. Lewis at war, I discover a number of images of the man: a 2nd lieutenant in the Somerset Light Infantry; a war poet—one of the Lost Generation and an atheist, and in many respects not at all out of company with many of that generation. As did those of the elder generation (those who began the war), Lewis sought an explanation for what had happened to the world and to himself during the Great War.

As has often been pointed out in biographies of Lewis, he wrote that in his mind he was able to dismiss the war to such a degree that some people would disbelieve him, would think it an impossible mental feat, and would even consider him to be living a fantasy (*SBJ* 158). The remark is the posture which has been taken at face value: Humphrey Carpenter, for instance, wrote of Jack's war service that, "though he found it horrific he was not deeply shaken by the experience. He had, after all, lived with the knowledge of the war for more than three years before going out to the front" (8).

Hemingway well knew it is easy to make assertions about one's human subject without the valuable scrutiny of those who stood with and walked through time alongside that subject, knowing him personally, closely—both long and *honestly*. To this end, it is an advantage that Warren recorded his distrust of a number of his brother's recollections, stating that there were facts that Jack would not admit. Too, Lewis himself admitted posturing on other issues (*SBJ* 192). Others distrust some of Lewis's accounts of himself. George Sayer records the remarks of Sir Donald Harman, a schoolmate of Jack's who regarded Jack's views of their mutual school days as "unbalanced and exaggerated. This is not to say that some of the practices and customs he complains of did not exist; they did, but Lewis has blown them up out of all proportion" (qtd. in Sayer 85). Jack himself is reported to have said, in reading his own version of his school, Malvern, that it was not a true account (Sayer 86).

But there is more to Jack's posturing, as the contexts of WWI and its soldiers' experiences reveal when they are examined closely and set properly beside the details of Lewis's war experience. If Lewis balked in his autobiography, the effects of the war upon his imagination are nevertheless pitched straight in his early poetry—in *Spirits in Bondage* and in his other early poem, *Dymer*. What we see is Lewis traumatized by war; specific events shattered his early beliefs and assumptions about life; he then attempts to rebuilt those shattered assumptions, and his early poetry is that attempt. Otto Dix attempted to deliver himself of his trauma by drawing and painting the actualities of war. Painting was in part the simple process to chronicle war and give trauma a voice. For Lewis, it is not painting but poetry. In such cases, their respective arts serve even as one of Hemingway's characters, Brett in *The Sun Also Rises*, said of their code: "it is what we have instead of God" (245). Lewis the atheist had his poetry instead of God. As with Dix, the Lewis that we discover in his early life, in his early poetry, and in his later imagination, we must see in light of his war.

The image of Lewis in this book precedes and contradicts most other images that the name C. S. Lewis evokes: as an adult, he was first a soldier; as a writer, first a war poet; as an adherent to reasoned beliefs, first an atheist. My intention is neither to explain the philosophical or theological shape of his literary imagination. Nor is it to trace his Christian pilgrimage. Nor is my purpose to rehearse his general biography, his school years, his entrance to Oxford which, quite apart from the war's centrality in that event, has also been repeatedly presented to us. My sole purpose is to explore 2nd Lieutenant Lewis. My hope is that this Lewis will be set in context with all the others.

WORKS CITED

Audoin-Rouzeau, Stephane, and Annette Becker. *14–18: Understanding the Great War*. Trans. Catherine Temerson. New York: Hill and Wang, 2002.

Carpenter, Humphrey. *The Inklings*. New York: Ballantine, 1981.

Craig, Joanna Hildebrand. e-mail. 7 Dec. 2001.

Fussell, Paul. *The Great War and Modern Memory*. Oxford: Oxford UP, 1975.

Gilchrist, K. James. "2nd Lieutenant Lewis." *VII: An Anglo-American Literary Review*. Vol. 17 (2000): 62.

Hemingway, Ernest. *True at First Light*. London: Arrow, 1999.

Holmes, Richard. *Acts of War: The Behavior of Men in Battle*. New York: Free, 1989.

Keegan, John. *The Face of Battle*. London: Penguin, 1976.

McGreevy, Linda F. *Bitter Witness: Otto Dix and the Great War*. New York: Peter Lang, 2001.

Sayer, George. *Jack: A Life of C. S. Lewis*. Wheaton, Ill: Crossway, 1994.

Thompson, David, and Geoffrey Warner. *England in the Twentieth Century (1914–79)*. London: Penguin, 1991.

Tillyard, E. M. W. and C. S. Lewis. *The Personal Heresy*. Oxford: Oxford UP, 1939.

CHAPTER 1

Optimism's Demise

IN 1916 A NOVEL BY H. G. WELLS appeared which told the story of an Englishman on the home front: *Mr. Britling Sees It Through*. In the opening pages, the state of Britain just prior to WWI is being described by Mr. Britling who speaks from his comfortable English countryside home. He and his guests have already discussed Ulster Home Rule and the Irish acquiring Mauser rifles from the Germans, an event they decided is a German issue, not an Irish one. But the real danger, Britling sees, may come from the English themselves:

> "People may be too safe. You see we live at the end of a series of secure generations in which none of the great things of life have changed materially. We've grown up with no sense of danger—that is to say, with no sense of responsibility. None of us, none of us—for though I talk my actions belie me—really believe that life can change very fundamentally any more forever. All this"—Mr. Britling waved his arm comprehensively—"looks as though it was bound to go on steadily forever. It seems incredible that the system could be smashed. It seems incredible that anything we can do will ever smash the system. . . . We English are everlasting children in an everlasting nursery."
> (46–47)

Britling is a book that interested C. S. "Jack" Lewis, a young Irishman who knew its themes even if he had not read it by May of 1917 when he was in officer training in Oxford (*CL* 306). In March of 1914, the period near to that

described in the novel, Lewis was at school in England, away from his Belfast
home. He wrote to his father, Albert Lewis, that the news was full of the Ulster
conflict, but those in England did not seem to grasp matters well, not knowing if volunteers being called for were for or against Home Rule (*CL* 52). As
Thompson and Warner explained, "by 1914 the Liberals were ready to coerce
Ulster into submission in order to grant the Irish Home Rule; the Unionists
were equally ready to provoke mutiny in the British Army rather than let
Ulster go" (32). The sense was pervasive that Ireland would explode. The nov-
elist Alec Waugh, who himself would fight and be captured in The Great War,
recalled his school headmaster's "farewell address" in which was mentioned
"the bad news in the morning papers. . . . I thought he was referring to the
threat of civil war in Ireland" (qtd in Fussell 25). There were other upheavals:
and "for all these reasons British national life in 1914 was subject to many
schisms and tensions, and even the future of constitutional government seemed
in jeopardy" (Thompson and Warner 33). The irony was that "the trouble was
expected in Ulster rather than in Flanders. It was expected to be domestic and
embarrassing rather than savage and incomprehensible" (Fussell 24). Jack
Lewis and his brother Warren were exempt from compulsory service because
they were Irish. In actuality, they would both serve. Warren served by choice.
Jack entered through an officer training corps in an attempt to delay his call
to the front until the war had ended. Thus, Jack began his service by the safest,
not the nearest way. Warren had chosen a military career, begun at the Royal
Military College at Sandhurst when war began in August of 1914. But Jack,
being about three years younger than Warren, would have preferred (indeed,
most people in Britain expected) the war to end before Jack would arrive at military age. Jack further hoped that he would remain in Mr. Britling's pleasant
England, at Oxford specifically. For all the upheaval in Britain, England seemed
certain, stable, full of the old, good things that kept it a fastness of tradition
against an increasingly disorienting modern world. Indeed, after the horrors
of the war were over, Warren expressed what many felt. He noted that "the
whole state of the world now is enough to make any sane man dispair [sic].
Everything which is worth living for is disappearing or has disappeared. If only
the pre-war world could have lasted my time" (*LP* VI.93, #1387). This feeling of security, of stability, of Britling's unchangeable England seems to have
been mere illusion, as various historians have contended.

     The stable days were gone. If The Great War did not kill the melioristic
and seeming innocence of the nineteenth century, it placed the toe tag unequiv-
ocally upon its corpse. The English nursery, as Britling put it, was closed, and
for Jack Lewis the approach of war began to confirm that the certainty, the opti-
mism, the meliorism had been a deception. Fussell observed that "the Great

War was more ironic than any before or since. It was a hideous embarrassment to the prevailing Meliorist myth which had dominated the public consciousness for a century" (8).

Jack's and Warren's letters to their father, as well the family records compiled by Warren as *The Lewis Papers*, all convey an image of a generally happy family. At its head was a solicitor in Belfast who built a comfortable house (if the plumbing was temperamental) away from the city in a mildly fashionable area. The *Papers* present both direct and indirect sketches of the Lewis relatives with whom the Lewises met during various holidays; general domestic bliss is apparent if not also an awareness of family idiosyncrasies and the minor wrangles they at times precipitated. In his autobiography, Lewis wrote that on his father's side his ancestors swayed according to their emotions while his mother's family were folk more centered in their intellect (*SBJ* 3). But for all the bliss, his early days moved in ways not unlike Britain itself before the war: "the day-by-day approach to a catastrophe by an unsuspecting victim" (qtd. in Fussell 24). A sense of doom (implicitly behind Britling's comments) was seen as an undercurrent at the time and was due to many things, among them Irish rumblings, Germany's rising power under an eccentrically brash if strictly disciplined Kaiser, and women's rights. In Thomas Hardy's poem "Channel Firing" the speakers—the dead in a country churchyard—despair over the arms race which the British and German navies are running, evidenced by the ships practice-firing in the channel and promising to make "red war yet redder" (Hardy, 1750). And in "Convergence of the Twain," Hardy considers the *Titanic* a vessel of inordinate pride that "the Spinner of the Years" sends to the ocean floor where the "moon-eyed fish" wonder at "this vaingloriousness down here" (1751). Hardy's description of the ship's complete ruin combined with the poem's republication in 1914 carries the sense of pride-inspired doom that August 1914 would thereafter take on, not least for Ford Maddox Ford. His novel *The Good Soldier* has the ominously recurring date of August 4th to mark its circus of social, marital, personal, and mental demise. Of the time Winston Churchill remarked how "the terrible Ifs accumulate" (qtd. in Tuchman epigraph).

To what degree the uncertainty of world events before the war affected the young Lewis is a matter revealed largely in his early letters where political and, later, war issues are topics. The teenage Lewis discusses such matters with a precociously astute manner that is present in the stories he created as a child: "Animal Land" and "Boxen." Yet while he addresses politics and the prospect of war in his letters, it is clear that Jack does not *feel* anything deeply on these issues nor does he understand what the approach of the war's horrors may mean. His comments seem imitatively appropriate statements on topics which adults discuss with seriousness. He discusses such issues with a lightness and adolescent assurance, one moment joking, the next somehow serious. Not world events, then, rather, those things which bring a sense of uncertainty into Lewis's world were his school Malvern and the death of his mother.

The horrors of the schools Lewis attended is a well-rehearsed topic in Lewisiana. In his autobiography Lewis described at length the levels of that hell: floggings, which were a punishment for a mistake in geometry, and the half-mad wranglings of Oldie, a headmaster. The letters Jack wrote to his father from the school are a boy's plea for removal from a prison whose warden was to die in an asylum. Warren, however, found his brother's account of Malvern (a school Warren had also attended) inaccurate:

> Here I feel it my duty to make some comment upon his criticisms of the school, as expressed in his letters of the time as well as in *Surprised by Joy*. . . . I find it very difficult to believe in the Malvern that he portrays. (Memoir 4)

Warren lists facts that "Jack seemed reluctant to see or admit" (Memoir 5). This is a significant observation from someone who knew Jack better than did anyone else, and it marks an important tendency in Jack that is central to his response to war. In his autobiography Jack describes Malvern as a place less desirable than a freezing and sodden trench in France. He paints Malvern with more horrible detail than he sketches his war service. Further, in *Surprised by Joy* he covers his war experience in chapter XII ("Guns and Good Company") while devoting two chapters, VI and VII, to his schooling.

Prefacing the war and before his experiences at his schools, one event above all others brought Lewis a sense that the world is uncertain and even hostile. His account of his mother's death is a record of much beyond its mere facts. It shows Lewis, as he struggles through the trauma, developing a pattern of coping that will appear again as he grapples with the trauma of the war. Lewis recalls how despite his cries from the effects of a bad tooth and a headache, his mother could not help him. Physicians were with her. He could hear people talking, going in and out of rooms; at the end of what must have seemed an interminable time, his father, Albert, came to him crying and attempted to convey to his young mind what was happening: his mother had cancer (18).

It was but the beginning of that grief: his mother slowly died; the boys slowly lost her, and their world became strange with the house being invaded by new odors, whispering persons, and sounds in the night, things that carried to the boys a pervasive sense of hostility. He recalls feelings which he and his brother shared: that they were somehow responsible. What emerged was an uncommon closeness between brothers in the midst of crisis: two terrified boys in a grim world growing closer in their mutual need of one another (*SBJ* 19).

With the death of his mother, his sense of certainty, of a stable world, passed just as it was already beginning to pass for the rest of Europe (*SBJ* 20). She died in 1908. It was not many years beyond her death that the proverbial Edwardian weekend would close, but many refused to see it despite the portents.[1] H. G. Wells's character, Mr. Britling (representing, as the name suggests, Britain at the time), continues another of his monologues, and in the very moment he delivers a discourse on how "The world grows sane"—that Germany would have to be insane to start a war—the explosion occurs not in Germany but elsewhere (76). As Lord Esher wrote in his diary after the funeral of Archduke Ferdinand, "There never was such a break-up. All the old buoys which have marked the channel of our lives seem to have been swept away" (qtd. in Tuchman 14).

NOTE

1.   The existence of an idyllic period called variously the Edwardian afternoon or weekend, as part of the larger "Myth of the war" as Samuel Hynes has termed it, has been contended by Hynes and others but also by Martin Stephen in *The Price of Pity: Poetry, History and Myth in the Great War* (London: Cooper, 1996). For Lewis and his brother at least, there was indeed a deep security in life up to the year that his mother died, an event shattering Jack and Warren's security.

WORKS CITED

Fussell, Paul. *The Great War and Modern Memory.* Oxford: Oxford UP, 1975.

Hardy, Thomas. "Channel Firing." *The Norton Anthology of English Literature.* Volume 2. M. H. Abrams, ed. Fifth edition. New York: Norton, 1986.

Hardy, Thomas. "Convergence of the Twain." *The Norton Anthology of English Literature.* Volume 2. M. H. Abrams, ed. Fifth edition. New York: Norton, 1986.

Keegan, John. *The Face of Battle.* London: Penguin, 1976.

Lewis, W. H. Memoir. *C. S. Lewis Letters.* Ed. W. H. Lewis. New York: Harcourt, 1966.

Baker, Chris. "A: Tommies Recruitment in 1914–1918." *The British Army in the Great War.* available <http://www.1914–1918.net/recruitment.htm> 6 August 2001.

Thomson, David and Geoffrey Warner. *England in the Twentieth Century <1914–1979>.* London: Penguin, 1991.

Tuchman, Barbara W. *The Guns of August.* New York: Ballantine, 1994.

Waugh, Evelyn. *A Little Learning.* Boston: Little, Brown, 1964.

Wells, H. G. *Mr. Britling Sees It Through.* London: Hogarth, 1985.

CHAPTER 2

A Prospect of War

ON 9 JANUARY 1914 RESULTS OF AN EXAM were published relating that Warren Lewis had won a place in Sandhurst, and on 3 February he crossed from Ireland to England with Jack (*CL* 47). Jack went back to Malvern for one more term while Warren began work at the Royal Military College. For the Lewis family it was the beginning of the war as far as it would affect them personally. W. T. Kirkpatrick had been tutor to both Albert Lewis and Warren and would also tutor Jack. Kirkpatrick had written to Albert even before Warren took exams for Sandhurst that the boy should be headed towards some career, but the army would not be an easy road. Nevertheless, Warren had made up his mind about a military career (*CL* 46). Although Warren was set directly on a course that would lead him into the war, for Jack at his school—as for many in England at the time—the approach of war was a distant abstraction. Both a war and the Ulster situation remain topics in Jack's letters. As to war, he explained to his father that in returning late to school after a holiday, one of his school masters joked that he and the students had feared Jack had been a casualty of war, apparently referring to war in Ireland as this event occurred in May 1914. Jack observed to his father that any war would not be a matter for levity, as everyone would eventually see (*CL* 56). Like so many in England and not least like Wells's Mr. Britling, Jack may have been expecting civil war in Ireland, not a world war in Europe.

At Sandhurst, Warren could not help but think about the approach of war. The prospects of war and of facing battle would become more immediate for him before going to France than they would for Jack over the next three years he spent in England studying. Warren, as the unpublished papers of the Lewis family show, was carefully tracking world events during the summer of 1914. He notes, for instance, the conflicts and ultimatums between Serbia and Austria, that Austria will soon be at war with Serbia. The next day he notes that Russia is moving its military forward (*LP* IV. 203–204). Instead of the usual one year's preparation, Warren underwent only nine months of training (*CL* 1012) as Britain hurriedly prepared for war. The details of that training, some of which Warren regarded as absurd, he recorded in part for his father. They were exercises that Jack would eventually experience and entailed the usual drills in moving units efficiently (marching), inspecting units, studying strategies, firing weapons, and attending various lectures, during some of which Warren became so bored, his diary records, that "I was reduced to playing naughts and crosses with Parkin: if Elliot continues to lecture, I see that I shall shortly have to send home for a box of toy soldiers" (*LP* V.281).

Details of military training that Jack would encounter will be given later, alongside discussion of Jack's entrance into the war. What is more important to understand here is that the psychological preparation for war was quite different for the two brothers. The military academy prepared one psychologically for war quite differently than did the home front.

John Keegan, who for many years taught at Sandhurst, describes the military paradigm at the college:

> The deliberate injection of emotion into an already highly emotive subject will seriously hinder, if not indeed altogether defeat, the aim of officer-training. That aim, which Western armies have achieved with remarkably consistent success during the 200 years in which formal military education has been carried on, is to reduce the conduct of war to a set of rules and a system of procedures—and thereby to make orderly and rational what is essentially chaotic and instinctive. It is an aim analogous to that—though I would not wish to push the analogy too far—pursued by medical schools in their fostering among students of a detached attitude to pain and distress in their patients, particularly victims of accidents. (18)

The object is to standardize the whole of military operation and, hence, individual soldiers' responses to battle, to create a "corps" (as in *corporation*), by focusing on "procedures which have as their object the assimilation of almost all of an officer's professional activities to a corporate standard and a common form" (Keegan 18–19). This "reductive" aspect in training military officers has an "important and intended . . . psychological effect," something considered "de-personalizing" and even "dehumanizing" by some, but which, Keegan points out, "is powerfully beneficial":

> For by teaching the young officer to organize his intake of sensations, to reduce the events of combat to as few and as easily recognizable a set of elements as possible, to categorize under manageable headings the noise, blast, passage of missiles and confusion of human movement which will assail him on the battlefield, so that they can be described—to his men, to his superiors, to himself—as "incoming fire," "outgoing fire," "airstrike," "company strength attack," one is helping him to avert the onset of fear or, worse, of panic and to perceive a face of battle which, if not familiar, and certainly not friendly, need not, in the event, prove wholly petrifying. (20)

Warren was to undergo just this type of education before reaching the front, with its clinical and detached mode of reference. Indeed, if a soldier's ability to displace instinct and panic failed and resulted in his hanging back during an attack, the penalty could be death. The British government has removed some of the stigma attached to young men shot under such circumstances, about 300 of them during WWI. In June 2001, a statue of a 17-year-old veteran shot for desertion was unveiled in Lichfield, but the decision to do so "is not a judgmental one. Rather the memorial asks us to recognize these deaths as another of the tragedies that warfare has brought about" ("UK"). It is an issue debated heatedly today, but the feelings in 1914 were decidedly against those who appeared to be cowards, even if plausible excuses might be made. After General Haig ordered in 1916 that more officers be shot for desertion (the majority were enlisted men), within two months "21-year-old Edwin Dyett, was shot at dawn in France. Dyett said he had got lost in no-man's-land but was convicted of desertion. A few weeks later a second young officer was executed" (Burke). After the war, however, no contingency existed for what the returning soldier was to do to recover more normal psychological responses—those which had been repressed on the battlefield—once he was demobilized and back at home where the "Sandhurst paradigm" is no longer operative.

Quite apart from the men at Sandhurst, many boys like Jack learned about the war from their brothers, from wounded men recuperating at home, and from newspapers, all of which often provided emotionally laden accounts of battle, not accounts marked by the clinically detached psychological training Sandhurst gave its soldiers.

However, in 1914 one emotion that pleased the military ran high both at Sandhurst and in town squares throughout Europe. True to highly patriotic sentiment, Warren reports (is it not with a sense of pride?) that one of his superiors complimented the men on their noble choice of career, and on 18 August records his hope: "with luck we shall go straight to the front" (*LP* IV.203–204).

Voices of patriotism dominated these pre-war and early-war days and sub-dued societal clamoring on other issues. One recruitment poster of the time expresses the sentiment perhaps better than the plethora of historical and lit-erary accounts: pictured is a German dirigible caught by a searchlight in the night sky over London (Parliament and St. Paul's dome are distinct features). The poster reads, "IT IS FAR BETTER TO FACE THE BULLETS THAN TO BE KILLED AT HOME BY A BOMB—JOIN THE ARMY AT ONCE & HELP TO STOP AN AIR RAID—" then, in smaller caps, "GOD SAVE THE KING." The poster speaks beyond the level of mere patriotism: here is duty, social guilt, emotional coercion, and a sense of futility in avoiding death. In the logic of the poster, it is all but inevitable that one will be sacrificed some-place, sometime before it is all over, and if dead, one's honor is best served if acquired by fighting. "In London young women paraded the streets, offering white feathers (symbols of cowardice) to any man still in civilian clothes" records A. J. P. Taylor (58), and in recruitment rallies, the plying of men's sense of duty did not stop at patriotic or even emotional appeals. Horatio Bottomley—bankrupt before the war but regaining his fortunes in his recruit-ing efforts, only to squander them all once more on "racehorses, women, and champagne"—introduced "Jesus Christ, the Prince of Peace" to his rallies and led "his audience to the foot of the Cross" when contributors to war funds "paid more than £200" (Taylor 36). One's religious observance is infused with patriotism. Rupert Brooke's poems would not appear until 1915, but their strains further ennobled the war until other voices, those of Siegfried Sassoon, John McCrae, and C. S. Lewis among them, began to call into question the wisdom of a war that silenced Britain's darling sons as it had silenced Brooke. Brooke's famous lines, ironically from his poem entitled "Peace," were a catchphrase once they emerged: "Now God be thanked who matched us with His hour" (144), but another of Brooke's poems goes beyond this mild, if pow-erful, inducement, polishing a soldier's death to a glowing phenomenon of a mind that yet "Gives somewhere back the thoughts by England given" (148). Perhaps the most familiar of Brooke's poems, "The Soldier," is with other patri-otic poems from Kipling peppered through one training manual for officers:

> If I should die, think only this of me:
> That there's some corner of a foreign field
> That is forever England. (Lake 184)

Against the pervasive patriotic stance, poets like Charles Hamilton Sorley expressed things differently: "Such, such is Death: no triumph: no defeat" and "When you see millions of the mouthless dead / Across your dreams in pale battalions go, /Say not soft things as other men have said, / That you'll remember" (89). Sorley's poems, and those from many other war poets who questioned or wrote against patriotic sentiments such as those found in Brooke's poems, were among a large and growing body of works expressing disillusionment with the war as it continued. Both Brooke and Sorley were dead by 1915, Brooke dying of a mosquito bite and resulting fever, Sorley dying in action.

Even before probing verses like Sorley's or Sassoon's gave voice to it, vestiges of disillusion existed in Britain even during the earliest days of the war. Evelyn Waugh relates that "my father read family prayers every morning. In August 1914 he abandoned this practice on the very curious grounds that it was 'no longer any good'" (68). Even well before the war, as has been shown, Hardy's works were compounding a sense doom and disillusion, as in "The Darkling Thrush," which sings in the gloom and aware of "Some blessed Hope, whereof he knew / And I was unaware" (Hardy 1744).

Despite the disillusion in some poets and perhaps in an occasional neighbor, in the early Lewis family dialogues on war, patriotism had a firm place. Warren, for instance, wrote to Albert concerning their Belfast neighbor, Mr. Greeves; Greeves would not allow his son Willie to join the army, which brings Warren to jest with mild disdain about Mr. Greeves's collusion with the Germans (*LP* IV.235–236).

As Warren trained for Army life, in September of 1914, Jack left Malvern to be tutored by W. T. Kirkpatrick at Great Bookham. There he found a place where, to use Yeats's words, "peace comes dropping slow." His literary nature developed fully under "Kirk," as Jack called his tutor. Not only do his literary abilities and tastes become well defined during this period, so do his *uses* of literature. To Arthur Greeves, Mr. Greeves' son and Jack's lifelong friend, he writes letters whose subjects are chiefly literature and music. The boys discuss their literary discoveries and current readings and offer consequent appraisals of works they read. They share their original compositions and spend extensive time discussing new book orders and the very bindings of books. Among such discussions are other moments like these:

> You ask me whether I have ever been in love: fool as I am, I am not quite such a fool as all that. But if one is only to talk from firsthand experience on any subject, conversation would be a very poor business. But though I have no personal experience of the thing they call love, I have what is better—the experience of Sappho, of Euripides of Catullus of Shakespeare of Spenser of Austen of Bronte of, of—anyone else I have read. (*CL* 146)

and

> I keep my friendship with you only for the highest plane of life: that I leave to others all the sordid and uninteresting worries about so-called practical life, and share with you

those joys and experiences which make that life desirable [. . . .] But seriously, what
can you have been thinking about when you said "only" books, music, etc., just as if
these weren't the real things! (*CL* 205)

In other places he indicates the same sense (*CL* 187 and 245), and each
instance reveals Lewis's persistence in viewing a fictional world and its characters as Real, viewing literary experience, despite its vicarious nature, as existing on the same plane as one's own actual experience. In the second example
above he prefers the fictional world and its characters over the real world and
its actual people. Kirkpatrick, writing to Albert, notes that

> his tastes and predilections are solely in the direction of books and learning. He has sin-
> gularly little desire to mingle with mankind, or study human nature. His interests lie
> in a totally different direction—in the past, in the realm of creative imagination, in the
> world which the common mind would call unreal, but which is to him the only real
> one. (qtd. in Hooper xxii)

One may put this tendency in Jack down to the idealism of youth; certainly
youth is in the mix. But his tendency to view life as literary is something he sustained throughout the war and long after, when he was writing *The Problem
of Pain*, for instance, and, earlier, in *Allegory of Love*. Of the latter book, Lewis
said he had treated the courtly love tradition as if it were nearly solely a matter discovered in books but had eventually learned something of the reality that
lay behind the phenomenon (Carpenter 266). His view matured only toward
the end of his life after he married Joy Gresham. Similarly, in *The Problem of
Pain*, Lewis treated suffering and sorrow in the world in a fashion somewhat
removed from real conditions of suffering. In the same way that his views on
love changed by falling in love and marrying, so too his view toward pain and
suffering changed through the death of Joy Gresham. After she died, Lewis kept
a journal, later published as *A Grief Observed*. Because it shows Lewis confronting the realities of grief which his earlier theories could not fathom, the
journal should serve as an appendix to *The Problem of Pain*. But these books
come from an older Lewis. For the young Lewis at Kirkpatrick's, for the 2nd
lieutenant standing in the trenches, life was something vicariously experienced
through literature; he would approach war similarly.

Warren, training at Sandhurst and adopting official perspectives on the war,
approached war matters very much more matter of factly than did Jack. Jack,
on the other hand, was learning of it in a very different way, a topic discussed
in some depth by Lewis scholars. Of Jack's life at this time, Humphrey
Carpenter noted that Lewis had ample time to adjust to the idea of war:
"Though he found it horrific he was not deeply shaken by the experience. He
had, after all, lived with the knowledge of the war for more than three years

before going out to the front" (8). Indications are that Lewis regarded his war quite differently than Carpenter suggests. It is certain, indeed, that throughout his years at Kirk's, Lewis, like everyone else, became familiar with the idea of war. In large part it came by saturation, from the circumambient air of war-talk and from newspaper articles (however far they were to be believed). Lewis recalled how the prospect of a war began as mere rumor among students that—as they discussed whether England would be in the war or not—increased to the stature of a minor apocalypse (*SBJ* 131).

One expects to find such a recollection in *Mr. Britling Sees It Through*, which expresses precisely Britling's disbelief that England will enter any war at all. Yet of war-talk, Jack takes a milder interest than did, perhaps, others, and he notes that while so many discuss it, they know very little about such matters even so (*CL* 137).

Beyond newspapers, other sources made him familiar with some of war's grave possibilities. One literary source was the first text he would study at Kirkpatrick's, and it was one, by his own confession, that would act profoundly upon his imagination immediately upon his entering the trenches. To Arthur Greeves Jack wrote that he had become quite moved in reading Homer's *Iliad* (*CL* 71). Moments of undeniable beauty exist in the epic, in its compendium descriptions of the Greeks' homeland and way of life, and not least in its language. There is also this in plenty:

> this man
> dismounted to face him, aye! but only met
> a spear-thrust square between the eyes, unchecked
> by his bronze helmet rim. Through bronze and bone
> the spearhead broke into the brain within
> and left it spattered. Down he went. (Homer 254)

War in this particular aspect was still a reality: the British still trained men to use the long, 1907-model sword bayonet fixed to their Enfields, of which Warren writes home to his father that Jack should be told "his brother killed a great big German with his sword yesterday, etc., etc." (*LP* IV.309).

Another source for Jack's increasing familiarity with the war came by way of men who returned home wounded. Of the Smythe family—friends of the Kirkpatricks—one boy, Gerald, returned home wounded by early November 1914: his wound left him without an arm. Gerald apparently sounded to Lewis like an incompetent soldier in relating events of the Front to Mrs. Kirkpatrick. Jack was, however, comforted in the news that the moment of wounding did not cause great pain (*CL* 88). Gerald later returned to France (*CL* 111). Another Smythe, Osbert, also returned home three times due to wounds (*CL* 218). Jack's cousin, Richard Lewis, was also wounded (*CL* 204) with what the soldiers called a "cushy" or a "Blighty wound": it would not cause death but was severe enough to bring them home to "Blighty"—to England.

Yet other, more remote encounters familiarized Jack with war. As he traveled between England and Ireland on holidays, his travels were not without some threat of German subs, one of which sank the ship *Kilcoan*, which had been designed by Albert's brother, Joseph. There were also airships which dropped bombs, contraptions that Jack reasoned were rather inane and would only hurt civilians in an attempt to demoralize them—but that would depend upon the courage of those affected by the bombs (*CL* 106).

Zeppelins were used just as Lewis thought, to deliver "terror to the people of London" (Banks 281). London was attacked by the airships "twelve times between May 1915 and October 1917" (Banks 281). His location in Great Bookham, just south and slightly east of London, allowed Lewis to tell his father that they had, according to some observers, seen airships in the process of bombing Waterloo Station. Although the sky lit up, they could hear no explosions (*CL* 148). Evelyn Waugh tells how

> An anti-aircraft gun was posted at the Whitestone Pond and made the great noise when Zeppelins were overhead. No bomb fell within a mile of us, but the alarms were agreeable occasions when I was brought down from bed and regaled with an uncovenanted picnic. I was quite unconscious of danger, which was indeed negligible. On Summer nights we sat in the garden, sometimes seeing the thin silver rod of the enemy caught in converging search-lights. On a splendid occasion I saw one brought down, sinking very slowly in brilliant flame, and joined those who were cheering in the road outside. (94–95)

Of course, as the war continued, Albert's fears for his sons increased (and, indeed, would naturally remain for the duration of the war). His fears were not merely for Warren. Jack was approaching military age and, further, was in England which—rumors circulated—might be invaded by Germany (*CL* 85 and 85n). H. G. Wells spoke for Albert and many other fathers in casting Mr. Britling's hopes for his son, Hugh: "He was ashamed of his one secret consolation. For nearly two years yet Hugh could not go out to it. There would surely be peace before that" (281). Jack attempted to appease his father, saying in essence that the war couldn't endure, that Germany was overextended and would inevitably confront Britain's naval fleet (*CL* 85). His comments were not made with any actual confidence in Britain's navy or Germany's overwhelming preoccupations on both the Eastern and Western Fronts. Rather, he seems to have written to intercept any intent on Albert's part to have Jack come home. Jack writes to Arthur that as yet such a plan had not been discussed, and he was quite content at Kirkpatrick's; to go home would mean involvement in religious matters, which would to all indications bore him (*CL* 87).

Whatever his actual views were towards the war, Jack was nevertheless gaining a sense of what its consequences might mean. Although he at times jokes with his father (for instance, hoping that some of the people near his home in Ireland would go to France: they might be better people for being shot), in other moments he takes up a serious tone. In one instance, he refers to Kirk's philosophy that war will ultimately allow only cowards to survive, a view in direct contrast to Darwin's ideas about the better vestiges of the race surviving. What such a scenario means for future generations Jack does not like to contemplate (*CL* 88).

Jack also shared his father's inevitable concerns for Warren's safety. In an attempt that could hardly succeed, but which reveals an important aspect of his character, he writes to ease his father's mind that if Warren can survive the war (which Jack describes in darkly gothic terms), he will be a better person upon his return (*CL* 91). His words could not have comforted Albert. That letter shows Lewis's tendency to philosophize, keen in the young man early in life and something that gained power in him while he was under the influence of Kirkpatrick. It leads Jack to abstract reasoning over matters not simply literary but more pertinent: his father's anxieties. He writes to his father, for instance, about the misfortune of having Warren entering the war, an event neither Albert nor Jack can do anything about: Jack reasons, it would be best to simply mentally dismiss the reality of the situation as it cannot be changed (*CL* 90).

The reality is, however, that a father's fears over his son going to war can hardly be dismissed. Kirkpatrick knew this trait in Jack, which allowed the young man to philosophize and ponder phenomena in a way detached from reality. Both Warren and Albert, of course, could not also have failed to note it. The awareness of the trait lies behind Warren's advice to his father on Jack initially being sent to Kirkpatrick's: "There would be no one there except Mr and Mrs K for him to talk to, and he could amuse himself by detonating his little stock of cheap intellectual fireworks under old K's nose" (*LP* IV.156–157).

Yet Warren's letters reveal that Jack's suspicions about his brother were correct: that Warren would become a more serious being through war. Warren was sent to France on 4 November. In mid-December, he writes to Albert of the terrible feeling the front gives: "you cannot imagine what it means to hear shells bursting and see the lines of motor ambulances coming back from the trenches" (*LP* IV.253). He was serving in No. 4 Company of the Army Service Corps, a supply unit that remained behind the lines but which was occasionally shelled. As the war progresses, Warren's disparaging tone deepens, and in describing a magnificent sunset in April of 1915, he can see only beauty's odd juxtaposition with the immense vestige of death

> Last night there was a glorious sunset—all crimson and gold, and not a gun to be heard
> anywhere: somehow it suddenly struck me how silly the whole thing is—I don't know
> if you can understand what I mean—but on a lovely spring evening, why should some
> five million men be concentrating all their energy on the destruction of another five
> million? (*LP* IV.308)

In this letter, Warren expresses a sentiment parallel to that which Sassoon expressed as he attempted to comprehend the vastness of the war:

> I leant on a wooden bridge, gazing down into the dark green glooms of the weedy lit-
> tle river, but my thoughts were powerless against unhappiness so huge. I couldn't alter
> European history, or order the artillery to stop firing. I could stare at the War as I stared
> at the sultry sky, longing for life and freedom and vaguely altruistic about my fellow-
> victims. But a second-lieutenant could attempt nothing—except to satisfy his superi-
> or officers; and altogether, I concluded, Armageddon was too immense for my solitary
> understanding. Then the sun came out for a last reddening look at the War. (82–83)

Jack, still in England, also begins to see things more darkly. Writing to Albert and thinking of the war and the report of Kitchener's death, he considers that matters had grown darker (*CL* 204). Worse would come: that letter was written two days before the beginning of the Battle of the Somme (1 July 1916)—still the worst day in British military history with some 59,000 casualties, 20,000 of them killed outright, among the Allied troops along a mere 14 miles of the Front.

Jack's darkening vision towards the war certainly came in part from Warren. A note of Jack's records that on 9 July 1915 he returned to Kirkpatrick's in Bookham after a short absence (*LP* IV.326); Warren had arrived from the Front on leave, stopped at Bookham, and on 4 July the two Lewis brothers had returned home to Belfast for a short visit (*CL* 135). No doubt they talked much about the war during Warren's leave. While the newspapers provided their own, often antiseptic, accounts of the war, the information civilians winkled out of returning veterans often concerned what it was actually like at the Front. Jack records in a diary for 19 July that he "had ghastly dreams about the front and getting wounded last night" (quoted in Hooper, xxi). Certainly this is in part a reaction to the inevitable discussions the brothers had. Not long after the nightmare, he offers himself to act as a wounded soldier for a woman who had volunteered for medical service and needed to practice placing bandages. On 28 July he writes to his father he had spent an evening being tended for various wounds (*CL* 140–141). Even before this time he had been thinking about how the war might involve himself. Jack had written to his father in June, before Warren's short leave, that although he still might wish the war to end before

forced to enter it himself, it would not be the best way to enter if he were merely an enlisted man. But—it is a grim fact—he sees that, should the war end
before he enters it, many competitors for a place at Oxford will have been
removed (*CL* 131). The concerns are directly on issues of survival.

The important distinction to make here is that Warren was conditioned by
Sandhurst in entering war, followed by a more hostile education, one found
only at the Front. Jack's early education in war, on the other hand, came only
by way of the wounded he met, the newspapers he read, the talk of war from
those who spoke without authority on the subject—and, more significantly,
from talk with Warren, who did, indeed, speak with some authority. If Warren's
letters from France to his father indicate anything of the discussions the brothers had between themselves, then they had rummaged through the spectrum
of war talk: the politics, the strategies (not only those concerning the war, but
personal strategies for Warren's securing leave while Jack was on holiday from
his studies), and the actualities of the Front, its bleak visage, devoid of plant
life, the uneven ground, and a dead boy seen by Warren: "I shall never be able
to forget—a boy lay asleep on a bank and the mess by his head was his brains"
(*LP* V.109–110). Exactly a year from the time of his leave with Jack, Warren
mailed a package to his father which contained some souvenirs from the Front
(*LP* V.106); later he brought home a shell fragment that nearly killed him and
embedded itself in a tree (*LP* V.219).

As the war went on for Warren, Jack continued his studies. Against not only
their own hopes but also against Europe's, the war drew on. It looked as
though it would, indeed, last until Jack was of age for conscription—his prepa-
rations for Oxford exams became inextricably mixed with concerns for his participation in the Army. If he had three years to adjust to the idea of war, as
Carpenter relates, they were increasingly grim years as far as the prospect of war
was concerned and did in no way ease Jack's mind towards involving himself
in it.

WORKS CITED

Banks, Arthur. *A Military Atlas of the First World War*. Barnsley: Cooper, 1998.
Brooke, Rupert. "Peace." *The Works of Rupert Brooke*. Ware: Wordsworth, 1994.
———. "The Dead." *The Works of Rupert Brooke*. Ware: Wordsworth, 1994.
Burke, Jason. "War leader had officers shot 'to goad troops.'" *The Guardian*. available:
    http://www.observer.co.uk/uk_news/story/0,6903,436494,00.html 7 August 2001.
Carpenter, Humphrey. *The Inklings*. New York: Ballantine, 1981.
Fussell, Paul. *The Great War and Modern Memory*. Oxford: Oxford UP, 1975.
Hardy, Thomas. "Channel Firing." *The Norton Anthology of English Literature*. Volume 2. M.
    H. Abrams, ed. Fifth edition. New York: Norton, 1986.

———. "Convergence of the Twain." *The Norton Anthology of English Literature*. Volume 2. M. H. Abrams, ed. Fifth edition. New York: Norton, 1986.

———. "The Darkling Thrush." *The Norton Anthology of English Literature*. Volume 2. M. H. Abrams, ed. Fifth edition. New York: Norton, 1986.

Homer. *The Iliad*. Robert Fitzgerald, trans. Garden City: Anchor, 1975.

Hooper, Walter. Preface. *Spirits in Bondage: A Cycle of Lyrics*. New York: Harcourt, 1983.

Keegan, John. *The Face of Battle*. London: Penguin, 1976.

Lake, B. C. *Knowledge for War: Every Officer's Handbook for the Front*. London: Harrison, 1916.

Lewis, C. S. *The Pilgrim's Regress*. Grand Rapids: Eerdmans, 1979.

Lewis, W. H. Memoir. *C. S. Lewis Letters*. New York: Harcourt, 1966.

Sassoon, Siegfried. *Memoirs of an Infantry Officer*. London: Faber, 1965.

Sorley, Charles Hamilton. "Two Sonnets: II." *The Penguin Book of First World War Poetry*. London: Penguin, 1996.

———. "When you see millions of the mouthless dead." *The Penguin Book of First World War Poetry*. London: Penguin, 1996.

Taylor, A. J. P. *The First World War: An Illustrated History*. New York: Perigee, 1980.

"A: Tommies Recruitment in 1914–1918." *The British Army in the Great War*. available <http://www.1914-1918.net/recruitment.htm> 6 August 2001.

"UK unveils memorial for World War I deserters." *The Sun Sentinal*. available <http://www.-sun-sentinel.com/news/nationworld/sfl   621deserters.story?coll=sfla newsnation-front> 7 August 2001.

Waugh, Evelyn. *A Little Learning*. Boston: Little, Brown, 1964.

Wells, H. G. *Mr. Britling Sees It Through*. London: Hogarth, 1985.

Winter, Denis. *Death's Men: Soldiers of the Great War*. London: Penguin, 1979.

CHAPTER *3*

Model Trenches

LEWIS WROTE IN HIS AUTOBIOGRAPHY THAT HIS decision to serve in the war was not a matter of pride to him (*SBJ* 158). Indeed, he attempted various means to avoid serving. Lewis, his father, Kirkpatrick, and Warren all involved themselves in the issue of Jack's service, even if Warren could only offer advice in his letters from France. The main question was: Should conscription be impossible for him to avoid, how best could Jack be situated for both the university now and after the war? During the Christmas holidays of 1915, Jack and Warren were at home on what Warren then thought might be his last leave, for the war during the previous spring had intensified, making all men's presence on the Front essential. Jack was home from 21 December and returned to Kirk's on 21 January 1916. On 8 January *The Times* published details of "provisions with respect to Military Service in connection with the present war"—conscription—but which excluded young men "who were resident in Great Britain for the purpose only of their education" (qtd. in *CL* 159). Albert duly notes the word "education" and what it meant for Jack's endeavor to attend Oxford (*LP* V.87). Whereas in August of 1914 crowds of men were packing the streets outside enlistment offices throughout England, with their numbers increasing in September, by October the number of volunteers had dropped by about two-thirds. The Military Service Act was introduced on 27 January 1916. Voluntary enlistment ended, and all British men "were deemed to have enlisted" if between the ages of 18 and 41, residing in Great Britain, married or not (Baker). Important to the Lewises was that Irish men were initially excluded. The Lewis family records show vacillation in determining just how the Act applied to them. Jack writes to his father in February, asking if Albert is certain that the Act applied also to him (*CL* 163)—Albert as an solicitor would see any loopholes that existed for the Irish. Yet later Jack seems to have come to a resolve. To Arthur he writes that Jack has seemingly time left before he turns of age and will be sent to France (*CL* 171).

When England was moving toward including Ireland in the Military Service Act, Kirkpatrick wrote to Albert that Jack is a most suitable candidate to enter Oxford, but should he enter, only months later he will be of military age; should the Irish come to be included, Jack might have to go (*CL* 178). More broadly, Kirk ponders how severely the universities will be affected by the Act (*CL* 179).

As early as 1914 the universities were seen by General Haig as mines that could be delved for their wealth by the recruitment offices: "send out young Oxford and Cambridge men as officers [. . . .] They understand the crisis in which the British Empire is involved" (qtd. in Winter 63). In 1916 Haig's idea to "send" was, indeed, a matter for the British government to decide, left no longer to the individual. Jack's service appears settled in Albert's reply to Kirk: Jack had decided to serve but would attempt to enter Oxford meanwhile (*CL* 179). In June of 1916 Jack hears from his father that the exact terms of the Act do not apply to him (*CL* 199)—he may apply for exemption because he is Irish. Even then Jack considers gaining a commission which, perhaps, might allow him to serve at home in Ireland. About this time Jack received a letter from a fellow student he knew at Malvern who indicates that he was conscripted and asks Jack what he will do. The letter leads Jack to ponder actualities of service, especially the value of having a friend in the service if one were to enter (*CL* 206–207). As a last resort, he might follow in the path of his brother and attend Sandhurst, but should he gain a commission by that means, the military might just hold on to him after the war ends, and returning to Oxford would be out of the question. Jack asks Albert if there were any connections among their acquaintances who might help (*CL* 203). Kirk, on the other hand, suggests that Jack could prepare for the foreign office by learning a variety of languages—Italian, German, and Spanish—if he is unable to gain admission to Oxford. Vacillation continues. Albert indicates that Jack has refused to apply for exemption, and Jack writes in definitive tones to Arthur in July of 1916 that he will do nothing about the army until after entrance exams for Oxford have been completed, after which he would enter service by some undecided means (*CL* 205). It seemed to finish the discussion.

But not quite: on 8 November 1916 Jack writes to his father that conscription was being applied to the Irish also, something that might encourage manliness in some of their relatives (*CL* 250). By 19 November he has changed his mind and asks Albert to look once more into a possible exemption (*CL* 255). Thus, in December, Jack and Kirk explore the possibility of exemption, going so far as to consult a solicitor, who advises Jack to write to the Chief Recruiting Officer in Guildford, which he does. The reply is both a relief and a warning: on the one hand Jack is exempt, but he must register for the exemption immediately (*CL* 261).

Jack's next step was to take the Oxford exams, by which he was elected a scholar in classics at University College. His dreams of entering Oxford, even then, remained clouded by the prospect of military service. In a letter to Jack after he had gained election to Oxford, the Master of University College asked about his intentions for military service and observed that all the college men who are physically able are committed to service in some capacity. Albert divines the remark for its true sense: "So now I have to start to look for a commission for Jacks. Failing that, I am afraid that he must either chuck Oxford or go into the ranks. Apparently it is a moral impossibility for a healthy man over 18 years of age to go into residence at Oxford" (*CL* 264).

In consequence, Jack planned to enter the service by way of the Oxford Officer Training Corps (O.T.C.), through which he could gain a commission (*CL* 267). He had but to prepare for a series of exams before actually arriving at Oxford, and (although he failed one exam—that in algebra) Jack arrived in Oxford in April of 1917, taking a room at University College. Lewis recalled in his autobiography that his primary interest was not how to enter the army but how to enter Oxford (*SBJ* 186). The O.T.C. allowed him to remain at Oxford while he prepared for the taking of a commission as an officer and joined an officer cadet unit.

Various endorsements were required in order to enter the O.T.C. Lewis's military file survived the bombing of London during the Second World War during which many records were destroyed. His application for the O.T.C. is signed by C. S. Lewis, Albert Lewis, W. T. Kirkpatrick, Arthur C. Allen, Headmaster of Lewis's school, Cherbourg, and by John C. V. Behan, Dean of University College, Oxford (WO339/105408), whom Lewis described as having no facial hair and being in his mid-twenties (*CL* 296).

A letter of reference from a school House-Master, R. Porch, also exists in the file testifying to Lewis's fitness of character for officer status. Whereas the enlistment application indicates that Lewis was joining the Senior Division of the Officer Training Corps, beside the entry "Service in Officer Training," the record indicates that he served one year in the Junior Division of his school's

O.T.C. The letter from Porch says nothing of this, indicating merely that Lewis was a member of School House, Malvern, and that his "conduct was entirely satisfactory" (WO339/105408). However, Jack remarks in a letter to Albert written after admission to the O.T.C. that the Senior Division of O.T.C. was much better than that which he had met in school; there was none of the mistreatment by one's superiors (*CL* 299). In his autobiography where he discusses Bloodery (service younger boys at school paid their elder boys), Lewis mentions that the job was inflicted upon the boy most disliked (*SBJ* 95); Jack recalled that he could hardly keep up with the work he received in the system. Such service would not only have conveyed something of daily military regimen but would also have reinforced to Jack the value of entering the service as an officer as opposed to entering as an enlisted man.

But in what capacity should he become an officer? A note at the bottom of the O.T.C. application, signed by G. H. Claybole, Lieutenant and Adjutant for the Officer Commanding Oxford's O.T.C., reads, "Likely to make a useful officer but will not have had sufficient training for commission to an O.C.U. before end of *June.*—INFANTRY" (WO339/105408). The emphatic notation of infantry is significant: if sent to France, he might serve in and be sufficiently trained only to lead an infantry unit as apart from, say, an artillery unit (which requires strong mathematical skills) or an RAF unit (Lewis never learned to drive a car).

There was, however, service in other capacities: in Signaling Corps, Command Depots, Regimental Depots, and Supply Depots among them. Warren, for instance, was in a unit behind the lines which supplied shells to artillery units. While service in a similar unit might be feasible, Jack's military record indicates that he had no ability at signaling.

Lewis's war record also indicates his "General Efficiency" was "Good," and in "Musketry," he was at least adept at a "miniature and 200 yards Range" (WO339/105408). Paul Cornish, a weapons expert at the Imperial War Museum, indicated that this means Lewis could fire a Lee Enfield rifle and hit a target at 200 yards and on a miniature—probably an indoor—range. However, Jack's own statements contradict indications of his proficiency. Even after he had been in France, Albert attempted to convince his son to transfer to a machine gun section, thinking that such a change would place his son in a relatively safer situation. Jack wrote to Albert that although he had been shown repeatedly how to fire his gun, it was still effectually a mystery (*LP* V.278). Statements like this exasperated Albert, who marked it down as Jack's infuriating willingness to let fate take its course. As Albert wrote to Warren, (i.) I certify that the above particulars are correct and complete. I request that I may be admitted to an Officer Cadet Unit with a view to being appointed to a commission as stated in (2) above.

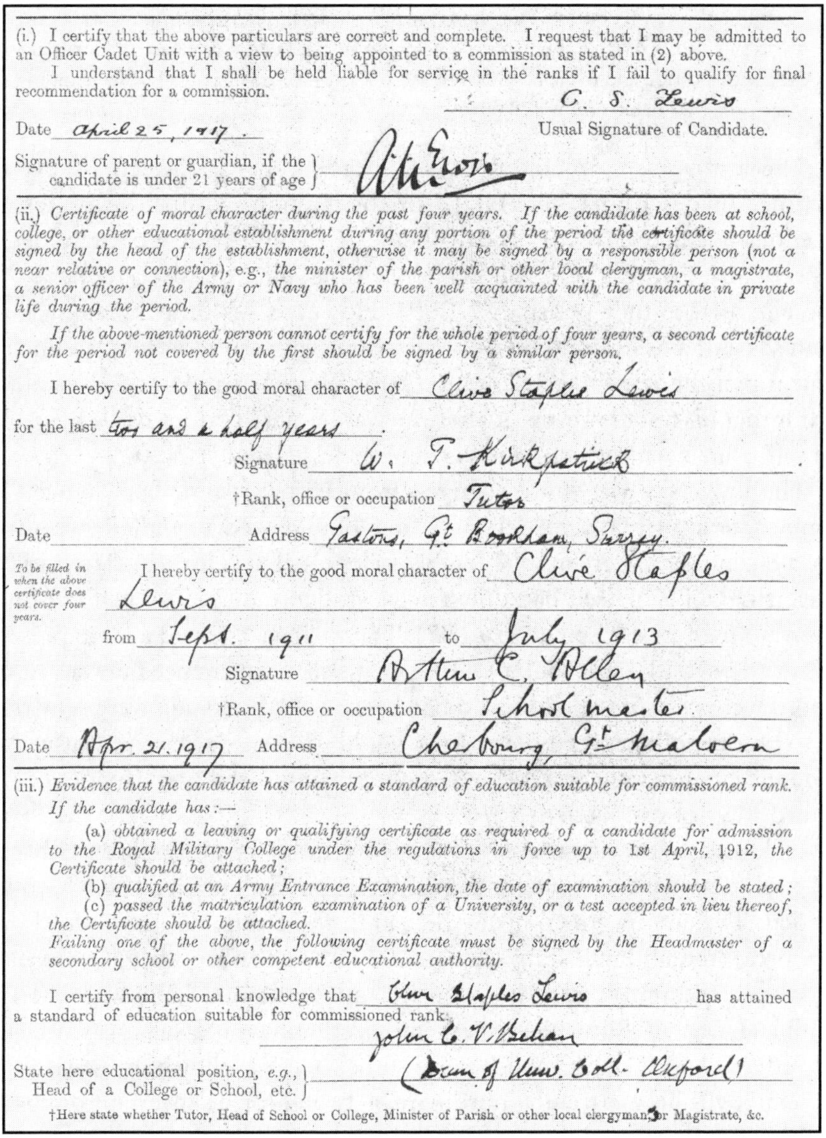

I understand that I shall be held liable for service in the ranks if I fail to qualify for final recommendation for a commission.

C. S. Lewis

Date *April 25, 1917*.

Usual Signature of Candidate.

Signature of parent or guardian, if the } candidate is under 21 years of age }

(ii.) *Certificate of moral character during the past four years. If the candidate has been at school, college, or other educational establishment during any portion of the period the certificate should be signed by the head of the establishment, otherwise it may be signed by a responsible person (not a near relative or connection), e.g., the minister of the parish or other local clergyman, a magistrate, a senior officer of the Army or Navy who has been well acquainted with the candidate in private life during the period.*

If the above-mentioned person cannot certify for the whole period of four years, a second certificate for the period not covered by the first should be signed by a similar person.

I hereby certify to the good moral character of *Clive Staples Lewis*

for the last *ten and a half years*.

Signature *W. T. Kirkpatrick*

†Rank, office or occupation *Tutor*

Date

Address *Gastons, Gt. Bookham, Surrey.*

To be filled in when the above certificate does not cover four years.

I hereby certify to the good moral character of *Clive Staples Lewis*

from *Sept. 1911* to *July 1913*

Signature *Arthur C. Allen*

†Rank, office or occupation *School master.*

Date *Apr. 21. 1917* Address *Cherbury, Gt. Malvern*

(iii.) *Evidence that the candidate has attained a standard of education suitable for commissioned rank. If the candidate has:—*

(a) obtained a leaving or qualifying certificate as required of a candidate for admission to the Royal Military College under the regulations in force up to 1st April, 1912, the Certificate should be attached;

(b) qualified at an Army Entrance Examination, the date of examination should be stated;

(c) passed the matriculation examination of a University, or a test accepted in lieu thereof, the Certificate should be attached.

Failing one of the above, the following certificate must be signed by the Headmaster of a secondary school or other competent educational authority.

I certify from personal knowledge that *Clive Staples Lewis* has attained a standard of education suitable for commissioned rank.

John C. V. Behan

(Dean of Univ. Coll. Oxford)

State here educational position, e.g., } Head of a College or School, etc. }

†Here state whether Tutor, Head of School or College, Minister of Parish or other local clergyman or Magistrate, &c.

Figure 1. Lewis's enlistment papers. The record of Lewis's enlistment with an Officer Cadet Unit includes signatures of C. S. Lewis, Albert Lewis, and W. T. Kirkpatrick. (The National Gallery (PRO) WO339/105408)

with his usual self depreciation he scouted the idea [of entering a machine gun unit]. He said that he had had the mechanism of a rifle explained to him a hundred times and that he knew nothing about it yet. Of course, I believe that is what he himself would

have described as "codotta." But the attitude he seems to have taken up towards the
war is this—in as much as he hates the whole business, but has to be in it, he will just
drift with the tide and make no effort to reach a safe—or comparatively safe—landing
place on either bank. (*LP* V.278)

The atmosphere at Oxford was something Lewis reveled in, even in
wartime. In describing his Oxford of the Training Corps, he writes dis-
paragingly of men arriving from other O.T.C. units but especially decries
those of the Flying Corps whom he views as men crassly celebrating the
moments before they perish (*CL* 299). However, his exuberance in letters
about Oxford's beauty and his hopes for the future are very clear, and he rec-
ognizes that the war-time changes to Oxford are but temporary. He writes to
Arthur that his friend must visit after the war because Oxford was a husk of its
real self, a husk with which Lewis is nonetheless elated (*CL* 304).

The university was quite changed from its peace-time appearance. The
numbers of students were depleted, and blue-coated wounded, who were
convalescent cases, were installed in his college's Hall (*CL* 295). That college,
University College, itself had only twelve students (*CL* 298); half the buildings were used as a hospital (*SBJ* 187). The military asserted a large presence
in Oxford beyond those young O.T.C. members inexperienced in war. Also in
Oxford were men of the ranks who had been at the Front and were now training to become officers themselves. Jack would write that given the unusual, un-
academic environment and his own preoccupations, this first experience with
Oxford was not productive (*SBJ* 187).

Jack had lived the three years before arriving at Oxford with only
Kirkpatrick, his wife, and one other boarder whom Kirk tutored and whom Jack
avoided. The amount of company he had in these early days at Oxford must
have presented an interesting change. He lamented that Arthur, who had a
weak heart and remained at home in Ireland, could not find a way to escape
that life (*CL* 299). But while Jack seemed veritably in heaven at Oxford, Jack
disliked an Oxford acquaintance at this time, one Edgell, whom Lewis found
intolerable for his apparently inordinate piety and for his incessant discussion
of close relatives killed in the war (*CL* 301). Although Edgell's irritating
reminders persisted as to what might await Jack in France, Lewis glows over
the university as an ideal: the size of the buildings, the paneling, the floors (*CL*
297).

He regrets that Arthur cannot share the beauty of its scenery, especially its
spires viewed at night, with him (*CL* 301). Oxford had become for Lewis the
center of an Ideal England he had begun to enjoy at Kirk's: the rural England
with a rich, literary tradition (*CL* 89). This ideal England would become for
many soldiers as they endured conditions at the Front a vision of a distant heav-

en. It would become no less than that for Lewis who would eventually write of it idyllically in his earliest poems.

However ideal the setting was, not his studies but his duties with the O.T.C. increasingly occupied his time. The O.T.C. men spent time in model trenches that had all the features of a "real" trenches including graves (*CL* 315). The graves were a feature Lewis found to be excessive and believed his commanding officer was perhaps touched.

Lieutenant Colonel J. Stanning (WO339/105408) may not have been as touched as the young men supposed, and the graves not as excessive as they seemed. Jack's sense of his C.O. comes only from his own and his comrades' inexperience. Constant reminders of death awaited them, and the presence of the artificial graves were a means by which, to apply Keegan's point discussed in the introduction, the men might learn to regard death with clinical detachment (Whose grave? Who knows?—it's just another like those we saw at Oxford . . .). Whether such training actually worked to diffuse the horrors of war for soldiers is another matter. In France often the dead went unburied for months. Indeed, bones of soldiers turn up in the soil of France today. While still at Kirk's, Jack had heard from the Smythe boy, who had lost his arm in France, that Indian troops were in the habit of not burying their dead (*CL* 101–102). While Lewis doubted this account, it is a fact that the dead were often left unburied; it was not from any ethnic custom but due to regular shelling of areas where bodies lay, something that also accounted for the disappearance of many of the corpses. One notorious example is at Thiepval: the monument erected there after the war lists the names of some 70,000 men whose bodies are scattered along the Somme. The areas near Verdun hold perhaps many thousands more whose bones are today discovered regularly by forestry workers and hikers and then are interred at an ossuary. It was common to lose corpses as battle ensued, and even if buried, corpses were often repeatedly ripped once more to the surface by shells and pulverized in the process. That April of 1917 when Lewis entered Oxford, the very ground around the French village of Monchy le Preux, to which Lewis would be sent, was itself being filled with the corpses of horses and men in fierce battles for the town. His commanding officer was but preparing the men for the realities that would meet them in France.

Jack very much enjoyed the month of May 1917 at University College despite the intrusions of officer training. By the end of the first week of June, however, his happiness at Oxford underwent revision. On 7 June he joined a cadet battalion, something the military could now require him to do. If Jack seemed to make less noise about his fate, Albert and Warren were more than irritated.

As Albert expressed in a letter to Warren on 12 June 1917, his consterna-
tion with the change came in part from Jack's having to move out of University
College but more from the little time his son had been able to study (a month)
while in the O.T.C. Further, Jack's presence in Oxford had cost Albert money.
As far as Albert could see, his son's college career had been ended by the military (*LP* V.222). Jack informed his father on 8 June that the cadet unit he was
attached to was moved into Keble College (*CL* 316). Warren, too, was out-
raged—less so about the situation at Keble than Jack being required to join a
battalion (*LP* Vol.V.223). Whereas the Conscription Act exempted the Irish
(and thus Jack), men in the O.T.C. were now considered subject to military
command, regardless of nationality, something Warren noted with chagrin (*CL*
315). While Jack might have, in peacetime, withdrawn from the O.T.C., he
now found himself firmly in the army. If so, Albert as well as Jack knew it was
best that he entered as a commissioned officer, not as a private.

His new room at Keble was undecorated and shared with a roommate,
something more akin to what one expected of the military. Between moving
and having now to wear a uniform, Jack felt put upon (*CL* 317). If the accom-
modations were less desirable than those he had at University College, at
Keble he met men who would remain in his memory for life. With one of them
he formed a pact, an agreement that would influence how he lived the rest of
his life. To his father he mentions that his main companion is one Somerville,
who was at King's College, Cambridge, a quiet man whose interests, like
Lewis's own involved books (*CL* 317). This was Martin Ashworth Somerville,
who had been at Eton College from September 1912 to Easter of 1917; his
father, Annesley Ashworth Somerville, was on staff at Eton College and later
became MP for Windsor (Hatfield). Martin would become a 2nd Lieutenant
in the 6th Battalion Rifle Brigade (attd. 1st/10th Bn.), London Regiment
(WO339/98419). At this time Jack seems to have been closer to Somerville
than to his roommate, Edward Francis Courtenay Moore, or "Paddy." While
he regards Somerville favorably (*CL* 319), his remarks are less positive toward
Moore, who is "a little too childish" he explains to Albert (*CL* 317). To
Arthur Jack writes, the same (*CL* 319). It may—or may not—be telling that
in Moore's military record is a statement by Paddy's aunt, Edith Askins, which
includes an incidental remark that even as Paddy prepared to leave for the Front,
he was in the habit of calling his mother "Muvvy" (WO339/97704). Yet Jack
would tell Warren years later that Mrs. Moore and her son did not get along
(Carpenter 8).

In addition to Paddy, the other men, all of whom would be commissioned
as 2nd lieutenants in their respective battalions, were Alexander Gordon
Sutton, 2nd Battalion Rifle Brigade, of Reading; Thomas Kerrison Davey, 6th

attd. 1st Battalion Rifle Brigade, of Wraxall Court, Somerset (CWG); and Denis Howard de Pass, 12th Battalion Rifle Brigade (*CL* 402). These six men, Lewis included, went frequently to the home of Paddy's mother, Janie K. Moore (*LP* VI.44–45). She had moved to Oxford to be near Paddy while he was still in England.

Within Lewis studies the friendships that Lewis held with these men have been variously interpreted. Some see them as being marked by a closeness with Paddy far above that which Lewis shared with the other five officers, even though Lewis's remarks indicate the opposite. George Sayer, for example, asserts that Lewis "revised his opinion of his roommate" and eventually believed better of Moore (126). Carpenter hits closer to the mark in writing that "Lewis did not particularly care for his room-mate" (7). From the timbre of Lewis's letters, I come to believe that Paddy held significantly less favor than did Somerville. Yet Somerville was to serve in Palestine, and Lewis lost touch with him. Moore was sent into the 2nd Rifle Battalion. Both men were out of reach for close friendship. When Jack later joined a battalion, he instead became very close friends with yet another officer, Laurence Bertrand Johnson. Before going to France and still training at Crown Hill by Plymouth, Lewis writes to Arthur that talks with Johnson had brought about a change: Lewis increasingly philosophized (*CL* 341). Johnson, who had lived in Hampstead, was in the junior O.T.C. at the City of London School, then in the Inns of Court O.T.C. before taking a commission in the Somerset Light Infantry (WO339/83704). He entered Oxford as a scholar at Queens College. It is Johnson, not Paddy Moore or Somerville, who became Lewis's chief male friend in the war.

Another very intense friendship begins at this time, and it was one more significant to Lewis than was his relationship with Johnson. Jack's relationship with Mrs. Moore quickly became very close. As Warren recorded of Jack's preference for Mrs. Moore, "My father's pocket-book contains a wry note of this order of priorities: the situation did not reach full development until much later, but its character may have been apparent already" (8).

Having met her one or two times in June (*CL* 322), and having stayed a week with the Moores in August (*CL* 334), by September when Albert asks to borrow a book from Jack, he is told it will be sent later: Mrs. Moore was reading it (*CL* 335). This is the first of many such moments where Albert discovers himself somehow second to Mrs. Moore in relations to Jack. And her influence is, after the war, significantly weightier than is Jack's memory of Paddy. Her importance is seen in Jack's pet names for Janie, or Mrs. Moore— "D." and the inexplicable "Minot"—as well as in his recalling their moments together. In 1922, after returning to Oxford and attending a meeting of the

Martlets (a literary group to which he belonged) the place they met, he found was the room he first had upon arriving at Oxford: "D [Mrs. Moore] had been in this room" (*AMR* 125). Not Paddy, his old friend killed in the war, but Mrs. Moore. When he arrived in France, Jack wrote to Arthur (who was also corresponding with Mrs. Moore, Jack being the catalyst of his communication with Mrs. Moore) that he relished the idea that his two favorite people were mutual communicants. At Jack's request, Arthur was never to inform Albert that he had received correspondence from either Mrs. Moore or from Jack (*CL* 348). Warren, years later, recalled of this time that as "Jack started to display a marked preference for Mrs. Moore's company," it was immediately upon Jack's return to Oxford after the war that things "developed more strongly" (12). More pointedly, at the time Jack was training at Crown Hill, Jack writes to Arthur that

> Since coming back & meeting a certain person I have begun to realize that it was not at all the right thing for me to tell you so much as I did. . . . try & forget my various statements & not to refer to the subject . . . I still have no business to go discussing those sort of things with you. (*CL* 339)

The "certain person" is undoubtedly Mrs. Moore, as an editorial note in Lewis's *Collected Letters* agrees (*CL* 339, n.132). This letter was written to Arthur only after Jack had informed his father that a persistent cold continued and "Mrs. Moore took my temperature and put me to bed, where I am writing this letter" (*CL* 337). Most likely Arthur destroyed the letter which communicated the "taboo" elements Lewis becomes chary of discussing, even as Arthur later expunged various other letters from Lewis in which he discussed each other's sexual preferences, masturbation, and flagellation.[1] That single letter would likely have settled forever any remaining question on the nature of the relationship. As many Lewis scholars have pointed out, Jack's loss of his mother early in his life is a central factor in his relationship with Mrs. Moore. I would say reciprocally this is so—that mother/son relationship became an important aspect for Janie also after Paddy was killed. Yet beyond that relationship, Mrs. Moore was quite obviously dazzled by Jack. She writes to Albert, "Your boy of course, being Paddy's room mate, we knew much better than the others, and he was quite the most popular boy of the party; he is very charming and most likeable and won golden opinions from everyone he met here" (qtd. in Wilson 53). "But from no one more than from Janie Moore herself," as A. N. Wilson observes (53). Carpenter does make a slim correlation between Mrs. Moore and romance in discussing a young Belgian girl, a refugee in England, but "before any real romance could begin [Lewis] met Mrs. Moore" (7). While Carpenter later remarks on their deportment as "mother and son"

(8), a sexual interest seems a radical element from the early days of their relationship, and this aspect would be, I believe, compounded by the physical and
psychological effects of the war upon Jack as well as upon Mrs. Moore.

The fulcrum of the earliest relationship is a mutual promise between Lewis
and Paddy, overheard by Paddy's sister, Maureen—that should either boy die
in the war, he who survived would care for the other's parent (CL 337). It was
that pact to which Warren refers in explaining the relationship: "He may have
felt also some sense of responsibility, a duty perhaps of keeping some war-time
promise made to Paddy Moore. Be that as it may, Jack now embarked upon a
relationship with Mrs. Moore which was almost that of son and mother" (12).

Outwardly, indeed, they are mother and son. Yet, as has been pointed out
by other scholars, it is difficult to imagine the independent Albert allowing
Paddy to care for him should Jack have been killed—even without the fact that
Albert would have had Warren. As Carpenter further observes of a remark made
by Jack years later—that Paddy and his mother seemed not to get along well—
"probably Jack would have looked after her whether Paddy had come back or
not" (8).

Before leaving for France, Jack's time at Keble was marked by other events
that are perhaps common among men newly entering college, and perhaps also
common among men who knowingly may be headed for death. In the same
letter to Arthur Greeves in which he describes his room at Keble, Paddy
Moore, and other friends, Lewis also relates that in visiting a student's rooms
at Exeter College, he became intensely drunk, during which time he made his
way around the room offering money in exchange for the opportunity to whip
them; what he laments is that he has revealed something to these men that
Lewis had only revealed to Arthur (CL 319). The group of men caused a dis-
turbance sufficient for the Dean of the college to send notice that the student-
host's guests must depart. Lewis came to in his own room, but how he got
there he did not recall (CL 319). An editorial note to this letter indicates that
the student-host, Madhavji Gokuldas, was a member of Brasenose College, not
Exeter (CL 319 n. 102). The next morning another partygoer, one Butler,
probed Lewis's confused memories of the previous evening, especially of Jack's
interest in inflicting pain and pursued him on the subject (CL 320). The long
conversation which ensued showed Lewis that his interest had a name, and in
further exploring the fetish, the two young men looked into a French source
to examine a biographical listing for Vicomte de Sade. At the mention of this
book to Greeves, Lewis went on to discuss as usual his current reading, among
which were volumes by Spenser, Johnson, and a 300-year-old book written by
a magician—somewhat unreadable because it was moth-eaten. Lewis enjoyed
simply holding it because of its age (CL 320).

Lewis's military training continued through the next four months and involved much of what Warren had experienced years before Jack encountered the same drills. Jack describes becoming fit exercising in the hot weather (*CL* 322) and in a training excursion into the Wytham Hills in September, during which it rained and made their training ground and trenches a morass of mud (*CL* 335). Their trenches were not the only such works in England. Some "famous" trenches were dug in Kensington Gardens that were created

> for the edification of the home front. These were clean, dry, and well furnished, with straight sides and sandbags neatly aligned. R. E. Vernède writes his wife from the real trenches that a friend of his has just returned from viewing the set of ideal ones. He "found he had never seen anything at all like it before." And Wilfred Owen calls the Kensington Gardens trenches "the laughing stock of the army." (Fussell 43)

A very different reality awaited Lewis in France, but his training would have followed the War Office's syllabus for military preparedness.

Many training manuals were published during the war which would have been based on the War Office's syllabus. That which I have used is by a Captain B. C. Lake. Appearing in 1916, this manual gives a strong sense of not only the military exercises, strategies, and weapons that Lewis would have been presented with in his training but also the military paradigm implicit at the time; it contains both standard instruction and patriotic poems from Rudyard Kipling and Rupert Brooke. It also includes advertisements for military gear that men could purchase before going to the front, among which are boots and uniform items.

What was Lewis's training? He was to become an officer not only able to lead men into battle but also to govern their lives and duties in the trenches, in reserve, on relief, and in working parties. Officers were to lead men by example and teach everything in the soldiering profession to new recruits entering the trenches as replacements for those killed. This included anything from caring for and using a rifle, digging trenches, and caring for one's feet, to estimating distances for firing accurately at the enemy. An officer must be able to move a company of men "with the shortest delay in any given direction in any formation that is required" (Lake 7), hence the continuous drilling when out of the line. At night in the trenches, an officer walked up and down the trenches to make certain of many things, including that his men were at their posts and not sleeping (a serious offense), that their equipment was well cared for, and that none had disappeared in a raid.

Central areas of training for an officer were these: discipline, drill, musketry, tactics and field warfare, topography, trench warfare, billeting, machine guns, interior economy and military law, physical drill, and signaling (Lake 1–5). Yet when one compares the manual to the events described in numerous diaries and letters from soldiers, one gathers that to go strictly "by the book" did not prepare soldiers for realities of the Front. Descriptions and diagrams of how to build trenches, the placement of latrines and their proper drainage are, of course, ideal, and in the mud of Flanders and the Somme the idea of creating something near the textbook's model must have been a bitterly laughable notion to enlisted men and officers alike.

Lewis's own lack of suitability as an officer would have been compounded when he was placed in the conditions at the Front. A few points will help to illustrate the disparity. Whereas an officer must be able to teach his men the proper care for and use of their rifles, Lewis, as previously related, wrote to his father that he could not understand the use of his weapon (*LP* V.278).

As a lieutenant, Lewis would not have carried a rifle; however, in one battalion diary is an account of an officer who fired some 200 rounds with a rifle while alongside his men during an attack. Lewis would have carried a military-issue pistol, likely one or another model of a Webley or a Colt revolver, but other officers chose to purchase pistols privately—or acquire one from a wounded officer. Siegfried Sassoon privately purchased his pistol, an "Old Model," 1900 Browning, in London in 1916 and had it engraved with his name. It was to replace the Colt revolver he had been issued and which he felt was a distinct danger to himself; it was largely ineffectual and "clumsy" (Bownes). Yet, as the manual explains, an officer must "know and be able to explain to a platoon" every element of using the rifle, including judging distances, and "must pass a severe test in" the "control and direction of fire" and "the instruction of a recruit" (Lake 1–2).

In terms of trench warfare, an officer "must have a knowledge of" everything from the use "of commonest bombs and explosives" (including leading a grenade party) to directing "a working party," and "loopholing and revetting" (that is, the placement in a trench of protective steel plates having a hole through which a rifle is fired and the repair of trenches) (Lake 2–3). These are things which Lewis refers to in his letters and are duties that his battalion diary indicates he was performing while in France. Yet the brevity of his training and indications in his autobiography convey a sense that Lewis can hardly have been very proficient in these life-and-death operations. Lewis, deficient in both mechanical prowess and mathematical ability, would have been at odds to become a fit officer in the months he was trained. Some of his training he found decidedly lax in points. He describes leading men under his command to a parade area, handing them over to an instructor, and then going walking for some hours. His concern is not about the lack of training; it is that his intellect will suffer (*CL* 338). These events occurred at Crown Hill, near Plymouth in Devon.

Later in his war experience, Lewis would also miss a month of training that the rest of his battalion was to receive. Beyond the accumulated lapses in training, Jack's physical abilities and manual dexterity created difficulties: he wrote that as a child he suffered from a lack of dexterity, which he said arose from having only one joint in his thumbs, a condition he shared with his father and brother. While it allowed him to use pens, pencils, and paintbrushes without undue effort, he was unable to use a weapon, sporting equipment, or other such tools (*SBJ* 12).

If he was competent as an officer, he was only mildly so and was undoubtedly not at all an uncommon officer in that case; certainly he would not be the worst officer whom his men would meet.

Perhaps it was because Albert understood these matters that he continued to nurse hopes that Jack would transfer into a different battalion—specifically, into an artillery battalion. Albert supposed that, with their men well behind the front lines, artillery units were safer than units posted right in the front lines. Certainly men in the front line encountered heavier and more regular shelling than did those behind, but the concept can be deceptive. Walter Hooper remarks that "Artillery was the great killer of the First World War; it is thought that artillery fire caused up to 70 per cent of battlefield deaths. But whereas the infantry were in close contact with the enemy, the artillery were firing from some distance behind them, and their position was perhaps somewhat safer" (*CL* 322n). Throughout the war, the "great killer" was the machine gun, accounting for 33.49% of casualties, most of whom would have been in the front lines or in the midst of an attack. One has only to read the accounts of the Somme (in, for instance, Martin Middlebrook's *The First Day of the Somme*) to grasp this weapon's ominous presence in the war. Next, gas caused 31.49% of the overall casualties; once developed, it could be fired via shells well behind the lines. Artillery (fragments—shells containing high explosive which causes the steel casing to explode into splinters) caused 8.94% of casualties. Shells (shrapnel—shells usually containing lead, but sometimes steel, balls which by a delayed fuse burst downwards from the shell canister yards above the ground) accounted for 15.08% of casualties. Aircraft that spotted artillery below dropped bombs on enemy artillery emplacements and, through wireless communication, directed their ground artillery to fire on them.

Great War veteran and Oxford scholar C. M. Bowra told of a related experience. Behind the lines one morning, he decided to skip breakfast although he was passing through the mess tent and took only coffee with him. When he was some yards away, an enemy shell hit the mess tent, killing everyone inside (Bowra 75). Warren remarked, in a letter of 8 June—the very day Jack wrote to his father that he had joined a cadet battalion—how his unit, while seldom nearing the front lines was itself hit by 5.9-inch shells (*LP* V.219). Despite the obvious danger, Albert continued to believe that Jack would be safer in an artillery unit. While in France Warren kept abreast of Jack's doings and, despite his own experiences with German artillery, advised his father on 20 June 1917 to get Jack into an artillery battalion—believing that massive barrages were no longer used (*LP* V.225). He later reversed this advice, hearing from others that an artillery unit was not safer than an infantry unit (*LP* V.246). Just as the men vacillated over Jack's means of entering the service, they were indecisive over just what sort of battalion he serve with. But as far as Jack was concerned, the matter was closed once he was in officer training (*CL* 291).

Even so, to his father's increasing annoyance and anxiety, Jack refused to seek the safest means of service. He understood clearly and explained to his father that his lack of abilities in mathematics would not, for instance, get him into an artillery unit (*CL* 322). Once in France, he offered another argument for staying in the infantry: if, he reasoned in effect, it was true that men in the artillery had fewer casualties, perhaps that was because there were fewer men standing at cannons than those who stood in the trenches (*CL* 347). The infantry could not, then, be any more dangerous. To the infantry he would go.

NOTE

1. Walter Hooper had most of these passages restored. See *Collected Letters*, x. George Sayer agrees concerning Lewis's letters about Mrs. Moore, that they "were certainly destroyed by either Jack or Arthur" but merely remarks that Jack "must have discussed his love or infatuation for her with Arthur in Belfast" (128).

WORKS CITED

Baker, Chris. "A Tommies Recruitment in 1914–1918." *The British Army in the Great War*. available<http://www.1914–1918.net/recruitment.htm> 6 August 2001.

Bownes, David M. "Sassoon's Pistol." *The Royal Welsh Fusiliers Museum*. 11 July 2002. http://www.rwfmuseum.org.uk/nb.html#SASSOON'S PISTOL. 1 August 2002.

Bowra, C. M. *Memories 1898–1939*. Cambridge, MA: Harvard UP, 1967.

Carpenter, Humphrey. *The Inklings*. New York: Ballantine, 1981.

Cornish, Paul. Telephone interview. London: Imperial War Museum, 23 May 2002.

Fussell, Paul. *The Great War and Modern Memory*. Oxford: Oxford UP, 1975.

Hatfield, Penelope. Letter to author. 6 June 2002.

Hogg, Ian V. *Dictionary of World War I*. Lincolnwood, IL: NTC, 1997.

Lake, B. C. *Knowledge for War: Every Officer's Handbook for the Front*. London: Harrison, n.d.

Lewis, C. S. *The Pilgrim's Regress*. Grand Rapids: Eerdmans, 1979.

Lewis, W. H. Memoir. *C. S. Lewis Letters*. New York: Harcourt, 1966.

Sayer, George. *Jack: A Life of C. S. Lewis*. Wheaton: Crossway, 1994.

Wilson, A. N. *C. S. Lewis: A Biography*. New York: Norton, 1990.

Winter, Denis. *Death's Men: Soldiers of the Great War*. London: Penguin, 1979.

CHAPTER 4

Preparing a Defense

THE FACE OF THE WESTERN WORLD HAD changed distinctly by the time Lewis formally entered his training. We may return to *Mr. Britling*:

> This war is pounding through Europe, smashing up homes, dispersing and mixing homes [. . .] it is killing young men by the million, altering the proportions of the sexes for a generation, bringing women into business and office and industry, destroying the accumulated wealth that kept so many of them in refined idleness, flooding the world with strange doubts and novel ideas. . . . (257)

For Wells's Britling, the changes were inevitably brought home as his son, Hugh, prepared for war. Their conversation undoubtedly reflects thousands of conversations throughout Britain during the war years and likely bears close relation to conversations between Jack and Albert—indeed this passage from Britling seems close to Lewis's own mental debate as he made his decision to go to war:

> "I *don't* want to go," said Hugh with his hands deep in his pockets. "I want to go and work with Cardinal [at his studies]. But this job has to be done by everyone. Haven't you been saying as much all day?. .. It's like turning out to chase a burglar or suppress a mad dog. It's like necessary sanitation. . . ."
> "You aren't attracted by soldiering?"
> "Not a bit. I won't pretend it, Daddy. I think the whole business is a bore [. . . .] I expect my share will be just drilling and fatigue duties and route marches, and loafing here in England. . . ."

> You can't possibly go out for two years," said Mr. Britling, as if he regretted it. A slight
> hesitation appeared in Hugh's eyes. "I suppose not," he said.
> "Things ought to be over by then—anyhow," Mr. Britling added, betraying his real feel-
> ings. (Wells 245)

Hugh was "still trying to read a little chemistry and crystallography," his areas
of study, "but it didn't 'go with [military] life'" (Wells 246). Jack's dilemma
as a would-be scholar was not only how to finish his education but how to cope
with the war's intrusion into both his academic pursuits and, more significantly, into the tranquility of his world. Like Mr. Britling's son Hugh, Lewis finds
a disparity between his two lives as soldier and budding scholar:

> Accordingly I put the war on one side to a degree which some people will think
> shameful and some incredible. Others will call it a flight from reality. I maintain that
> it was rather a treaty with reality, the fixing of a frontier. I said to my country in effect,
> "you shall have me on a certain date, not before. I will die in your wars if need be, but
> till then I shall live my own life. You may have my body but not my mind. I will take
> part in battles but not read about them." (*SBJ* 158)

Yet the issue is not as merely academic as Lewis intended to convey. The
phrase "but not read about them" is telling. Reading causes one to think, and
to think beyond what one reads. If his was a "treaty" with reality, then much
ground is allowed the war, with Lewis's position being no less a retreat, mentally, into a secure citadel. From before the time his mother died, Lewis had
written, drawn, and lived within his reading and thinking about imaginary
worlds. Warnie and Jack's co-creation of Animal Land and Boxen comprised
the making of worlds set apart from the realities that home meant for the two
boys. Lewis said that these romantic (in the old sense) tales remained quite separate from his present world; they remained gothic tales essentially (Gilbert and
Kilby 98–99). While some of these creations preceded the time of his mother's death, they also continued through that time of trouble. Lewis emphasized
that their essential nature was distinct from simple wish-fulfillment (*SBJ* 15).
They were deeper and—interesting to note in relation to his faulty recollections
of the horrors of his school days—involved what Tennyson called "the passion
of the past" which was contingent upon memory, but for Lewis also involved
that distinct sense of inconsolable longing he defined as "Joy" (*SBJ* 16–18).
The point is this: the creation of a distinct and articulated mental separation
from reality, the creation of a realm of ordered tranquility, was a method
Lewis used in contending with trauma. He used this means of coping during
the time of his mother's death, and he continued to use it as war approached.
In remembering the traumatic events of his war service when he had moved
years beyond them, he also used this same means of coping with those dark realities. Lewis justified his treaty with the war thus:

> If this attitude needs excusing I must say that a boy who is unhappy at school inevitably learns the habit of keeping the future in its place; if once he began to allow infiltrations from the coming term into the present holidays he would despair. [. . .] No doubt, even if the attitude was right, the quality in me which made it so easy to adopt is somewhat repellent. (*SBJ* 159)

Significantly, this passage springs from discussion of his unhappiness at schools, something not only replayed at length in Lewis's autobiography, but which is also rehearsed in his writing of *The Magician's Nephew* decades after the war. One scene in particular recalls both his unhappy school days as well as his mother's slow movement towards death: the protagonist, Digory, stuck at a horrible school, is found hidden away and crying because his mother is in the midst of dying (3).

What was the "quality" in Jack that allowed him to make his treaty with the realities of school, of his mother's death, of war? It is precisely the quality that Kirkpatrick observed in young Jack, as previously related, whose "interests lie in a totally different direction—in the past, in the realm of creative imagination, in the world which the common mind would call unreal but which is to him the only real one" (qtd. in *SIB* xxii). In consequence, Kirkpatrick wrote to Albert a letter noting the radical nature of this propensity in Jack, that Jack would do well enough as an author or in the university, but the boy seemed unsuitable for anything else in life (*SBJ* 183).

For Lewis, then, surviving the war—not only physically but mentally and emotionally—would mean removing himself from realities as the war increasingly began to assert itself ever more personally. And war did assert itself from numerous angles of attack. For example, after he had taken his exams to enter Oxford, he returned home believing the exams were a failure and expecting compassion from his father—compassion for a young man headed to war and from which he might well never return (*SBJ* 186). He was staring at what he believed was not only the death of his dreams but death itself. By this time Jack had pondered the prospect of his own death increasingly as he roomed with men who lost relatives in the war, saw the wounded at Oxford, talked with his brother at home on leave. It will be recalled that in July of 1915, well before his entering O.T.C. but when the war had run on nearly one year, Lewis wrote in his diary that he experienced nightmares concerning the war. The day which led up to the nightmares involved conversations on the war, plus Warnie, in France, had written him, saying little but that there was little enjoyment or what we call creature comforts in serving (*CL* 136–137). Jack may also have heard something about soldier's wounds from Gundreda Ewart, a Lewis relative who worked as a VAD, a nurse, in France and who had arrived home on leave (*CL* 310 N. 86).

Set against these realities was Lewis's mental world. It was a world very much like that he would find in reading George Eliot's novels. It was not a world without pain, not without turmoil, but the idyllic, rural England—the England of a long literary and romantic tradition—with which he increasingly identified himself. It is a world, as Fussell puts it, that was "static"—"where the values appeared stable and where the meanings of abstractions seemed permanent and reliable" (21). If the war shattered that world's assumptions, Lewis would encounter the same shattering of his assumptions, those which Britling experienced as the war became a glaring reality. Not least, war came home to Britling in the form of a telegram announcing the death of a son. Lewis, like many other soldiers, would cling to the notion that an Ideal England existed someplace. Lewis's England remained within the literature he read and existed (as did love at one point in his youth, as he had expressed to Arthur) solely within his intellect, which he took as firm reality. It is not an altogether unknown reaction: Siegfried Sassoon's world was divided between that of the rural England of a "fox-hunting man" and the war, whose literature presented a polarity, a "pointed juxtaposition," as Fussell termed it (92), that served to accent the change war brought with it. Lewis wished to remain in the secure world that was, in reality, being demolished both in its physical manifestations and assumptions. It did not exist but in his literature.

It is precisely because Jack's emotional survival was inextricably linked to his intellectual life that he feared sliding into a softer mindset, as Roland Leighton, Vera Brittain's fiancé, similarly feared:

> Hitherto I have been chiefly occupied in putting the men through section and company drill and attending lectures on Field Engineering—digging trenches etc. On the whole I like the life immensely. To be continuously busy in this way is a great joy—especially when the busy-ness is of immediate utility. The only thing I fear is that chameleon-like I may be taking on the commonplaceness of my restricted military surroundings. (Bishop and Bostridge 34)

To Arthur Lewis wrote that he feared the same: becoming an unthinking creature in the midst of all the military duties. He asks Arthur to continue writing to him about their shared intellectual interests (*CL* 320–21). At a deeper level the request is a plea for help in keeping the war at bay emotionally, not merely intellectually. Interestingly, Jack also indirectly expressed a supposition about those who settle into a belief in God: that theology was no help in keeping a sharp and interesting mind, which philosophy or metaphysics would accomplish (*CL* 342). At this point in Lewis's thinking, religion provides no help in keeping a treaty with reality. As I previously mentioned, Hemingway's character Brett said in *The Sun Also Rises* said of the characters' shared, post-war paradigm, "it's what we have instead of God" (245). At this time, Lewis had not God; he had an ideal world with its collective assumptions, a world found in literature.

Lewis's treaty with reality, then, has two purposes. First, it was to protect his intellectual citadel, which included his romantic and literary vision of the world. Second, by sustaining that citadel, he could indirectly sustain his emotional self. By these means, as he had done when a child facing the trauma of his mother's death, he could also protect himself from the trauma of war. To lose the first was to lose the second, and thence to be subsumed with realities that might overwhelm the mind and emotions. And, as he could not help but contemplate, his fears of keeping his intellect and emotional selves alive were inextricably mixed with fears of keeping his physical self alive; that a fear increased as the realities of death asserted themselves in France.

Stationed at Keble, but during a weekend stay at the now-empty University College, Lewis went exploring the empty rooms and came across a set, unlocked, of Arthur Norwood Carpenter, a scholar from Canada who was sent to France as a lieutenant (*CL* 324 n111). Lewis explored Carpenter's room, the photos, the furniture, and in describing the scene to Greeves he writes that items were still sitting as the occupant had left them, and Lewis wondered who the owner was and if he were still living (*CL* 111).

In practical terms, Lewis outlined the obvious possibilities: that he had just so many weeks, then he would join a unit. He planned to gather some poetry he had been writing and publish it; then, should he die in the war, he would at least have had his 30 seconds of fame (*CL* 321). In these calculations undoubtedly Lewis was thinking of Rupert Brooke, dead by 1915, whose poetry swept the country and moved many young men of England to enlist.

Lewis's talk at this time of modern poetry is also a telling feature of his intellectual citadel and his treaty with reality. Still in training, Jack wrote to Arthur about conversations on poetry he listened to, some involving Rupert Brooke, but that he had no sea legs when it came to verse and poets of that day, concluding that "I suppose our steady nibbling at older works is a safe-guard against 'crazes'" (*CL* 342).

"Safe-guard" is the appropriate term, for Lewis's mental citadel was threatened also by Modernism's seeming instability, and his opposition to anything modern was to become deep seated and life long. As late as 1954, in his address *De Descriptione Temporum*, he continued to attack Modernist paradigms. But in 1917, as Lewis headed to France, T. S. Eliot's "The Love Song of J. Alfred Prufrock" appeared, a poem which Lewis would demean by parody. Lewis wrote that he had attempted over decades to comprehend Eliot's line which cast the sky "Like a patient etherized upon a table" (Eliot 3): The result: "I simply wasn't able" (*Poems* 1). His steady nibbling at older works, was, indeed, his tie to a stable, certain world. The Modern world was in contrast increasingly angular, disjointed—lamenting, but occasionally celebrating when not merely describing, the world's uncertainty and human disconnection. The Modernist ways of viewing reality were new and disturbing, as were the paintings of Duchamp, the music of Stravinsky, the poetry of Eliot, the fictions of Joyce. As Samuel Hynes has expressed it, people generally

> had believed, or had *wanted* to believe, that English society was fundamentally stable, and that it was evolving in a progressive direction [. . . .] And now suddenly war had come and had brought that dream of order to an end. It came not simply as an interruption of peace, but as a contradiction of the values that they had thought made Europe one civilization. (4)

Even before the war, Modernism's unsettling nature was becoming quite clear to many. Such works as Stravinsky's *The Rite of Spring* (1913) and Duchamp's "Nude Descending a Staircase (No. 2)" (1912) are two works that called into question the perceived stability. Lewis himself would later write in *Pilgrim's Regress* of Modernism as a giant, whose eye-beams were like X-rays, allowing everyone to see the innards of everything his visions passed upon. The guard of the Modern prison, the giant represented the Modern, scientific paradigm, which for the novel's protagonist, John, produced only horrors, not least as he saw the internal illnesses of another prisoner and his own internal organs at work (60–61).

In this work, which appeared in 1933 after Lewis's conversion to Christianity, it was not only Modernism in its clinically detached, naturalistic world that he described—a world Lewis would see as devoid of higher values that lie beneath purely physical phenomena. He was also describing things he saw in France. It is a critical point. That the war is tied in Lewis's mind directly to the Modern reveals that his reaction against Modernism was decidedly more than, as Humphrey Carpenter called it, a "profound dislike" (51). Rather, his reaction to Modernism had far more to do with his fears and with his means of self-preservation which I have described than it had to do with matters of taste. Yet Carpenter noted that the sections of *Pilgrim's Regress* in which Lewis revisits his childhood "combined with the attack on contemporary ideas" and "did not escape the notice of the critics," one of whom Carpenter quotes as saying, "it is the romanticism of homesickness for the past, not of adventure towards the future, a 'Regress' as he candidly avows" (53).

The war Lewis was about to enter would, however, present to his imagination all of the phenomena with their inherent ironies that Modernism held high above the old, secure world. The modern world was increasingly represented by its weaponry: machined, breach-loading cannons (set anachronistically upon wooden wagon wheels) hurling shells amazing distances with unprecedented accuracy. Larger cannon of this war sat upon rail cars, fired 1800 lb. shells from behind the German lines 10,250 yards, into Liège, Belgium, and later the "Kaiser Wilhelm Geschutz" long-range gun fired shells of 264 lbs. up to 131 miles into Paris (Hogg 113). Beyond the amazing phenomenon of the machine gun was the development of gas as a weapon and the "ineffective" phenol helmets intended to protect against it (Hogg 135, no.3). Finally able to escape the earth and to fly, humans could use aircraft to kill one another. Modris Eksteins (photo opposite 222 in Eksteins) has termed it a "Cubist war"; such a world and its requisite war did not make sense; it obliterated the stable, the comfortable, the known, the certain. Science was at its height in both development and proliferation. But it is Modern science in its increasing separation from higher values that Lewis comes to regard with chagrin.

Wesley Kort has much to say on Lewis's reactions against Modernism as well as his significance to postmodernism, much of which relates to the war. Such issues will be discussed in their place, after Lewis's war experiences have been examined, but as Kort says, the "disenchantment of the world, while it takes it sharpest turn between the wars, stems from assumptions of habits of mind characteristic of modern rationality" (35). The assumptions and habits of mind central to 2nd Lieutenant Lewis rather set him *against* Modernism. His habits of mind, his collective assumptions, are decidedly of the old, secure world that was steadily being dismembered by a modern war. Central to Kort's thesis is Lewis's ability to speak to the modern world. This is certain, yet Lewis is interested in moving individuals in the world away from those "habits of mind and characteristics of modern rationality" towards what he felt was a more ordered existence, towards what he perceived were more stable assumptions about life and the world. It was this new, modern war he was entering that would compound in Lewis his sense of how disenchanting the modern world would become. It was a war that would shatter the assumptions he had built about the world, which he had built carefully from his childhood through his reading and early literary creations.

WORKS CITED

Bishop, Alan, and Mark Bostridge, eds. *Letters from a Lost Generation: First World War Letters of Vera Brittain and Four Friends.* London: Abacus, 1999.

Carpenter, Humphrey. *The Inklings.* New York: Ballantine, 1978.

Eksteins, Modris. *Rites of Spring: The Great War and the Birth of the Modern Age.* New York: Anchor, 1989.

Eliot, T. S. *The Waste Land and Other Poems*. New York: Harcourt, 1962.

Gilbert, Douglas, and Klyde S. Kilby. *C. S. Lewis: Images of His World*. Grand Rapids: Eerdmans, 1973.

Hemingway, Ernest. *The Sun Also Rises*. New York: Scribner's, 1970.

Hogg, Ian V. *Dictionary of World War I*. Lincolnwood, IL: NTC, 1997.

Hynes, Samuel. *A War Imagined: The First World War and English Culture*. New York: Collier, 1990.

Kort, Wesley A. *C. S. Lewis Then and Now*. New York: Oxford UP, 2001.

Lewis, C. S. *The Abolition of Man*. New York: Collier, 1986.

———. *The Pilgrim's Regress*. Grand Rapids: Eerdmans 1979.

———. "A Confession." *Poems*. New York: Harcourt, 1964.

Wells, H. G. *Mr. Britling Sees It Through*. London: Hogarth, 1985.

CHAPTER 5

Friendship and the Front

ALTHOUGH LEWIS'S MILITARY TRAINING WAS DISTINCTLY LESS than what it should have been for an officer who would lead men into battle, the expectations set upon young officers were not reduced by the War Office nor by the unparalleled conditions at the Front. Hastily trained, officers were set in deplorable situations and yet required to keep the men under their command firm in matters of military regimen, use of arms, and tactics. But more: they had to show new arrivals how to survive, something those never before in the trenches would not have discovered in training manuals. The situations in the trenches placed immense pressure upon officers and soldiers alike. Lewis had been in O.T.C. but seven months, from April to October 1917, when he joined his battalion. He would leave for France in November, with periods of leave in between.

Upon receiving his commission, Lewis received four-weeks' leave before he joined his regiment (*CL* 321). Before this longer leave was awarded, he had already been able to pay a four-and-one-half-day visit home in August (*CL* 329). The travel time involved left him a visit with his father that lasted only from Thursday to Saturday (*CL* 334). When the later, month-long leave was given, Jack spent three weeks of it not at home with his father but with the Moores (*CL* 335). Jack left on Saturday 29 September with Paddy Moore and remained at the Moores' home in Bristol until 12 October. Albert was in the meantime anxiously awaiting his son's arrival. In the end, Jack finished the month's leave with but a very short visit home (*CL* 336). He had put off his father saying he would remain with Paddy and would sometime send notice when he would arrive in Ireland (*CL* 336); when he did so, it was not until 3 October (*CL* 337). He gives reasons for the delay, among which was a cold that

> went on so merrily that Mrs Moore took my temperature and put me to bed, where I am writing this letter (Wednesday). (*CL* 337)

He eventually visited his father from Friday 12 October until Thursday 18 October, when he left to join his battalion at Crownhill, South Devon (*CL* 3380). It became clear through such events that Lewis not only preferred the company of Janie Moore to his father's, as Warren later noted in his memoir (12), but Jack was becoming increasingly estranged from Albert. The nature of the relationship remained opaque even to Warren, and in the years after the war, when Lewis returned to Oxford to set up house with Mrs. Moore, affairs would be kept, as Warren remarked, "concealed from my father of course, which widened the rift between him and Jack" (12). When once Warren asked his brother about it, Jack told his brother sharply to mind his own business (Carpenter 11), an unusual response. At the time of his training, however, the relationship with Mrs. Moore would intensify independently from whatever friendship Jack had with Paddy Moore.

The company Lewis found in his military unit was not as bad as he perhaps expected, albeit he had more talk upon mundane topics than he enjoyed. He thought a couple of the men might do, but they shared little in common with Jack. His main concern remained the lack of intellectual stimulation (*CL* 338).

One important relationship began during this time that was to influence Lewis's memory of the war both positively and negatively. The intellectual importance of the Laurence Johnson friendship we may note through two accounts. It was that relationship he discussed in a letter to Greeves, already mentioned, which explained the influence Johnson was having upon him, specifically their philosophical discussions (*CL* 341–342). The importance of the relationship remains in the memorial to the man that Lewis's autobiography contains; there Lewis describes Johnson's intellectual prowess that was mixed with the enthusiasms of the young men for poetry. The two men argued over Johnson's tastes for Theism when the two were not in the trenches (SBJ 191–192).

Given the philosophical grounding of his relationship with Johnson, above the ruthless wielding of logic that Jack shared with Kirk (and which Johnson was also known for), it is not surprising that after the war Lewis took his initial degree in philosophy, not in the literary pursuits in which he matured as a scholar. It also says something of the importance for Lewis of establishing the *right* assumptions in everything—a central a theme in *Surprised by Joy* as in his letters both during the war and after. Such is what he and Johnson argued: what were the *right* assumptions to hold about life? He began to look to Johnson for direction in shaping those assumptions, which says much about the high regard Lewis had for him as does the tribute Lewis wrote to him in his autobiography.

Laurence Bertrand Johnson was a fellow 2nd lieutenant and a scholar elect of Queen's College, Oxford (CWGC). Commissioned on 15 April 1917 (*CL* 341), he would die a year later to the day standing beside Lewis in battle.

In all, Lewis felt himself fortunate in his companions, as he wrote to his father. He enjoyed the company of the men in his unit, a mix of working-class with a greater number of upper-class men. Paddy Moore, who was sent to a different unit, the Second Rifle Battalion, found that men in his unit were not such enjoyable company and the work he faced was apparently more difficult (*CL* 344).

At one point before being posted to France, it appeared that Lewis would instead be sent to Ireland to keep the Irish in line should the rumors of the Germans supplying them with aid prove true. Lewis hoped then for a more temperate job at home. It was news that could not but have raised Albert's frantic hopes that this son would be kept away from the Front (*CL* 344). Yet the strain between father and son would go decidedly to the worse and create a simmering resentment in Jack. When he learned that he was to be posted to the Front after 2 days' leave, he notified his father by telegram to visit him at Mrs. Moore's home in Bristol (*CL* 345). Albert did not understand the grave import of Jack's telegram and asked Jack merely to write again to explain (*CL* 345 n152). Jack was forced to write in lamenting tones a letter to Albert explaining that he had received his father's telegram, that he would send his father another, clearer telegram, but still in disbelief that his father could have misconstrued the first message (*CL* 345). In his letter Jack observes the obvious fact that a leave of only 48 hours would have been take up almost entirely by travel (*CL* 345–346). But he implores his father not to fret about him, supposing (erroneously) that he would remain in England for a while before going to France (*CL* 346). On 16 November he again telegraphed his father that he was to report to Southampton by 4:00 on 17 November and that he would go from there to France; if he were coming to see Jack, Albert should wire immediately (*CL* 346). Albert did not see his son before he sailed for France from Portsmouth. As noted by Warren, Albert could not but seem to have let Jack down in the midst of important moments for the boy (12); the event served only to cement Jack's emotional attachment to Mrs. Moore. It is not that Albert was unfeeling. Writing to Warren, he mentions that

> I had a scribbled line from "IT" [Jack] yesterday. Of course he tries to make things light for me, but the suddenness of the thing, and his own sense of want of training have I am afraid depressed him a good deal. (*LP* V.244)

Jack's movements toward the Front would have taken him into France through La Havre. He would then have moved by stages to the lines. In a style akin to that of Robert Graves, he recalls with the irony inherent in many soldiers' experiences a part of his initial journey in France. Lewis and three other officers shared a portion of a coach on a slow train that moved through freezing weather outside Rouen no faster than a person could run. In passing through a tunnel, a sudden clamor erupted, after which the men discovered their door had fallen off. Being suspected by the train's commander of tampering with the door, Lewis and his fellows are berated. Lewis observes the illogical conclusion of the commander: why would men in the midst of winter want to prepare for a freezing and seemingly interminable journey by taking the door off their train carriage? (*SBJ* 194–195). Such stories typified the fabled illogical nature of the military and its consequent machinations.

In a letter written shortly after arriving in France, Lewis reported that he was in a secure town which would have served as a staging area. He also wrote that he was to receive an injection against infections rife in the trenches, and in the afternoon would have 48 hours off duty (*CL* 346). A note by Walter Hooper in the *Collected Letters* indicates this town is Monchy le Preux (*CL* 346 n154), which is an impossibility. Monchy did not serve as a base or staging area as it was on the front line. In the spring of 1917, just when Lewis was entering Oxford, the Germans were being pushed from Monchy in fierce fighting during the Battle of Arras. Although they were driven out, the German's new front line remained about 500 yards from the village proper, immediately east of Monchy. Their front line trench was a stone's throw from that of the British (WO297/2176). Not only had Monchy been shelled by the British as they drove the Germans out, but once expelled, the Germans themselves commenced shelling the village as the British tried to set up posts in it. As historian Colin Fox described it, "The thousand or so yards to the east of the village became for the next two months the arena where many regiments [. . .] fought to gain the prize—uninterrupted observation over the Douai Plain—which might justify the expense of Monchy" (44). The Germans, having lost the village, shelled it with a vengeance. Fox relates one example: when a British cavalry unit was to enter the village just after the enemy had been forced out, the Germans set a barrage to fall in a large square around the horsed soldiers. The German guns tightened the square, destroying everything within it. One observer who went into Monchy just after the bombardment described the scene he met when rounding a bend in the road and going into Monchy:

> I stopped. The sight that greeted me was so horrible that I almost lost my head. Heaped on top of one another and blocking up the roadway for as far as one could see lay the mutilated bodies of our men and their horses. These bodies, torn and gaping, had stiffened into fantastic attitudes. All the hollows of the road were filled with blood. This was the cavalry. . . . Nothing that I had seen before in the way of horrors could be even faintly compared with what I saw around me now. Death in every imaginable shape was there for the examining. (qtd. in Fox 40–44)

A year after these events, when Lewis arrived in France, Monchy was far from being a secure town in which to keep soldiers. Monchy would have been at that time quite unsafe, without a building undamaged and continually under fire. Later in the war, when the Germans once more overran Monchy, followed by the Allied advance which pushed them out once more, the village was, as photographic evidence indicates, the ruin that Lewis described in his poem "French Nocturne (Monchy le Preux)" (*SIB* 4).

Figure 2. The ruins of Monchy le Preux (IWM Q7028)

Lewis was, in writing of the secure town, most likely in a staging town west of Arras—perhaps Rouen, or perhaps further towards the front: Amiens. Even later, when Jack would write from the town of Arras, he would describe it as having been shelled, which this staging town was apparently not to any distinct degree.

Albert, who kept Warren informed of events concerning Jack, was correctly interpreting events: the injection hinted to Albert that Jack was to be sent immediately into the trenches, a thought that nauseated him (*LP* V.244).

British law required each battalion to keep a regimental diary. Many of these have been published, whereas originals may be found in the Public Records Office at Kew. The diary for Lewis's battalion of the Somerset Light Infantry, the "War Diary or Intelligence Summary" (WO95/1499), provides the best record of Lewis's unit during his time in the trenches.[1] While Lewis's military record indicates that he was in the 3rd Infantry Battalion of the Somerset Light Infantry (which continues to be asserted as late as 1 April of 1920 when Lewis relinquished his commission) (WO339/105408), Walter Hooper records that Lewis was moved from the 3rd to the 1st battalion on 20 November (xxx). I have not discovered this date in Lewis's military record. That he was in the 3rd battalion is verifiable from O.T.C. documents at Keble College, Oxford. There is, however, no doubt that Lewis landed in the 1st Somerset Light Infantry as a letter of 21 November indicates (*CL* 346). The "Arrival Report" which Lewis filled out on 22 May 1918, after being wounded and shipped to Dover from France, indicates he was in the "1st Somerset Light Infantry-11th Brigade, 4th Division" (WO339/105408).

As to which company Lewis was in we can be certain. The Commonwealth War Graves Commission indicates that Laurence Bertrand Johnson was in "B" Company of the 1st Somerset Light Infantry. The military training manual explains the structures: "A brigade of infantry consists of 4 battalions under a brigadier" and consists of "roughly 4,000" men, with a battalion consisting of four companies (Lake 25). The division moves by groups of sixteen: "A company consists of 4 platoons, numbered 1 to 16, throughout the battalion, and is commanded by a major or mounted captain with a captain on foot as second in command" (Lake 25). The platoon itself is divided into four sections, likewise numbered 1–16 within a company, and "is commanded by a subaltern, with a platoon sergeant. Within a platoon are sections, commanded by a subaltern [an officer like Lewis], with a sergeant as second in command" (Lake 25). Lewis would have been in charge of a section of men, with a sergeant as his second in command.

Because Lewis spent much time with Johnson when they were out of the trenches, as *Surprised by Joy* indicates (191–193; 201), and because Lewis and

Johnson were standing together during an advance when a shell killed both Johnson and Lewis's sergeant Harry Ayres, one might erroneously gather— as I did at one time—that these men served in the same company; Ayres was Lewis's sergeant; Johnson himself commanded his own company (*SBJ* 191), Company B as the War Graves Commission indicates. However, upon first entering the trenches, Lewis writes, he reported to his captain, P. G. K. Harris, and this man was not only someone Lewis knew but is identified as the captain who commanded "H" Company, later called in the battalion diary "Light" Company (Majendie 120). Lewis was, thus, in "H" or "Light" Company. How events brought Johnson, in B Company, and Ayres and Lewis, in Light Company, to be standing beside one another becomes clear and will be explained later in examining their advance on the village of Riez.

I assume that readers are at least somewhat familiar with conditions encountered in the trenches and will talk about these conditions with little explanation. As to the arrangement of trenches Lewis would have encountered, Fussell provides straightforward description:

> There were normally three lines of trenches. The front-line trench was anywhere from fifty yards or so to a mile from its enemy counterpart. Several hundred yards behind it was the support trench line. And several hundred yards behind that was the reserve line. There were three kinds of trenches: firing trenches, like these; communication trenches, running roughly perpendicular to the line and connecting the three lines; and "saps," shallower ditches thrust out into No Man's Land, providing access to forward observation posts, listening posts, grenade-throwing posts, and machine gun positions. The end of a sap was usually not manned all the time: night was the favorite time for going out. Coming up from the rear, one reached the trenches by following a communication trench sometimes a mile or more long. It often began in a town and gradually deepened. By the time pedestrians reached the reserve line, they were well below ground level. (41)

Other descriptions provide a sense of the experiences one encountered in the line during a day with typical enemy activity:

> Enormous noise. Continuous explosion. A deserted landscape. Complete immobility of everything. Men were eating, smoking, doing odd jobs but no one was fighting. A few were peering in periscopes or looking through loopholes. I tried, but could see nothing but upturned empty fields. Then suddenly there was a terrific crash which flung me yards. I picked myself up and did my best to laugh. Near by a man lay with a tiny hole in his forehead and close to him another limped with blood pumping out of his leg. Both were carried away. A casualty was not a matter for horror but replacement [. . .] That was how I first saw the war. (qtd in Winter 82–83)

The battalion diary records that on 28 November part of Lewis's battalion was being relieved from trench duty, but some units stayed in the line:

"Reserve Coy. were not relieved and moved to 'F', 'C', and 'H' strong points. Remainder of Battalion moved to MONCHY DEFENSES on relief which was complete by 7–15 P.M." (WO95/1499). Lewis wrote that he reached the trenches on his 19th birthday (*SBJ* 188). That day, 29 November 1917, was the day after his company had moved into the trenches to relieve another unit at the strong points indicated above, the remainder of the battalion going into trenches by Monchy ("C" strong point is shown on the trench map just south of Monchy back from the actual front line (see map National Archives (PRO) WO297/2176). If Lewis moved with his unit into the line during this relief, he would have joined his company in the Monchy trenches on the night of 28th November, not on his birthday, the 29th. Yet it appears not altogether uncommon that a new man might join a company after it was already situated in the line, as may be evidenced by Lewis's recollection of his first night:

> The world presented itself in a very ridiculous form [. . . .] As I emerged from the shaft [leading down] into the dugout and blinked in the candlelight I noticed that the Captain to whom I was reporting was a master [. . .] at one of my schools. I ventured to claim acquaintance. He admitted in a low, hurried voice that he had once been a schoolmaster, and the topic was never raised between us again. (*SBJ* 194)

The event is not so odd as it may appear upon first glance and was likely repeated in other dugouts during the war. R. C. Sherriff's play, *Journey's End*, presents a similar picture. Indeed, while the new arrival to the unit in that play, Raleigh, is considerably naive in many respects, yet even so presents a slight likeness of an inexperienced, young Lewis arriving in something so unearthly and disorienting as that dugout in the trenches at night:

> RALEIGH *comes groping down the steps and stands in the candle light. He looks round, a little bewildered. He is a well-built, healthy-looking boy of about eighteen, with the very new uniform of a second lieutenant. . . .* (Sherriff 16).

Raleigh meets Osborne, a more experienced officer, who mentions, in their initial small talk, the Captain: Stanhope, a man who happened to be not only a hero at Raleigh's school but who was close to Raleigh's sister. Stanhope carries a photo of her. It becomes clear that since the days the men knew one another at school, the exhausted Stanhope had taken to drink inordinately and refuses to take his leaves, staying on with his unit. He has, inevitably, lost many of the young, inexperienced men sent to him. "You see," Osborne explains to Raleigh, trying to prepare the young officer for meeting a very different Stanhope than the school hero he once knew, "he's been out here a long time. It—it tells on a man—rather badly—. . . . If you notice a—difference in Stanhope—you'll know it's only the strain—" (Sherriff 19). When Stanhope arrives at the dugout, he curses over the condition of the trenches they have occupied from the previous unit, lights a cigarette, curses as he tells the cook to forget his soup and to bring the whisky. Stanhope then notices the new officer:

> RALEIGH: Hullo, Stanhope!
> [STANHOPE *stares at* RALEIGH *as though dazed.* RALEIGH *takes a step forward, raises his hand, then lets it drop to his side.*]
> STANHOPE [*in a low voice*]: How did you—get here?
> RALEIGH: I was told to report to your company, Stanhope.
> STANHOPE: Oh. I see. Rather a coincidence. (Sherriff 23)

The next scenes in the play explore the tension created by Raleigh's presence; not only must Raleigh be educated in the ways of the trenches—that he must take his pistol, his gas mask, that he must identify incoming shells by their sound and take appropriate action—but as he stands by, he observes the alienated character Stanhope has become. Stanhope regrets Raleigh's presence not because he is witness to the person the war has made him but because he will likely lose another young man. This man has a name and a face he knows; he will be responsible to Raleigh's sister for this young officer. Of course, in the end Raleigh is killed. The reaction Lewis received from his captain, the one-time schoolmaster Harris, may have sprung from a similar emotional basis.

His first night in the trenches would have been, most likely, an education while at the same time a test of Lewis's mettle. Robert Graves recalled his own introduction to a new unit, already in the trenches:

> We went up to the trenches that night. [. . . .]
> My first night, Captain Thomas asked whether I would like to go out on patrol. It was the Regimental custom to test new officers in this way, and none dared excuse himself. During my whole service with the Welsh I had never once been out in No Man's Land, even to inspect the barbed wire; the wire being considered the responsibility of the Battalion intelligence officer and the Royal Engineers. (129)

The purpose of this patrol was not to inspect wire but to see if a forward point in the German line was occupied. They went, "wriggling flat along the ground," for "ten yards at a time," waiting ten minutes before moving again (130). Among the undulations of the that waste land filled with sharp-edged shell fragments and the tearing points of barbed wire, he recalls, "I snatched my fingers in horror from where I had planted them on the slimy body of an old corpse" (130). They found the position in the German line unoccupied. Graves later reflected upon the changing conditions of an officer's worth:

> Having now been in the trenches for five months, I had passed my prime. For the first three weeks, an officer was of little use in the front line; he did not know his way around,

had not learned the rules of health and safety, or grown accustomed to recognizing degrees of danger. Between three weeks and four weeks he was at his best, unless he happened to have any particular bad shock or sequence of shocks. Then his usefulness gradually declined as neurasthenia [mental and emotional strain] developed. At six months he was still more or less all right; but by nine or ten months, unless he had been given a few weeks' rest on a technical course, or in hospital, he usually became a drag on the other company officers. After a year or fifteen months he was often worse than useless. (171)

Setting up the wire was a standard duty, like conducting a raid or the observation of the enemy, which was no less dangerous than these other duties. As a veteran explained in an interview,

One of the first things I learned was erecting barbed wire defenses. This job consisted of a team of six. Three were carriers of posts and coils of barbed wire, two were post erectors, and the posts had to be driven into the ground by a heavy wooden mallet, and after a few thumps of this in the still of the night, the Germans would open fire with machine guns. This made us drop flat and wait until the machine gun had stopped firing, and then we would jump up and carry on thumping a few more posts in. Two men would then pick up a coil of wire and put it on a pole so it revolved, and then they would dance round the post, and it was my job, as NCO, with thick leather gloves on, to wrap the wire round the posts. The whole job took from two-three hours, more than half of which was taken lying flat on the ground, dodging machine gun bullets. (Quinnell)

"The usual tour in the front line was four days," the Comanding Officer of the Somerset Light Infantry, V. H. B. Majendie writes, "with similar periods in Brigade support or reserve. Each Brigade had, as a rule, twelve days in Divisional reserve, which were spent either in the Schramm Barracks in Arras, or in the Bois des Boeufs or Wilderness Camps on the Cambrai road" (62).

In the months before Lewis's arrival at the Front in late November, soldiers had been set to work in renovating trenches that were in ill repair because of hard rains in October. The ground in some places near Monchy were described as "marshy," and as unoccupied, made a gap in the British line. Thus a new trench was dug to help alleviate this situation: Dale trench was constructed and fitted with pumps to keep it clear of water (Majendie 63). The month of November, "was fairly fine," with December delivering "cold, with a continuous frost and some snow" (Majendie 63).

The cold was something easily described but difficult to comprehend. Wilfred Owen describes his experiences of the winter of 1917. His platoon was without dugouts and

had to lie in the snow under the deadly wind. By day it was impossible to stand up or even crawl about because we were behind only a little ridge screening us from the Bosche's periscope.

> We had 5 Tommy's cookers between the Platoon, but they did not suffice to melt
> the ice in the water-cans. So we suffered cruelly from thirst.
> The marvel is that we did not all die of cold. As a matter of fact, only one of my
> party actually froze to death before he could be got back, but I am not able to tell how
> many ended in hospital. I had no real casualties from shelling, though for 10 minutes
> every hour whizz-bangs fell a few yards short of us. Showers of soil rained on us, but
> no fragments of shell could find us. (158)

The day of November 29, hours before Lewis arrived in the trenches, was
a "Fine day" during which the men worked on the trenches and "Considerable
enemy shelling took place. Barrages were put down at 1 P.M., 3–30 P.M., and
6–15 P.M. 2 other Ranks wounded"; the next day, Lewis's first day in the line,
the enemy "shelled the trenches heavily practically all day [.] A few Gas Shells
were put over about 8–30 P.M. and a number of 5.9's. Capt. R.A.A. Chichester
was wounded about 9–30 P.M." (WO95/1499). "Above normal" shelling
continued into the first day of December, with a heavy German barrage hitting Monchy; nevertheless, Lewis's account generally agrees with the battalion diary regarding the amount of shelling he experienced during this time in
the line:

> we had a pretty quiet time. Even then they attacked not us but the Canadians on our
> right, merely "keeping us quiet" by pouring shells into our line about three a minute
> all day. (*SBJ* 195)

Majendie writes that this "winter in the line was on the whole uneventful: the
artillery on both sides showed considerably [sic] activity, and gas shells were
freely used. The German trench mortars were, as usual, rather a source of
annoyance, but as a general rule they were kept in subjection by our guns" (63).
However, the absurdity of higher command, often cast in surreal proportions
by writers of the war, is evidenced in some reality just at the time Lewis
entered the trenches:

> At the end of November certain "quiet periods" were ordered; during these periods
> no gun was permitted to fire except in case of emergency. The idea apparently was to
> mystify the enemy as to our intentions; it is not known if the desired result was
> obtained, but the Germans invariably replied to such "quiet periods" by particularly
> heavy shelling, and the infantry were distinctly adverse to the procedure. (Majendie 63)

Albert, still nursing hopes that he might get Jack transferred, wrote in late
November 1917 to a member of Parliament, Colonel James Craig, for assistance in moving Jack to an artillery unit. It began another round of vacillation
on the family's part as to where Jack would be safest, compounded by Craig's
reply that Jack himself would need first to request a transfer (*CL* 347). Albert
wrote to Jack, whose reply was, as discussed previously, that he was attached

to the men in his unit (undoubtedly Johnson was a chief figure here), that the
artillery men were really no safer than men in the trenches, and that it would
be inefficient to train a man, set him at his duties, only to remove him and train
him for something else (*CL* 347–348).

Map 1. Monchy le Preux French map, corrected to 19 November 1917, ten days before Lewis
arrived in them. (National Archives (PRO) WO297/2176; reproduced from the 1917 Ordnance
Survey)

The officer training manual conveys a similar sense of things: "the post is
a definite appointment, and transfers should be as infrequent as possible"
(Lake 25). Lewis's attachment to his men, however, should not be set down
as him simply putting a good face on the poor likelihood he might transfer. The
bonds between soldiers were crucial, and often, as various scholars have asserted, their sense of "duty," not to an abstract ideal, but of one man to another,
was the only thing that brought men to cohere during moments of fighting,
moments when a panicked individual's sense of self-preservation could otherwise destroy a unit's cohesion. In the impossibly trying conditions of the
Front, men often needed one another just to sustain a relative sanity. Before
entering the battle of the Somme, one captain recorded, "I have had two
chances of leaving my Dublin fusiliers—one to take sick leave and the other to
have a staff job. I have chosen to stay with my comrades. Somewhere the
choosers of the slain are touching as in our Norse story they used to touch with

invisible wands those who are to die. I am calm, but desperately anxious to live"
(qtd. in Winter 56).

A number of current scholars of WWI have emphasized assumed homosexual aspects of soldiers' friendships. While such relations certainly existed and
have done in all wars, indications are that homosexual relationships were less
prevalent than intensely strong, brotherly-fatherly, mutually protective attach-
ments. While one may examine Rupert Brooke's relationships with such a view,
as has been done, to presume a homosexual aspect in Lewis's friendships is to
misconstrue the nature of them. As do many men, he quite simply held no
propensity for homosexuality yet would discuss it openly as he did in his autobiography among other places (*SBJ* 89). He readily conceded its existence in
war time:

> In war-like societies it was [. . .] likely to creep into the relation between the mature
> Brave and his young armour-bearer or squire. The absence of the women while you
> were on the war-path had no doubt something to do with it. (*Four Loves* 93)

This he wrote decades after his war service. Wesley Kort, in a dismissive sweep,
remarks that "Homophobia seems to increase as Lewis matures" (11).
Difficulties ensue if one treats the subject of the sentence with proper etymol-
ogy: Lewis, even late in life, did not become irrational in fearing homosexu-
als. But at issue is whether Kort's approach on the topic fits with the context
of Lewis's wartime world. Kort fails to consider the fact that Arthur Greeves
confided to Lewis his homosexual leanings—or that Lewis also confided in
Arthur about his own propensities for masturbation and sadism; such sexual
matters were regular features of the boys' letters while Jack was at Malvern. Yet
Arthur's propensity did not affect Lewis's friendship with Greeves in the least,
a close friendship lasting until Lewis died. But this analysis is still not to treat
the more common attachment between soldiers, a considerably different phenomenon than home-front friendships.

Rather, a brotherly-fatherly relationship typifies Lewis's wartime friendships,
an attachment illustrated and defined in numerous works: fiction, war diaries,
memoirs, letters. R. C. Sherriff's play *Journey's End*, and Remarque's *All
Quiet on the Western Front* depict this type of connection, for instance. Stanhope
and Raleigh figure in the former, Katz and Paul in the latter. In Virginia
Woolf's novel *Mrs. Dalloway*, the crucial relationship between Evans and
Septimus Warren Smith is remarked:

> There in the trenches [. . .] he developed manliness; he was promoted; he drew the
> attention, indeed, the affection of his officer, Evans by name. It was a case of two dogs
> playing on the hearth-rug [. . .]. They had to be together, share with each other, fight
> with each other, quarrel with each other. (86)

This is not homosexuality; neither were so many actual relationships. Denis Winter's *Death's Men: Soldiers of the Great War* closely documents numerous non-fictional accounts of this type of attachment between soldiers. In one case a soldier recalls that

> the war years will stand out in the memory of vast numbers who fought as the happi-
> est period in their lives. And the clue. . .we were all comrades. ..we saw love passing
> the love for women of one pal for his half section. (qtd. in Denis Winter 55)

Lewis was particularly attached not only to Johnson, but also to his sergeant—his second in command, through whom he passed orders to his men, but who had been at the front longer than Lewis had been. "Dear Sergeant Ayres" took Lewis—"a futile officer," a "puppet"—and instructed him in his duties as a soldier, those things which a book for officers could not teach the young Lewis, who outranked the older sergeant: Ayres "turned this ridiculous and painful relation into something beautiful" and "became to me almost like a father" (*Joy* 196). He relates an important, front-line lesson, where he proposed lobbing grenades at some Germans who allowed themselves to be seen moving along one of their trenches. Ayres replied that Lewis could, indeed, order such action, but the Germans would simply be returning the favor (*SBJ* 194). Another sergeant might have followed the suggestion as an order, let the young, inexperienced officer have his way, and watched the Germans retaliate and kill men. Harry Charles Ayres, 32, was from Keyford Gardens, Fromme, Somerset (CWGC) and was one of the men of whom Lewis remembered fondly, saying that between the educated and professional men on the one hand and the country workers on the other hand, they could have found no better company and conversation (*SBJ* 193). Even outside his battalion he met something of this same comradeship. When first arriving in France, he was commandeered two different times by officers who took him on as they might have done with an old chum; in the second event, he was pulled after dinner and wine from his book and taken to enjoy a smoke and after-dinner drinks (*SBJ* 189).

Because Lewis provides extensive detail about his attachment to Johnson in *Surprised by Joy*, some may construe the relationship as homosexual. I would mark it as the sustaining friendship between soldiers who, in this case, also share like paradigms and interests. In *The Four Loves*, Lewis set the hallmark of such friendship as, "when two such persons discover one another, when. ..they share their vision—it is then that Friendship is born" (97). Such was his bond with Johnson; it is the formation and the confirmation of—in some cases a posturing in—mutual assumptions about life and intellectual matters, discussions on aesthetics and classical authors. Johnson was so important a figure to Lewis that he admits to and defends an intellectual pose that made it seem as if his assumptions about life approximated those of his friend (*SBJ* 192–193).

While we may dismiss a homosexual basis for this friendship, it is important to note Lewis admits to posturing. That he does raises questions regarding Lewis's transparency in other issues. It becomes important in evaluating the war's lasting impact upon Lewis, an issue that will be treated fully in its place. But I believe there is more to the bonds between soldiers generally and between Lewis and Johnson specifically than what Lewis can bring himself to admit. Such bonds were built less immediately on the pursuit of some resolve on a philosophical issue than on, as David Jones put it,

> practical utility. The group helped each carry the guilt of killing, allowed the pooling of verbal aggression which eased the burden of dependence and fear. . . . Above all, the group allowed a sense of purpose not present in the actual war situation and which permitted men to impose a sense of time upon days and years which seemed otherwise featureless and endless, by common discomforts and grievances, by deep fears and common laughter, by shared prejudice against other units and common authority, by sudden violences and long stillnesses. (qtd. in Denis Winter 55–56)

"The guilt of killing"—and perhaps also of having survived friends. The conditions of war were for Lewis, as for most soldiers, loathsome (*SBJ* 188). But when Lewis remarks that he was surprised to find he did not loathe it entirely (*SBJ* 188), we understand him better in light of Jones's statement. Lewis discovered a lightness as each soldier he encountered held the same view: the whole affair was horrendous and came between humans and their allotted roles in life; the commonality of this understanding made it somewhat easier to accept (*Joy* 188). Yet for Lewis, as I have asserted, discussions on philosophy, on literature, on beauty became one of his primary ways of coping with the war. They did not merely comprise a diversion; such discussions were also shaping the assumptions by which he would meet the war's horrors, and as such became also "practical utility."

The nature of soldiers' relationships were recorded long ago by an author with whom Lewis had recently become familiar: Homer. *The Odyssey*, for instance, contains numerous passages in which Odysseus and his soldiers openly weep when they hear songs recounting their friends killed in battle at Troy or weep when other men are lost, either to death or misadventure:

> but great Odysseus melted into tears,
> running down from his eyes to wet his cheeks . . .
> as a woman weeps, her arms flung round her darling husband,
> a man who fell in battle, fighting for town and townsmen,
> trying to beat the day of doom [. . . .] (Homer 8.586–590)

In another place, they "recalled [their] dear companions, wept for the men/that Scylla plucked from the hollow ship and ate alive,/and a welcome sleep came on them in their tears" (Homer 12.334–36).

And in yet another place, Odysseus is asked about his tears, and the question itself serves to reveal the depth of the bonds between soldiers,

> why do you weep and grieve so sorely when you hear
> the fate of the Argives, hear the fall of Troy?
> [. . . .]
> Did one of your kinsmen die before the walls of Troy
> some brave man—a son by marriage? father by marriage?
> Next to our own blood kin, our nearest, dearest ties.
> Or a friend perhaps, someone close to your heart,
> staunch and loyal? No less dear than a brother,
> the brother-in-arms who shares our inmost thoughts. (Homer 8.647–657)

This is Lewis's link with Johnson, whom he had planned to befriend for life (*SBJ* 192). Such a connection is quite distinct among others that humans share. Indeed, even the Sirens exploit the unique connection between soldiers by the promise in their song to Odysseus's men: that they also understand the horrors that men suffer in war, for

> Never has any sailor passed our shores in his black craft
> until he has heard the honeyed voices pouring from our lips,
> and once he hears to his heart's content sails on, a wiser man.
> We know all the pains that the Greeks and Trojans once endured
> on the spreading plain of Troy when the gods willed it so—(Homer 12.202–206)

After his return and once Odysseus has restored order in his home, his first interest is renewing his relationship with his wife:

> But the royal couple, once they'd reveled in all
> the longed-for joys of love, reveled in each other's stories,
> the radiant woman telling of all she'd borne at home,
> [. . .]
> And great Odysseus told his wife of all the pains
> he had dealt out to other men and all the hardships
> he'd endured himself—his story first to last—(Homer 23.342–351)

Yet—here is an irony one encounters in studying soldiers' experiences: while Odysseus begins with the Cicones, continues to the Lotus-eaters, and on to describe all the adventures he faced on earth and the underworld—adventures that are fantastic and unearthly, encompassing the mysteries of earth and afterlife—not one word does he tell Penelope of what he experienced at Troy. Those events he cannot share with someone who does not know the pains of war. In this we understand Siegfried Sassoon's reported observation that "a man who endured the war at its worst was everlastingly differentiated from everyone except his fellow soldiers."

The strength that men gained from one another was something Lewis knew long before he arrived in France, an important episode in his life which he correlated directly to his war experience: "Familiarity both with the very old and the very recent dead confirmed that view of corpses which had been formed the moment I saw my dead mother" (*SBJ* 195–196).

It is significant that Lewis recalled during the war his earlier experience with death. The war would also have recalled other associations with his childhood experience, as he related in a passage previously discussed: that Jack and Warren's lives became, in the midst of the invasive odors, sounds, and unfamiliar people in the house as his mother died, beset with a hostile tinge. What sustained the boys? It was for them as it would be when they became soldiers: friendship (*SBJ* 19).

In light of the parallel between war and the death of his mother, we understand better why, when Lewis had an opportunity to transfer into a less dangerous regiment, he refused on the grounds he needed to remain with his men (*CL* 347–348).

Through the winter months of 1917 and early 1918, as Lewis served in the trenches near the villages of Monchy and Fampoux, he would encounter the ghastly horrors he described to Dom Bede Griffiths as the second World War approached. Those horrors included for Lewis every misery a human could possibly face on earth (*Letters* 320).

NOTE

1. Two works based on this diary have been published: one is written by the commanding officer, Major V. H. B. Majendie, *A History of the 1st Battalion: The Somerset Light Infantry (Prince Albert's), July 1st 1916 to the End of the War* (1921). The other is *The History of the Somerset Light Infantry (Prince Albert's) 1914–1919* by Everard Wyrall (1927), which reports from the diaries of other battalions in the S. L. I. Both Wyrall's and Majendie's accounts have small points of disagreement with the original regimental diary, and an occasional error (usually in reference to maps), but are otherwise useful, especially when they provide details not recorded in the official diaries.

WORKS CITED

Carpenter, Humphrey. *The Inklings*. New York: Ballantine, 1981.

Fox, Colin. *Monchy le Preux*. Barnsley, England: Pen & Sword, 2000.

Fussell, Paul. *The Great War and Modern Memory.* New York: Oxford UP, 1975.

Graves, Robert. *Good-bye to All That.* New York: Doubleday, 1957.

Homer. *The Odyssey.* Robert Fagles, trans. New York: Penguin, 1997.

Hooper, Walter. Preface. *Spirits in Bondage.* by C. S. Lewis. New York: Harcourt, 1984.

Kort, Wesley A. *C. S. Lewis Then and Now.* Oxford: Oxford UP, 2001.

Lake, B. C. *Knowledge for War: Every Officer's Handbook for the Front.* London: Harrison, n.d.

Lewis, C. S. *Letters of C. S. Lewis.* Ed. W. H. Lewis and Walter Hooper. New York: Harcourt, 1993.

Lewis, W. H. Memoir. *C. S. Lewis Letters.* New York: Harcourt, 1966.

Majendie, V. H. B. *A History of the 1st Battalion: The Somerset Light Infantry (Prince Albert's), July 1st, 1916, to the End of the War.* Taunton, England: Goodman, 1921.

Quinnell, Charles. Interview. 17 July 2003. *Counter-Attack.* <http://www.sassoonery.demon.co.uk/veteran.htm#top> 17 July 2003.

Sherriff, R. C. *Journey's End.* London: Penguin, 1983.

Stallworthy, John. *Wilfred Owen: A Biography.* Oxford: Oxford UP, 1977.

Winter, Denis. *Death's Men: Soldiers of the Great War.* London: Penguin, 1979.

Woolf, Virginia. *Mrs. Dalloway.* New York: Harcourt, 1953.

CHAPTER 6

What Homer Wrote About

LEWIS WROTE THAT A SINGLE INSTANCE APPEALED to his imagination more than any other of the war, an event that remained more significant to him than other actualities he met in war. It was a moment carrying an implicit connection between the ways Lewis conceptualized his experiences on the one hand and articulated the realities of the front on the other hand:

> It was the first bullet I heard—so far from me that it "whined" [. . .] [It created] a little quavering signal that said, "This is War. this is what Homer wrote about." (*SBJ* 196)

The statement reveals his means of coping with confrontations and traumatic events; he viewed the event by way of literary allusion. The allusion touches nothing of the reality of the experience, and Lewis does not consider the reality of how that bullet might have affected him personally. His response at the time, and in the 1950s when he was writing of the moment, was simply detached from reality; the bullet is safely distanced from its personal implications. The reality is different: Homer's war was nothing akin to Lewis's war—except in that humans died. Remaining similarities are superficial. The British 1907 model bayonet, a "sword bayonet," 22 inches long, could inflict wounds like those seen in Homer: a head split from top to jaw. Yet other features serve only to distinguish this war markedly from Homer's war, its realities too var-

ied to be ignored especially by Lewis who (as a junior Kirkpatrick) would usually insist on logic being ruthlessly applied in all matters, here creating a finer
delineation between Homer's war and his own.

Stephane Audoin-Rouzeau and Annette Becker have discussed factors distinguishing this war from all previous wars. Not merely by the time Lewis had
entered the war, but

> already in 1914, at the beginning of the war, battle was much more violent than it had
> ever been before. And then military and civilian suffering gradually intensified the vio-
> lence over the duration of the conflict. This progressive intensification lent its own
> dynamic to the conflict; in the very first days and weeks of the war the practices of war
> took a brutal turn, not only on the battle fields but also for prisoners and civilians. Even
> for the ordinary soldier, the enormous explosions of violence that occurred in the sum-
> mer of 1914 immediately and scathingly refuted all the predictions that had been made
> in the years prior. (21)

Lewis's recollection shows his romantic side and his preference for an idealized,
older world (one, ironically, in which war was still romantic); his statement
reveals the nature of his collective assumptions and from what they were built.
He would not have been alone in romanticizing the war; Wilfred Owen's poem
"*Dulce et Decorum Est*" speaks in opposition to such widely held assumptions.
The realities of war, however, are too stark for romantic notions to remain viable
in facing them: this war saw the use of technologically advanced weapons
(many for the first time in history)—among them are the use of gas, the use
of enormous mines beneath enemy trenches, the use of barbed wire in war, the
use of aircraft (dirigibles and planes), the deliberate targeting of civilians, and
the first systematic attempts at genocide. Above all, the horrors of the fronts,
where armies stood for years at stalemate in a war of attrition—with massive
body counts of which many simply disappeared in the mud—were not simply
unknown in history, but could not have been imagined. This was not war as
Homer wrote about it.

Just before his statement on Homer, Lewis remarked on a number of horrible elements of the war

> the frights, the cold the smell of H. E. [High Explosive], the horribly smashed men
> still moving like half-crushed beetles, the sitting or standing corpses, the landscape of
> sheer earth without a blade of grass, the boots worn day and night till they seem to grow
> to your feet—all this shows faintly in the memory. It is too cut off from the rest of my
> experience and often seems to have happened to someone else. It is even in a way unim-
> portant. (*SBJ* 196)

This list is too detailed for him *not* to remember it well. His letter to Dom Bede
Griffiths, referred to above, also reveals that war's horrors and their personal

implications were still, even twenty years on as WWII approached, quite immediate in Lewis's memory. Perhaps, like many veterans, he did not *want* to
remember, but the memories are not as faint as he proffers them to us. And
the word "often": he must recall it *often* in order to say that it "often seems
to have happened to someone else." It is a ruse, and he has begun this part of
his autobiography with the same trick: "The war itself has been so often
described by those who saw more of it than I that I shall here say little about
it" (*SBJ* 195). No one intends to tell all, but like a character in Browning's
poems, we sometimes communicate indirectly more than we intend to say. If
Lewis said, in re-reading the section of *Surprised by Joy* dealing with his school
years, that it was all "lies" (Sayer 86), then we may take this reticence on the
war as a similar concealment, a pose. Don King has also noted that Lewis is,
as he terms it, "masking" these war experiences (53). Even so, we may take
Lewis's statement that it seemed to have happened to another person as a fair
appraisal. Indeed, the world of the Western Front must have seemed so vast a
departure from the society in Oxford which he had recently left and to which
he returned, and finding oneself in such an unearthly place as the front and
being involved in such horrific events, the sheer disparity of like experiences
and places would, indeed, create such a sense.

Otto Dix recalled his initiation to the trenches:

> The impressions on the way to the front were already frightful: the wounded and the
> first gas victims with sunken yellow faces were being brought straight back behind the
> lines. Then we went into the beastly trench system of the front, into the soft white chalk
> trenches of Champagne, where one was tormented by the stench of the dead all
> around, crouching all day in a muddy corrugated foxhole, at best emerging at night.
> The borderless and tangled net of underground positions . . . with their battle and con-
> nective trenches, their foxholes, their kilometer-long communication trenches. Endless
> and bleak, running this way and that before a pair of dark, shot-up broken-down pines,
> a white, grey, yellow landscape of death extended. (qtd. in McGreevy 37)

On Lewis's first day in the trenches, it will be recalled, he entered the lines
as a great amount of enemy shelling occurred and two men were wounded
(WD). If Lewis arrived in the line at night, he would not have experienced these
moments, but the following day, as the battalion diary records, "Enemy shelld
[sic] the trenches heavily practically all day. A few Gas Shells were put over
about 8–30 P.M. and a number of 5.9's. Capt. R. A. A. Chichester was wounded about 9–30 P.M." *(WD)*. It would have been a frightful welcome Lewis
received, and the fears for his own life would immediately have become no less
a part of his concerns than those he held for his men.

Being new to the line was no guarantee of safety. An unfortunate but not
uncommon example occurred in Lewis's own battalion. 2nd Lieutenant P. Buse

joined the Somerset Light Infantry on 23 April 1918. While his unit was relieving another battalion in the front line "under considerable Machine Gun fire [. . . ,] Capt. H. M. Boucher and 2nd Lieut. P. Buse were killed" (*WD*). He did not survive a single day in the line.

As one traces individual days that Lewis spent in and out of the line, a note should be made concerning a common statement in the battalion diary. Daily entries most often begin with remarks like "Fine day," which pertain strictly to the weather and have nothing to do with the amount of combat in the line. Thus, on Lewis's second day in the trenches, 1 December, the diary indicates, with what seems to be great irony, "Fine day. Enemy shelling still above normal" *(WD)*. Incidental though it may be, the irony is not unsuitable.

His first day began, then, with fine weather that could not be fully enjoyed due to the shelling. Also this day his battalion's artillery and machine guns were fired in conjunction with a unit of Royal Engineers, who fired gas shells and thermite with a trench mortar. The Germans, however, "put down a heavy barrage on MONCHY school" *(WD)*. On 2 December, Lewis's battalion relieved another in "the new front line" during a "bitterly cold" day, and the next "a little snow fell." For the next three days, he remained in the line as the weather continued "frosty" and "very cold" as the Germans fired gas shells around Monchy, poisoning two men on 4 December, and fired various High Explosive shells, killing three and wounding two other soldiers (*WD*). On 6 December, the 1st Rifle Brigade moved into the trench line, as they were during this period the usual relief for Lewis's battalion; relief was complete by 7:50 P.M. While the relief was being carried out, the Germans "put down a heavy barrage on Support and Reserve line" with the battalion "suffering only two casualties; 1 remaining on duty" (*WD*).

When out of the front line but remaining within reserve line trenches or in a camp near the reserve lines as Divisional Support, the battalion was employed in a number of ways. They could be on fatigue, which mean working. They might be employed in carrying wire, ammunition, and other supplies to the front lines. They could also be employed by Royal Engineers in revetting trenches that frost and wet continually persuaded to collapse. During this period out of the line, Lewis's unit spent much time making "concertina wire" that would eventually be used through a marshy area where a new trench, Dale Trench (in the upper left-center on the Monchy trench map), would be built with pumps and duckboards. This area of the lines had proved to be a persistent problem as it continually filled with water. Majendie explains:

> Reference has previously been made to the gap in the defensive line which existed West and South-West of the Twin Copses owing to the marshy ground. In spite of many unsuccessful attempts which had already been made, Divisional H.Q. decided to dig

a support line here, and Dale Trench was the result. By skillful construction, and a thorough system of pumping, it proved a success, and was kept clear of water.

This trench was strongly wired with barbed concertina; the greater part of this wire was made by the Battalion when in Brigade reserve in trenches just East of Feuchy Chapel cross roads, and carried up to Dale Trench. The actual erection of the wire was done entirely by the Battalion, and an excellent job was made of it. (63)

The unfortunate thing about this work, a difficult undertaking, with the wiring performed at night and often under fire, was that the next spring thaw collapsed many trenches, including the new Dale trench. However, the Monchy trench map, issued in December, clearly shows the new trench. Lewis and his men would certainly have visited this place numerous times. Wire holders used by these men are today employed by farmers in the area to hold their wire for cattle fences. Not only may bits of wire be found in the fields today, but two entire rolls—perhaps wire made by Lewis's unit—sit rusting at the southern edge of Twin Copse towards the area where Dale was dug by Infantry Lane.

The work at Dale was done, as Majendie indicates, to fill a gap in the British line, but also because in "the first half of December an enemy attack was expected" (63). During this time, "the Battalion, which was then in Divisional reserve in Schramm Barracks, Arras, 'stood to' every morning at 6:30 A.M. ready to move at a moment's notice" (63). The barracks, or "casernes" in French, predate the war and were a part of the buildings that were part of the Citadel in Arras. Today they remain much as they were during the war and are used if reserve forces are needed in the area.

On 10 December Lewis's unit moved back to Arras and occupied the Schramm barracks. The battalion stood to (were ready to move into the line) at 6:30 A.M., and when an the anticipated German attack did not come off in the morning, was employed in other work. On 11 December, the battalion practiced "Musketry on Butte de Tir range" and spent time cleaning their equipment (WD). On this day—with Lewis having been somewhere in the front line or in reserve since 29 November—the battalion bathed for the first time since he joined it. On other days in mid-December, the battalion continued to stand to early in the morning, were on fatigue all of some days and for some nights as well, with a trip through a "gas chamber" to practice fitting their masks. On other days they practiced artillery formations. They observed field firing practice by another unit and, on 16 December, a Sunday, participated in the usual "Church parade" (WD). The next day the battalion was ordered to "carry out a Field Firing Practice at 11 A.M. but this was cancelled owing to the weather which was bitterly cold with frequent snow showers. Some drills and trench lectures were substituted for the mornings [sic] work" (WD). Thus, while out of the line, the work was still fairly constant.

It seems that only while he was out of the line did Lewis write letters. His first letter home was written on 13 December. In it he apologizes to his father for not having written sooner, but his duties interfered with personal tasks. He remarked that he was "in billets in a certain rather battered town somewhere behind the line" (*CL* 348). He mentions that he was also reading one of George Eliot's novels, *Adam Bede*. He enjoyed it so well that he sought more of her novels to read while in France (*CL* 348).

Consequently, he also read *Mill on the Floss*, a work he would read in the line at Fampoux.1 The volume he read had been a gift from Albert to his wife. About his reading, he tells Arthur in a letter written on 14 December that it was impossible to read a work for any length of time, but the task could be done in snippets. He was working through not only Eliot's novels but would read other authors as well (*CL* 348–349).

Describing Arras vaguely, as "a certain rather battered town somewhere behind the line," was necessary for Lewis to do. Should a soldier's letter fall into enemy hands and state exactly where his unit was billeted, the result could be a massive barrage from the enemy on a battalion. Had he not been vague, the letter would simply have been subjected to the usual military censorship that soldiers' letters home encountered.

Arras had been devastated by German bombardment throughout the war, from 1914 on. In March of 1918, when the Germans attempted their last great offensive, they initiated a last intense bombardment of the area, devastating what little remained intact. Of 4,521 houses in Arras, only 292 were undamaged at the end of the war (Michelin 26). By December of 1917 when Lewis arrived there, the town had been shelled repeatedly and sometimes heatedly for nearly three and a half years.

Photos of Arras at the time present a close representation of the derelict town in Lewis's book, *The Great Divorce*. There the town is evoked not only in its features but by the means commonly used to move soldiers from the town: buses. At the beginning of the book, the protagonist stands waiting at a bus stop among the buildings, many empty, that suffered shell-chipped stone, collapsed roofs, and gaping windows (*Divorce* 1). He was certainly recalling Arras and the long intervals officers spent standing with their men in queues to embus for the front lines further north. There are photos from 1917 of buses bringing soldiers back to Arras from areas near the lines at Monchy.

The battalion's time in Arras continued with early-morning preparedness and work details until 18 December when "Battalion left for the line at 4 P.M." (*WD*). During the next day, the Royal Engineers put men to work, 3 groups during the day, 4 by night, and the "Usual patrols went out by night" (*WD*). On the 19th also the unit was issued rum from one of the well-known rum jugs marked SRD, indicating "Special Rations Division," but which soldiers said meant variously "Soon Runs Dry," "Seldom Reaches Destination," or similar quips.

Figure 3. Arras after the war (IWM Q49543)

Once in the line again, the battalion found that enemy activity continued. Heavy Minnies, a diminutive for particularly dangerous High Explosive shells called in German Flugelminwerfers (Saunders 30–32), were "fairly active," and gas shells fell on Battalion Head Quarters in Crater Subway (*WD*) which is located on Majendie's map no. 5 at 13.b.5 along the Arras/Cambrai road. While parties from the battalion continued to work for the Royal Engineers— likely on establishing Dale Trench—German shelling continued, sometimes coming in heavy barrages. On 21 December, H company's cook was wounded. "Frequent shelling of our front and support lines" occurred on 22 December, with "three direct hits in front line" (*WD*). Relief was carried out at this time, with the disposition of units thus: "1 company and Battn. Headquarters at FOSSES FARM; 1 company in 'C', 'D', and 'E' Strong Points, remainder in FORK and EAST RESERVE" (*WD*). The next day was quiet until 6–20 P.M. when a "heavy hostile barrage" fell on the lines, and two S.O.S. signals were sent up by Reserve Battalions and by men in 'C' Strong Point as well as those in the Monchy sector (*WD*). Monchy Sector trenches are those just north and east of Monchy. East Reserve Trench runs close on

Monchy's east edge, with Fork attached to its south end at Saddle Lane. It is perhaps on this or a subsequent evening from East Reserve or Fork Trench (as the sun set toward the south) that Lewis looked west at Monchy and wrote his poem about this village. Nevertheless, the usual counterbarrage returned compliments to the Germans. No casualties occurred among the British units. The next day, described as a "usual eventful day," had "nothing to report" (*WD*).

The event Lewis described in his autobiography may have occurred while his unit was still in the line, before moving back into reserve. Lewis related that Sergeant Ayres was reluctant to follow his proposal to fire grenades at Germans nearby (*SBJ* 194). We are told merely that Ayres advised against it to avoid getting similar treatment from the Germans. However, this does not mean that another section failed to observe the same enemy movement and fire on it, which the battalion diary indicates did occur. Saps, shorter lines that could stretch some yards beyond the front line into No Man's Land, were often set as a forward post and used for listening to the enemy as well as for the advance placement of a weapon. But why should Lewis not propose simply firing a rifle at the Germans? One text explains:

> [there] were numerous directives that emphasized the need to shoot the enemy, when the rifle could be brought to bear, rather than relying on the grenade, irrespective of how it arrived at the enemy's feet. The truth was that the average infantryman had more faith in explosives than bullets for dealing with the enemy and by 1917 he had more experience with grenades than with musketry (Saunders 119).

It appears that Lewis was proposing what he believed any infantryman would have agreed with. What he could not expect was the principle learned only in this odd war where opposing troops remained for long hours static in trenches set meters apart: it was a principle of mutual convenience, not a lofty aim of peace, which prevailed. Indeed, both sides, at times, participated in the game, as Lord Reith wrote: "Funny business this. The enemy throws some shells at our trench. We've got your range accurately you see. No monkey tricks. Home battery replied. We're got yours; trench line and battery position—both. No more nonsense. Live and let live" (qtd. in Winter 213). If Lewis did not make his suggestion around this time, someone else did. On 25 December the battalion diary records "Enemy seen walking about Saps, and fired on" (*WD*). Whatever the outcome of his proposal at that time, Lewis's official sense of duty was stirred up: in January as he took a course on the use of bombs and the various chemicals used in them.

What lies beneath this event, whenever it occurred, is a side of Lewis not looked at steadily by his biographers nor perhaps by Lewis himself—at least publicly. He was suggesting killing men. He was actively imagining the exter-

mination of humans and devising creative means of doing so. It is what a soldier does and what a good officer should do in being an example to his men.
Yet when grenades explode, they rip parts from bodies, and, if they do not kill
immediately, they can leave men maimed to live sometimes for hours or days
in agony in a forward line, out of reach of their men, where their cries could
be clearly heard by those who fired the grenades. Lewis would have known this
after even a short time in the line. In our historiography, we have tended to
examine only the soldier as victim, with some considering it a sign of their
humanism (Audoin-Rouzeau and Becker 2); we have missed the other role of
the soldier: that of executioner, and it is very difficult for many to see Lewis
in this light. But more: the war, in its "radical and radically new violence was
not only massively accepted by the belligerent societies but also implemented
by millions of men over four and a half years," and that violence is part of the
un-civilizing of the West, as it is a part of the un-civilizing of Lewis personally (Aundoin-Rouzeau and Becker 33). Many writers have discussed issues of
the "civilizing" experiences and requisite values that serve to create a stable society. In relation to the war and its soldiers, Gertrude Stein, for one, remarked
that young people needed just such a civilizing experience (which Stein believed
included an affair with an older woman); her view was that the war generation,
however, missed that necessary, civilizing process and were "lost" (Rood 366).
Lewis himself remarked one soldier, Wallie, was perhaps the lowest member of
his group, but perhaps also its best feature. Lewis writes admirably of Wallie's
creativity and enthusiasm for killing the enemy although plans he made could
be apparently dangerous to himself and to the unit (*SBJ* 193). Yet Wallie's
apparent civility and simple patriotism stood in odd contrast to his interest in
killing. Whether Lewis thirsted for killing as did Wallie is not to me a sign of
his being uncivilized; it is, rather, a sign that the extreme, radical violence of
this war was, if not in one moment then in another, acceptable. Lines that Lewis
would later come to write in his narrative poem *Dymer* reveal uncivilizing acts
that occur in war and more. The lines are not written with a detached mode
of observation, not from the view of a war photographer, as it were. Rather the
perspective is one of active participation in the events described (*D* 43–44). It
reveals what a man has done in war and the ways he has felt about what he has
done. More will be said about the brutality that Lewis was describing and the
guilt of killing when *Dymer* is discussed on its own. But events that Lewis was
experiencing were teaching him very well that the war in which he was entan-
gled was one quite apart from anything Homer wrote about and that
humankind was far different from what his assumptions had previously allowed;
he was learning that men were capable of doing things beyond what his earlier assumptions could fathom. He begins to be like them in important respects.

I believe that from the day in November he first entered the trenches, his assumptions about life, the world, and himself began to shatter.

Christmas day would not be celebrated by the battalion with any extravagance. "All working parties" were "cancelled, except carrying wire to Support dumps" with "Services" for those units posted at "FOSSES CAVE and Company Hd. Qrs." (*WD*). The cave is probably part of Fosses farm. The day after Christmas, the battalion relieved the 1st Rifle Brigade in the front line on the Cambrai Road sector, south of the Monchy sector, where they spent a couple of quiet days despite, on 28 December, enemy planes being active over the line: "1 [aircraft] brought down about 10 A.M. near 'C' Strong Point" and "gale and snow later in the day" (*WD*). 29 December saw "Enemy Trench Mortars very active" with "retaliation by our Artillery" (*WD*). As for many men new to the line, it would have been a strange Christmas season. It was compounded by an event not uncommon at the front, and in this case it occurred in Lewis's unit: "Dug-out of 'H' Company collapsed; 6 buried (4, killed, 2 Sergts. alive). 3 other casualties from Trench Mortars" (*WD*). Ernst Junger described a similar event: "At the third shot the occupant of the next hole to mine was buried by a terrific explosion. We dug him out instantly, but the weight of earth had killed him. His face had fallen in and looked like a death's-head" (100). That day, however, the battalion moved out of the front line and took up positions in reserve.

On 31 December, reportedly a very cold day, two companies—not Lewis's—were out on Royal Engineer working parties, likely rebuilding the collapsed dugout, with the remainder working on reserve lines. The battalion was paid this day, and Lewis wrote a letter to Arthur, in which he relates that the weather allowed the ground to soften (which would likely be why the dugout had collapsed on Christmas), and that he misses the walks they had taken together, a feature of his old, uncomplicated life at home (*CL* 349). He adds a wish that while he has a new friendship, he would not like to lose Arthur's friendship: "if we were all three—you know my meaning—together [. . .] we could be [. . .] without any clash of interests" (*CL* 349). The third person is Janie Moore. Mrs. Moore had also been pressing Lewis to let her read his poems, so in this letter Jack asks Arthur to find the notebook they are in and send them to her: it is something that Mrs. Moore has been insistent upon (*CL* 350). It is an interesting request, for his brother Warren wrote years later of Mrs. Moore that in two decades of living in the home he shared with Jack and her, he had never seen her reading (12). Indeed, the letters she wrote to the War Office, extant in her son's military record, ramble throughout with a meager vocabulary. Yet one recalls that when Albert wrote to Jack requesting a particular volume be sent home, he was told to wait: Mrs. Moore was currently reading it. If Jack was blinded by love for her, Mrs. Moore was reciprocally in love with Jack and knew that through his books she could make a stronger connection with his internal life; such things lovers do with one another. I do not believe she read the books but merely held them, and as Lewis came to understand her mind years hence, he would have understood she had not read them. At this point, however, he would have been playing with illusions, illusions which the enforced separations that occurred in the war perhaps encouraged.

January arrived with the battalion remaining in the reserve lines; many of the men worked with Royal Engineers on rebuilding trenches. On 2 January, the "remainder of battalion bathed" (*WD*)—only the second time Lewis bathed since arriving at the front at the end of November. 3 January saw the battalion move into Wilderness Camp, along the Arras/Cambrai road, into brigade reserve. The Wilderness Camp, while away from the lines, was not without incident and had been destroyed by enemy shelling at least once in the war.

At this time Lt. Colonel V. H. B. Majendie, who had been away on other duties, returned to command his battalion. In a letter where Jack proffers reasons to Albert for not transferring to a safer unit, Lewis wrote of his high respect for Majendie and that he would not like to be thought by Majendie as trying to avoid his duties just as he was becoming proficient in them (*CL* 348).[2]

On 4 January, Lewis wrote his father that the pay he received on 31 December was sufficient for his needs, that his father need not send money, and that, again, he was insistent upon staying with his unit. Not least, the shelling which went past Lewis and his men to land upon the artillery further back convinced him that he was as safe as he could be remaining in his present duties (*CL* 351). The batteries that were being themselves shelled may have seen this action that the battalion diary records: "A few Gas shells dropped near Feuchy Chapel Cross Roads about 6 A.M." (*WD*), an area well behind the line. Of his work, Lewis indicates he was learning about bombing, the details of which were difficult for him to grasp, but that he was otherwise content (*CL* 351).

This letter, one of the most important he wrote as regards what he was observing at the front, describes his surroundings in ideal terms and likely appeased Albert's worries, as Jack may have intended. He describes the dugouts as relatively cozy and set well into the ground, that they have the wood-frame and steel mesh beds that one may observe in various photos and at museums along the front today, but that they lack fresh air due to the fires for heat and preparing meals. He also mentions that he was nearly blown up while attempting to relieve himself (*CL* 351–352), a statement that could hardly have comforted his father.

Here is one place Denis Winter's interpretation may be mistaken, that concerning a soldier's sense of danger: "Men in war seem to have an irrational fear of being under fire with their trousers down" (104). The training manuals show the latrines—ideally—as a small sap extending a short distance from a trench line. During heavy shelling and during extremely wet weather (two situations often combined), the latrines were of little use, and a nearby shell hole was in such moments expedient. Lewis, of course, does not mention to Albert the increasing danger that thaws brought with them—collapsing dugouts and trenches. But he mentions that, as he had begun *Mill on the Floss*, he would like a biography of George Eliot.

Figure 4. A working party in a particularly tidy trench near Arras, with the entrance to a dugout seen at left. The men are installing scaling ladders. The objects which look like lollies, upside down against the trench wall at right, are "Toffee Apples"—round mortar shells. (IWM Q6204)

It was not until 5 January that the battalion celebrated Christmas Day; no parades (marching in formation) or working parties took place, and a concert was held in the evening. Two men were also awarded medals. The next day the weather turned more towards that which the Western Front was known for: "Heavy rain started at night, and thaw set in. [. . .] 8 Officers and 300 Other ranks on working party at night" (*WD*). The work was likely to repair trenches sagging with the moisture. On 7 January the battalion moved from Wilderness Camp into Arras, again occupying the Schramm barracks. Whereas some outdoor training took place, a heavy snow storm halted these events, and while a return to parades was attempted in the morning, heavy snow resumed in the afternoon and night of 9 January. On that day as well, Majendie and some other officers went north to examine the trenches into which the battalion would move upon their next period in the line. In preparation for this move, on 10 January, the battalion bathed and went to the "Follies" that night, the next day marching out of Arras to the "left sub-sector" of the front lines, having tea at "BOIS DES BOEUF [sic] Camp on way up" (*WD*). On the 13th, the "Enemy attempted to raid the Battalion on our Right about 5:30 A.M. Our front line heavily shelled—no casualties" (*WD*). Things continued quietly thereafter, with the weather growing colder until, on 15th, "Heavy rain fell in afternoon and evening. This heavy rain coming on after the severe frost and snow caused all the trenches to fall in" (*WD*). With the battalion moving back into reserve lines, the next three days were much the same with "Trenches full of mud and water and absolutely impassable. All movement taking place over open, "which was extremely dangerous despite the presence of a heavy mist and the mercy of "little activity on either side" (*WD*). The Germans, who throughout the war built superior trenches to those of the Allied troops, certainly were at work on their own trenches given the extreme conditions. Lewis recalls in his autobiography that during this period fatigue and the weather were the greatest difficulties. Like other soldiers, he had been so weary that he found himself waking from sleep while walking, and that the junk of war hidden in the mud—razor-edged shards of shells, the omnipresent barbed wire, and such—would let water into the rubber boots that the War Office issued to soldiers in the lines (*SBJ* 195).

It was a notorious season: "During the winter of 1917, when there was one degree of frost in London, there were fifteen in Arras. Hot tea froze in minutes and bully beef became chunks of red ice. Bread acquired a sour taste and boots froze solid in seconds if they were taken off" (Winter 93). Guy Chapman records other features of the season:

> The cookhouse disappeared. Dugouts filled up and collapsed. The few duckboards floated away, uncovering sump-pits into which the uncharted wanderer fell, his oaths stifled by a brownish stinking fluid. All too late came the issue of long gum boots, held as trench stores. There were only sufficient for the front line. Mobs of cursing men, burdened with the paraphernalia of the army, exchanged boots, in the dark, pinned in by the walls of the trenches. Fortunate the man who did not emerge from the hurly-burly with two left boots. [. . .] Then the front line garrison was reduced by half, and the cellars in the support village filled to the stairway. The front line melted and slid. It became impossible to move along it. Bent double, we reached isolated groups by newly discovered routes over the top [. . .]. (63–64)

At times other things appeared in the trench during thaws and heavy rain: "The trench is water-logged beyond hope. We are up to our waists in ooze. It is enough to make one despair. On the right flank a dead body is coming to light, the legs only so far" (Junger 53).

As action from the Germans began to increase, the main concern for Lewis's battalion was to repair the trenches as rain continued. Yet when trenches continued to collapse, companies were moved back to a support line, leaving but one company post ahead. As work continued, duck-boards were extended up to the front line. These wooden sidewalks, having widely-spaced slats, were to be used in the bottom of a trench, not set above ground. During this time "as the trenches were still impassable" (*WD*), they were set above the trenches in the open. Many men had never observed No Man's Land during daylight save during an attack or through a periscope. Now, in order to move into or away from the line, men moved over open ground in plain view of the Germans. The danger was not merely to those in the very front lines: on 21st January, "1 man was killed on duck-board behind Support line by a Machine Gun bullet about 6 P.M." (*WD*). Over the next few days as the entire "battalion were employed on working parties day and night," periodic activity occurred on both sides with men killed or wounded by machine gun fire. On 24 January two battalion companies bathed, the remainder bathing next day. Before bathing the men and their wool uniforms would have been cakes of mud. Ironically, the entire battalion was once more on working parties the next day—in the mud. On the 27th the battalion was relieved and moved back into divisional reserve at the Bois des Boeufs Camp, finding it still occupied by another unit. In consequence, tea was served to the battalion in the open: a dangerous place to drink tea, especially as enemy aircraft had been active through this week. The next night, after a day of "general cleaning up," as the War Diary relates, "Enemy aircraft bombed the back area during the night." Enemy aircraft continued to increase their activity, and two men were wounded by shell fire. The last two days of January saw the battalion preparing for a long stretch of training—six weeks during which they would stay in shape with sports and take part in various courses and practice. On 31 January, the battalion moved back to Arras, occupying Schramm barracks once more, but Lewis would shortly be leaving his unit for a month of unplanned rest.

NOTES

1.   The book, somewhat soiled, is in the Wade Collection today.
2.   Vivian Henry Bruce Majendie, who would come to write the history of the 1st Somerset Light infantry, retired from the army as a major-general in 1946 (*CL* 348). He was born 20 April 1886 and died 13 January 1960, and not only distinguished himself during the war, gaining the D.S.O., but also had been relatively important as a cricket player from

1907–1910, playing for the Somersets; his statistics are still on line at <http://www. cricket.org/link_to_database/PLAYERS/ENG/M/MAJENDIE_ VHB_01003706/>.

WORKS CITED

Audoin-Rouzeau, Stephane, and Annette Becker. *14–18: Understanding the Great War*. Trans. Catherine Temerson. New York: Hill and Wang, 2002.

Chapman, Guy. *A Passionate Prodigality: Fragments of Autobiography*. Leatherhead: Ashford, 1990.

Junger, Ernst. *The Storm of Steel*. New York: Fertig, 1996.

King, Don. *C. S. Lewis, Poet*. Kent, Ohio: Kent State UP, 2001.

Lewis, C. S. *Letters of C. S. Lewis*. Ed. W. H. Lewis and Walter Hooper. New York: Harcourt, 1993.

———. *The Great Divorce*. New York: Macmillan, 1946.

Lewis, W. H. Memoir. *Letters of C. S. Lewis*. New York: Harcourt, 1975.

McGreevy, Linda F. *Bitter Witness: Otto Dix and the Great War*. New York: Peter Lang, 2001.

Michelin. *Arras: Lens-Douai and The Battles of Artois*. Easingwold, England: Smith, 1994.

Rood, Karen Lane, ed. *American Writers in Paris, 1920–1939*. Detroit: Gale,1980.

Saunders, Anthony. *Weapons of the Trench War 1914–1918*. Phoenix Mill: Sutton, 2000.

Sayer, George. *Jack: A Life of C. S. Lewis*. Wheaton, Ill: Crossway, 1994.

"Vivian Henry Bruce Majendie." *ecb.co.uk*. 23 July 2002. Available: <http://www.cricket.org/ link_to_database/PLAYERS/ENG/M/MAJENDIE_VHB_01003706/>. 25 July 2002.

Winter, Denis. *Death's Men: Soldiers of the Great War*. London: Penguin, 1978.

CHAPTER *7*

Respite and Reflection

ON 1 FEBRUARY 1918 LEWIS'S BATTALION PRACTICED firing on the Butte de Tir range in the Arras area. Lewis, however, was not with them. On 2 February, he explained to Arthur, who had already heard the news from Mrs. Moore, that he was in a military hospital (*CL* 352).

He was in Number 10 Red Cross hospital in Le Treport, also known as Lady Murray's Hospital, which remained in Le Treport from June of 1916 to December of 1918 (Baker). Lewis was suffering from trench fever, or P. O. U. (Pyrexia Origin Unknown), a common ailment among soldiers serving in the trenches. It was first observed in December of 1914 and was initially a mystery to doctors: "Conveyed by lice" and, in early cases lasting "five or six days," another "strain emerged in 1917 in which the average duration of the fever became longer" (Hogg 216). Lewis, like other soldiers, was infected with lice, was weak from long hours marching and working in the mud, and bathed only once in about ten days. It was impossible for infantry in the trenches to keep clean. One soldier counted 103 lice on his clothes and body: "they looked like little translucent lobsters and fed twelve times daily by holding on to clothing with their six feet while they drank blood. They laid five eggs daily [. . .] and these lice were hard to remove, since they could survive on just one blood meal in ten days while their eggs could resist all cold" (Winter 97). Soldiers sat "chatting" one another—searching their uniforms for these vermin hiding in seams of shirts and pants; "thumb nails were used to crack visible lice followed by a candle run up the seams of garments" (Winter 97). Some men threw the lice into a lid set above a candle, where the vermin exploded in a puff of smoke.

Before Lewis suffered this bout of fever, Laurence Johnson, who had been in France long before Lewis arrived, also suffered "slight" Pyrexia (in September of 1917) and was sent to a hospital in Doulens (PRO WO339/83704). Lewis's case, one of the 1917 strains that Hogg described, was not slight and would keep Lewis in hospital at Le Treport for nearly all of February. During this period Lewis's battalion would be out of the line. Instead they would be training as well as participating in sporting events organized between battalions and divisions.

What this long period of rest meant for Lewis is quite beyond what we might initially gather, and it is a time lightly passed over in Lewis biographies. He was safe, being out of the line. He had ample time to read. He had time to write. But he also had time—much time—to think about what the war had meant to him so far and to ponder what it could mean to him in the future.

So far I have not shown much about what the lines were like at Monchy. But as Lewis lay in hospital, he would look back at what he had beheld while in those lines. Despite the mental distancing that his reading allowed him as it took his mind off the war, he nonetheless must have rehearsed his experiences periodically during those long hours of February. It is important to understand just what he had seen, the realities accumulated behind the mere facts of his daily routine.

It is also important to note that war had been significantly different for Jack than for Warnie, who once visited the artillery lines that his unit supplied with ammunition and had been shelled on occasion for a short time (*LP* V.219); a shell burst near him and the fragment that nearly killed him was pulled from a tree and was sent home to Albert. Yet Warnie saw significantly less of the war at its worst than did Jack. In one particular letter Warnie recorded for Albert a visit to ground over which a battle had recently ensued, and while there is disillusion in Warren's tone about the war and the future, one catches also a strain of novelty concerning the event—even in seeing the dead German boy: although moved by such scenes, they are "in reality the ordinary incidents in a successful advance" (*LP* V.109–110). Whether because of a difference in temperament in the two men or because of the difference in Warren's proximity to war's grimmer features, its effects on the elder brother are comparatively milder than its effects on Jack, though Warnie is most assuredly not unaffected. Jack, however, would write of no such things in detail until years later when he came to write his autobiography. Prominent among the images (both in

Surprised by Joy and in *Dymer*) would be the omnipresent corpses retaining eerie postures (*SBJ* 196).

Figure 5. German dead (IWM Q23677).

Soldiers of this war recorded some remarkable encounters with the dead, who were often in massive numbers in places of concentrated battle. On the first day of the Somme, 1 July 1916, 59,000 casualties occurred—20,000 of them killed outright—with the greater part occurring within the first four hours. These men fell along about a 15-mile stretch of the front. Of such dead, one soldier wrote,

> The dead are quiet. Nothing in the world is more still than a dead man. One sees men living, living desperately and then, suddenly emptied of life. A man dies and stiffens into something like a wooden dummy at which one glances for a second with furtive curiosity. One sees such things and one suffers vicariously with the inalienable sympathy of man for man. (qtd. in Winter 132)

Another observed

> The dead man lay amidst earth and broken timber. It seemed like a sacrilege to step over him but there was no evading the issue. Never before had I seen a man who had just been killed. A glance was enough. His face and body were terribly gashed as though some terrific force had pressed him down, and blood flowed from a dozen fearful wounds. The smell of blood mixed with the fumes of the shell filled me with nausea.

[. . .] A voice seemed to whisper with unchallengeable logic, "Why shouldn't you be next?" (qtd. in Winter 133)

Many of the bodies along the Somme remained in No Man's Land for years; they could not be brought in, and until the Allies overran the lines where they fell, they were left in the mud to be repeatedly blown up by shells, to be crawled over in night raids, and to appear in shell holes one hid in. As Denis Winter observed, "Seldom could front-line soldiers get away from these reminders of mortality for any length of time" (132). Ernst Junger also described his encounters, one occurring not far from where Lewis arrived on the Front:

> Jumping out of the trench in the early morning, I found myself in front of a huddled-up corpse, a Frenchman. The putrid flesh, like the flesh of fishes, gleamed, greenish-white through the rents in the uniform. I turned away and then started back in horror: close to me a figure cowered beside a tree. It wore the shining straps and belt of the French, and high upon its back there was still the loaded pack, crowned with a round cooking utensil. Empty eye-sockets and the few wisps of hair on the black and weathered skull told me that this was no living man. Another sat with the upper part of the body clapped down over the legs as though broken through the middle. All round lay dozens of corpses, putrefied, calcined, mummified, fixed in a ghastly dance of death. (21–22)

And elsewhere:

> Among the living lay the dead. As we dug ourselves in we found them in layers stacked one upon the top of another. [. . .]
> The sunken road and the ground behind was full of German dead; the ground in front of English. Arms, legs, and heads stuck out stark above the lips of the craters. In front of our miserable defences [sic] there were torn-off limbs and corpses over many of which cloaks and ground-sheets had been thrown to hide the fixed stare of their distorted features. (99)

Wifred Owen described what he found a perpetual scene:

> Hideous landscapes, vile noises, foul language and nothing but foul, even from one's own mouth (for all are devil ridden), everything unnatural, broken, blasted; the distortions of the dead, whose unburiable bodies sit outside the dug-outs all day, all night, the most execrable sights on earth. In poetry we call them the most glorious. But we sit with them all day, all night . . . and a week later to come back and find them still sitting there, in motionless groups, THAT is what saps the "soldierly spirit". . . . (Stallworthy 159)

Such are the visions Lewis had also been experiencing on a daily basis, for the Monchy sector was full of the dead after 1917 when the Germans were pushed from the village. Yet he would not write of it. Even Albert noted that the letter Jack wrote describing the trenches was intended to appease his fears for his son: it did not succeed (*LP* V 278).

The reality of warfare includes both the outward visions of horror but also their inward relevance to the beholder, which for Lewis encountering the dead included the point previously related, an association with his mother's corpse (*SBJ* 195–196). Lewis was not alone in that association: Max Beckman, in 1915, wrote, "When my mother died, the world seemed just the same to me as it does now. The mystery of corpses pervading everything. . ." (qtd. in Pratt n. p.). When Lewis recalled the death of his mother, it was for two things: its lasting images and its psychological impact. When he wrote of his and Warren's life frozen beneath the strangeness surrounding her death (*SBJ* 19), he was like Max Beckman in describing the war. There he found the inescapable and strange smells of the Front, the perpetual stench of rotting flesh, explosives, gas, rusting metal, blood, the whispering in the trenches at night that was essential to avoid the detection of the enemy. Likewise in the hospital with trench fever, Lewis recalled, it was not the discomfort of his bowels but rather his roommate's secretive and passionate liaisons with a nurse that grated on his nerves (*SBJ* 189–190). Everything he encountered at the Front was a greater disorientation than Lewis had previously known; these phenomena forced his mind back to the images and associations that surrounded his mother's death. It was during that earlier trauma that he had first shaped his means of coping.

That means of coping continued to come from literature. It is a topic to which his letters invariably turn if there are letters of any moderate length. As Denis Winter remarked of the ever-present dead, "Confronted with so many visible witnesses, the mind tried to defend itself by a steadfast refusal to think beyond the concrete and immediate" (132). Winter pushes this point by giving the example of a soldier who has looked upon and describes in a letter the various and hideous corpses—"Death in a thousand different masks"—but next sentence turns his thought: "Heaven knows when our next rations will arrive" (132). Lewis, writing in April 1918, is capable of a similar tricks, turning to the topic of obtaining books from an aunt just after he has described a piece of shell that remains in him (*CL* 368). The turn is perhaps the most common feature of his wartime letters.

His time in hospital is not, of course, all dark. Le Treport must certainly have been a welcome relief. Warnie and Albert are thankful Jack is away from danger for the time, as is Jack. Albert communicated a hope that his son might even be sent home, to which Jack sensibly replied that it was very unlikely. He does, however, direct Albert to the fact that he is for some time out of the trenches, a strong consolation (*CL* 354).

Again, Jack is writing to comfort Albert. To Arthur, however, he writes that he left off reading altogether due to an apparently severe reversal in his condition (*CL* 354); that was written at the same period as the above letter to Albert.

His time in hospital was, then, a mixed time. It gave Lewis unpressured time to read and to write letters when he was well enough to do so. It gave the leisure to ponder his experiences in France thus far, in a place removed from them. But a hospital was a place where death remained all around him. During this time he had further received news that Arthur's cousin had been killed in action on 23 December (*CL* 352). All of the experiences would distill at this time into something close to despair. To Arthur, in a moment preceding a long reminiscence of their walks together and occupation with opera and reading, he asks in doubtful tones, "Shall we ever be the same again?" (*CL* 355). He does hold out some hope: "However, we may have good times yet, although I have been at a war and although I love someone" (*CL* 355). He is despairing what Philip Larkin articulated: the loss of innocence (Fussell 18), which he was losing to the war and his relations with Mrs. Moore.

In this introspective letter to Arthur, Lewis considers that only their mutual interests in literature have remained (*CL* 355), and it is here that he pleads with Arthur that he should continue writing to him on this topic (*CL* 356). The request is principally a prayer that his paradigm should stand firm against the realities he was experiencing at the front.

In this regard, Jack's propensity at this time for George Eliot is telling. In Eliot is an ideal England—largely a rural England[1]—that many soldiers longed for; fraught though her work is with slight social unrest and conflicts between families and personalities, it is nothing near the shattering violence of the war; her novels describe collective assumptions that are essentially civilized. When characters violate those assumptions, the reaction is decidedly against them; hers is an ordered world. That Lewis, after reading *Counter-Attack*, believes its author, Siegfried Sassoon, to be a vile creature is precisely because Sassoon's poetry avoids the assumptions of English rural poetry of the time; it expresses instead the reality of conditions at the front. Lewis was not alone: as Fussell points out, Middleton Murray found "Sassoon's poems didn't behave" in the ways of the English rural tradition as "too many of them [. . .] neglected to indicate the pastoral norm by which their horrors were to be gauged" (236). More will be said on this in consideration of Lewis's own war poetry. But here we note Lewis's preference for the rural poetry of Edward Marsh's *Georgian Poetry* anthologies (*CL* 404), which he felt expressed the "normal" world. Guy Chapman recalled his own reading, strangely parallel to Lewis's own,

> I mused upon ancient walls—Arras was an echo of Oxford—and read Meredith, a queer choice, but Meredith's artificial world transported the reader from a reality thudding with gunfire. Arras was full of surprises [. . .] down to the Field Cashier's office unexpectedly discovered shell-broken and full of blood and wounded men. (171)

George Eliot's worlds, as Chapman found in Meredith's, are also distinct from the war's: Eliot's are lush and green; the front barren of vegetation. The war is a place not only of flying metal and clouds of gas settling into low places and forcing one out in the open to be fired upon but is also rife with diseases that may infect the slightest scratch and turn a limb gangrenous. Such worlds as Meredith's and Eliot's are those that, simply put, are civilized and lead one's mind away from what the Front presented daily:

> . . . stench of rotten flesh was over everything, hardly repressed by the chloride of lime sprinkled on particularly offensive sites. Dead horses and dead men—and parts of both—were sometimes not buried for months and often simply became an element of parapets and trench walls. You could smell the front line miles before you could see it. Lingering pockets of gas added to the unappetizing atmosphere. (Fussell 49)

One soldier wrote of getting his drinking water out of a shell hole until a German corpse was found in it (Winter 102). But these are merely the outward semblances of that other world, conveying nothing of the psychological trauma caused when such scenes are taken in daily doses, and, not least, it says nothing of the effects encountered upon losing one's friends to horrible deaths—nor of surviving one's friends.

But there is one other scene that Lewis no doubt witnessed and thought of, a scene that removed in horrible ways "such linchpins of cheerful normalcy" which might also include the daily work in the trenches in quiet moments (Winter 59); such scenes effected visions (and their consequent repetition in nightmares) that could drive men along a path to madness. On 22 December, as already related, the Germans shelled the trenches as Lewis's battalion was in the line, during which time they suffered three direct hits. The simple phrase "direct hits" conceals what this means when the men must dig up a bunker where a shell has landed, and one dug up one's own men as quickly as possible, hoping for survivors:

> Of corporal Everett we found no trace; he must have been struck by the shell and blown to atoms. Bennett was badly shattered and most of his head was gone, whilst Hollins, who had been sitting with his rifle between his knees, was unrecognizable and the twisted rifle was buried in the front of his body. (Vaughan 48)

One might say there is no evidence that Lewis ever observed such a scene. One passage (and there are plenty more) in his poem *Dymer* stand to a refute to such notions (43).

Men, in leisure moments out of the line or at work remember and replay such an event. Not willingly do they do so; the replay is often intrusive and involuntary. And thus they also recall for their glaring contrast—like the worlds of Eliot and Meredith—the world of home: "In the penny world, what hopes? There was a country called England somewhere. It has once possessed beauties, perhaps more beautiful in dreams than in reality" (Chapman 260). There is, for most soldiers, no place where these two worlds may meet. For Lewis in hospital, he could only attempt to push the war into the background through reading and writing. Yet of the long hours of that month which he spent remembering the life that he and Arthur had shared, which the war in its ghastly vestiges was obliterating, he says virtually nothing. In his autobiography he records only a few amusing facts about this stay in the hospital. One was how he and a roommate who hated women could by straightening their beds each morning keep an abrasive nurse from coming in and doing it and thus pestering the men. The nurse put it down to the men being chivalrous (*SBJ* 189–190).

While Lewis remained in Le Treport, his battalion continued in training and in sports. Majendie explains that competition throughout the army was begun; "the intention was that eliminating competitions should be held within battalions, brigades, divisions and corps, with the idea of eventually selecting the best platoon in the Army in France" (64). The competition, while carrying on even after Lewis rejoined his unit at the end of February, was never completed due to the German attack later in the spring. Nevertheless, competitions were performed in military maneuvers (bayonet and firing) and in less official venues (boxing and rugby).

Training, however, remained the main concern of the battalion. They left the Wilderness Camp and marched to Wanquentin where "a good training area was available, and most successful training was carried out, the value of which was fully apparent later in the year" (Majendie 65). It was evident that the Germans were preparing "an offensive of a very big scale, the only [unknown] points being the date and the exact locality" (65). While some of the training that the battalion performed was rushed and "prevented the greatest value being obtained," they yet practiced in "principles of fire and movement" as well as in "various phases of open warfare, gas drill, and gas discipline," this latter due to the "ever increasing use of gas shells by the enemy" (Majendie 65). In consequence, the men spent extensive time in their gas masks, or box respirators, which were worn while they marched, and, in some cases, while they slept (Majendie 66).

In mid-February, Lewis wrote to his father, and told him of the same officer he had met in his first night in the trenches, P. G. K. Harris. Harris, he related, was his captain and a man Albert may have remembered from Jack's school (*CL* 357). Harris, called "Pogo" by Lewis in his autobiography, seemed to Lewis to be almost one of the boys, someone from a *Jeeves* novel (*SBJ* 67), someone as Walter Hooper interprets it, "of uncertain temper" (*CL* 357 n.11). Lewis says that in running into Harris at this time, he found that he had less respect for his Captain, something Lewis also apparently felt in encountering others he had known in England (*CL* 357). However, the change in feeling may have been due to the shift in context, for now "Pogo" was quite removed from his duties as a schoolmaster.

Harris's military record indicates he was of sterner stuff than many supposed, distinguishing himself in his duties, earning the Military Cross in May of 1918 and a bar to that medal in November of the same year (PRO WO339/24756). A personal letter from Majendie recommending him to the War Office remains in Harris's military record. Even if Harris was exemplary as a commander, he must also have been markedly human. Majendie, in the battalion history, relates with evident amusement that Harris

> was standing at the top of some cellar steps collecting prisoners, when a German came up from below "Kamerading" with such enthusiasm that he collided with Captain Harris and knocked him down. Captain Harris sat down violently on top of a dead German, and in his efforts to rise put his hand on the dead man's face. This was too much for Light Company's Commander; he leapt at the offender and, mindful of his Oxford days, caught him such a left under the jaw that the unhappy German did not recover consciousness for a long time. (120)

One who has never been in war pictures a corpse in relatively pristine condition, a creation perhaps described by Evelyn Waugh in *The Loved One*—something like a manikin in uniform. This seems not to be the case, given Harris's reaction. Even if newly dead, a corpse could be a horrid thing to behold, let alone touch. And if dead for some time, something found on any part of the Front, a corpse could be utterly appalling, as one man relates:

> the bodies had the consistency of Camembert cheese. I once fell and put my hand through the belly of a man. It was days before I got the smell out of my hands. I remember wondering if I would get blood poisoning. (Winter 208)

This would easily explain Harris's extreme reaction. Harris suffered some unfortunate events in terms of his own health during the war: appendicitis in December of 1915, and he was wounded in "an accident in the Trenches on active service," in an unfortunate way, which left "the right testicle [. . .] slightly tender," a condition that rendered "pain upon hurried walking" (PRO WO339/24756). Such was the commander of Lewis's "Light" Company.[2]

As Lewis recovered he began to dread a return to duty and wished for his condition to again worsen (*CL* 358). He describes a walk he took around Le Treport and tells Arthur of his reading, primarily a biography of Cellini, and that he was on to another of George Eliot's novels (*CL* 360). Yet for all his reading, his return to the Front remained the foremost issue upon his mind. In a letter to Albert, whom he usually comforted, Jack writes with irony that he noted a positive view of the war was related proportionately to a person's location. The nearer one was to the trenches, the more hopeless things seemed to be (*CL* 362). As time for his return approached, he must have felt increasingly hopeless.

On 28 February, Lewis rejoined his battalion, who were still in training in Wanquentin and enduring "very cold weather" (*WD*). It would have been a severe change from the near month Lewis spent resting in hospital where he had enjoyed a real bed and a fire (*CL* 359). The battalion diary provides a general record of daily events from 1 March to 19 March when the battalion left Wanquentin and returned to Schramm barracks in Arras. During the time work details and "training continued," with Lewis's company winning the Guard Mounting and Company Drill. Laurence Johnson's "B" Company won the bayonet drills on 5 March and the Tug of War competition the next day. Drilling also continued on use of box respirators and "a scheme against Dummy Tanks" (*WD*). On 6 March, the battalion was ordered to be ready to move in 1 hour's notice, and while they remained on such readiness until 14 March, no order to move took place. On 11 March, an inspection took place, with a march past the Brigadier General on the training grounds. However, preparation for more significant events were taking place. On four days between 3 and 12 March, various officers went with Majendie north and east of Arras, near Fampoux, to examine the terrain and trench systems. Although Fampoux is only about five miles to the north of Monchy, the areas into which the battalion would next move were areas holding greater danger than Lewis had experience around Monchy.

NOTES

1.   In relation to the importance of rural England to the war paradigm, see Fussell, chapter VII: "Arcadian Recourses" which provides description of a significant aspect of the ideal England for which soldiers longed, but also provides a larger context for the poetry that Lewis would both prefer to read and to write.

2.   The battalion diary for 10 March, a period during which the men were still in training, indicates that "'H' Company earns the title of 'Light' Company," which it is called thereafter in the diary.

WORKS CITED

Baker, Chris. "The Stationary and General Hospitals of 1914–1918." *The Long, Long Trail.* 26 May 2003. <http://www.1914–1918.net/hospitals.htm> 2003.

Chapman, Guy. *A Passionate Prodigality: Fragments of Autobiography.* Leatherhead: Ashford, 1990.

Fussell, Paul. *The Great War and Modern Memory.* Oxford: Oxford UP, 1975.

Hogg, Ivan V. *Dictionary of World War I.* Lincolnwood, Illinois: NTC, 1997.

Junger, Ernst. *The Storm of Steel.* New York: Fertig, 1996.

Lewis, C. S. *Mere Christianity.* New York: Simon and Schuster, 1996.

Majendie, V. B. H. *A History of the 1st Battalion: The Somerset Light Infantry (Prince Albert's), July 1st, 1916, to the End of the War.* Taunton, England: Goodman, 1921.

Pratt, George. *No Man's Land: A Postwar Sketchbook of the War in the Trenches.* Northampton, Massachusetts: Tundra, 1992.

Stallworthy, Jon. *Wilfred Owen: A Biography.* Oxford: Oxford UP, 1977.

Vaughan, Edwin Campion. *Some Desperate Glory.* New York: Simon & Schuster, 1989.

Winter, Denis. *Death's Men: Soldiers of the Great War.* London: Penguin, 1979.

Man and Mouse

WHEN LEWIS REJOINED HIS BATTALION, IT WAS still in the midst of training at Wanquentin, not at Fampoux,[1] training which would continue up to 18 March, only after which did it move from Wanquentin to Arras, and then to Fampoux. The battalion diary further indicates that beyond their training, on 5 March and other days, they continued to be involved in various competitions: "'Light' Company competitions held"—that is, competitions deciding which company would be awarded the title of "Light" Company—"'H' Company won the Guard Mounting and Company Drill, while B Company won the bayonet competition" (*WD*). Lewis purportedly wrote to his father on 5 March, but the following events recorded in the War Diary—training, sports, and only after 20 March the return to the front lines—show this dating to be mistaken.

On 16 March, "Officers played the Sergeants at football, Officers losing 3–1. 'FOLLIES' performed in the evening" (*WD*). When such entertainment was provided, a soldier could gather that a stretch at the Front was immanent.

The long period of training ended on 19 March, the day the battalion left Wanquentin and arrived in Arras at 4:30 and billeted in Schramm barracks for one night. On the morning of the 20th, the battalion moved to "the front line of the Center Sector North of the SCARPE" river, being "conveyed from ARRAS to FAMPOUX by railway" (*WD*). Three companies were placed in the front lines, among which was "Light," Lewis's company. The front line was

in the center section of trenches north of the Scarpe, in what appears to be
Coral, Coot, and Cadiz trenches. The first night here was quiet. The next day
was not: "The German offensive began South of the SCARPE on the front of
56 miles. On our sector considerable shelling during day and night, many gas
shells being used. Several direct hits on our front line. 2 men were killed and
3 wounded" (*WD*). This offensive began the Germans' last efforts to win the
war; they would advance a considerable distance.

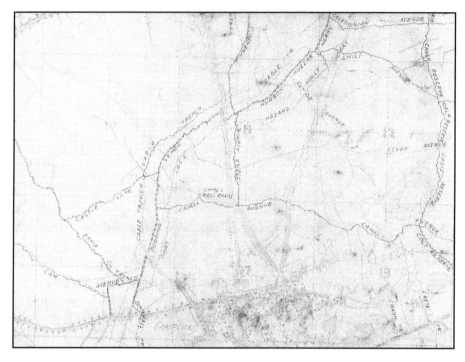

Map 2. Fampoux trench map as of 21 September 1917 (National Archives (PRO)
WO297/1839). A trench line would later be dug running south of Stoke near the capital "A"
on "Camel Avenue;" Lewis served part of his time in this trench. See the aerial photo, Figure 6.
Circles along the lines are dug outs.

From the point of the German advance, the war would become a more savage experience for Lewis and his battalion.

His battalion attempted repair of the trenches on the 22nd, and on the following day at dawn the front line where Lewis's company was posted was vacat-
ed. That afternoon German patrols entered the line but were "ejected" and
"believed to have been hit" (*WD*). Later another German patrol approached
the line but were repulsed by battalion firing. On 24th, the battalion was
relieved from the front lines and moved back into reserve in Sterling Camp,

Figure 6. Aerial photo of trench lines at the devastated village of Fampoux from 13 August 1918.
On 1 April 1918, Lewis in "Light" Company was sent from H.17.b.4.4 to "150 yards North
of Camel Avenue" into Stoke Trench (*WD*), the line between white arrows at top left and upper
center of photo. The white along the trenches is chalk that lies under the topsoil and was
brought up by digging and by exploding shells. The cross indicates north; light is from low in
the east, from the right. Trenches are zig-zaged, "crenellated," to stop shell fragments from flying long distances inside a trench line. (IWM Q47847)

which was along the road between Fampoux and the village of Athies, with
Laurence Johnson's "B" Company, however, being placed in Pudding Trench,
where, on 25th, "A" Company joined it. On 26 March "orders were received
at night to work on Army Line, just East of the Camp on both sides of the
SCARPE. Dumps [for ammunition . . .] were made in this line, and at 5 A.M.,
26th, the line was manned. Battalion Headquarters moved into the dug-out

in the embankment just North of the River" (*WD*). It is at this time Lewis wrote to his father a letter that has been incorrectly dated 5 March (*CL* 363). Given the context of the battalion training at Wanquentin on 5 March (they had not been in the line during Lewis's stay in the hospital), and given the nature of events he describes in the letter, it should be dated 26 March. He remarked to his father that he has moved back from the front lines after four days in them during which hostile activity has increased. He has been largely without sleep and on a work detail (*CL* 363). What he describes is likely what the battalion diary mentioned: the installation of the new battalion headquarters, the ammunition dumps, and the work done on Army Line, all of which are behind the lines.

This relief at Sterling Camp remained extremely tense despite its remove from the front lines. The men "stood to" while eating their breakfasts, but in mid-morning a "stand down" was given, and work begun overnight on the line just east of Sterling Camp was resumed. A single shell was reported to have fallen on the 26th: it landed on a hut used by another battalion killing 16 and wounding 41 men. That night, shelling increased and continued through the next morning. Early the next morning, at 2:45 A.M., an order came to move two companies into the same trench system Johnson's company was in, the 3rd System of support lines, but the order was cancelled soon after. The remainder of the day was quiet, as was that night, but at 3:00 A.M. on the 28th, "a very heavy barrage fell North and South of the SCARPE, together with a considerable quantity of gas. 3 direct hits on STERLING CAMP" (*WD*). About three hours later, orders came for the remaining two companies, "Light" (Lewis's) and "C," to join the other companies in the 3rd System lines. "Shelling was heavy on the FAMPOUX Road" (*WD*) with, again, considerable amounts of gas being used by the Germans, so the two companies moved up via an alternative path, losing one man in the process. "About 7–30 A.M. the Germans began their attack on our sector, but their progress was very slow," the diary records, yet holding the lines, which was accomplished by a number of other battalions, was a tenuous affair. "During the night"—one catches the euphemism—"a re-adjustment took place" (*WD*). The line was pushed back: "Rifle Brigade held new front line in STOKE from CAMEL to SCARPE. 'Light' Company moved back into Reserve line, 3rd. System. [. . .] Casualties—5 killed, 6 wounded, 1 missing" (*WD*).

The term "missing" was ominous in this war, as so many men had simply disappeared—physically—when hit or buried by a shell. Some who were buried later turned up again when another shell landed or were discovered while units dug a trench. Men who fell during an attack could remain in No Man's Land, unrecoverable, and their corpses subject to repeated barrages. In contrast, to be captured was, on the whole, to be out of danger, as Evelyn Waugh explained regarding his brother Alec who "had been posted to the front; the battle of Passchendaele was in progress—if the phrase can be used of that notorious operation—and huge casualty lists appeared daily. My parents were in perpetual anxiety for his safety" (114). Eventually the news arrived for the Waughs:

> The Easter holidays were darkened by the report that my brother was "missing" in the Ludendorf offensive. [. . .] Presently there was a telegram announcing that he was a prisoner. My father, even at the moment of victory, was haunted by the fear that the Germans would massacre their prisoners. (122–123)

Before long, Lewis would also encounter the term "missing."

As they moved into the new front line along Stoke and Camel to the Scarpe river, one man was killed. From this time forward, the daily entries in the battalion's War Diary increase in length respective to the increases in German activity. The almost continual shelling is the most remarkable feature of these days, continuous shelling stretching over long periods. It was a way to keep troops down. On 29 March the War Diary records "Heavy shelling early," with a party of Germans in Stoke Trench at 7:00 A.M. The officer who was commanding A company received an order to send a bombing party down Camel to expel the enemy, but this attempt failed. One of the very sad, but altogether common, events of the nature of this fighting occurred next: "Captain Parsons ordered Lieut. Prince to counter-attack with 2 platoons from PORT [trench] [. . .], and were told that they had to attack over the open and retake STOKE" (WD). This means they emerged from the trenches in daylight, being conspicuous targets making progress from a series of shell holes while under fire, as described: "The attack came under considerable machine gun fire and progress was slow. The enemy ran as soon as the attack developed, and STOKE was empty" (WD). These two platoons, from "A" Company, remained in Stoke, holding the recovered trench, but it cost them: "Casualties 1 Officer wounded and 27" other ranks wounded, with a lieutenant wounded and Captain Parsons, who ordered the initial attack, "killed later while trying to bring in wounded" (WD). Two platoons of Lewis's "Light" company were brought forward to replace the two platoons of "A" that had re-taken the trench. These platoons of "Light" company "remained here astride the FAMPOUX-PONT DU JOUR- Road" (WD). Later that afternoon, trenches at the top of the rise north and west of Fampoux—Pudding Trench—were "heavily shelled," with Second Lieutenant F. W. Perrett being wounded; their total casualties were 3 officers and about 80 other ranks. Of these days Lewis writes that a couple of his acquaintances were casualties, including F. W. Perrett, who was one of the men Lewis knew from England. Perrett was with

Figure 7. Men marching past a tank stuck on the road between Fampoux and Athies in April of 1917. Lewis would walk this road in March of 1918 (IWM Q6434).

him at school and was wounded in the eye by a fragment (*CL* 363). Lewis would meet up again with Perrett, but for now Lewis was seeing war quite apart from the romance that he formerly attached to it through reading Homer. It must have been in this period of heavy shelling that Lewis recalled in his autobiography how he met a mouse which, unafraid of Lewis, remained with him—both man and mouse shaking in their fear of being blasted (*SBJ* 195). The effects of continuous shelling were well described by Ernst Junger:

Now and then the ear was utterly dazed by a single absolutely hellish crash accompanied by a sheet of flame. Then an unceasing and sharp swishing gave the impression again that hundreds of pound weights were flying after each other through the air with incredible velocity. Then came another dud, plunging with a short, heavy thump that shook the solid earth all round. Shrapnel exploded by the dozen, [. . .] scattering their little bullets in a heavy shower, with the empty cases whizzing after them. When a shell went up near-by, the soil rattled down in a torrent, and with it the jagged splinters as sharp as razors rent the air on all sides.

[. . .] the brain links every separate sound of whirring metal with the idea of death, and so the nerves are exposed without protection and without a pause to a sense of the utmost menace. Thus I crouched in my little hole with my hand in front of my eyes, while all the possibilities of being hit passed through my imagination. (80–81)

Some men, well beyond shivering, were known to dart from their dugout into the shelling and certain death. For Wilfred Owen, it was thus:

My dug-out held 25 men tight packed. Water filled it to a depth of 1 or 2 feet, leaving say 4 feet of air.
One entrance had been blown in & blocked.
So far, the other remained.
The Germans knew we were staying there and decided we shouldn't.
Those fifty hours were the agony of my happy life.
Every ten minutes on Sunday afternoon seemed an hour.
I nearly broke down and let myself drown in the water that was now slowly rising over my knees. (156)

The end of March came with heavy shelling of Pudding and Port trenches on the morning of the 30th, during which one captain was wounded, followed by more shelling of these trenches that afternoon with several direct hits. "A" company relieved "C" company along the river, and the battalion enjoyed a quiet night. Early morning on 31st, however, brought renewed shelling on Pudding and the trench that continued from Pudding to the south across the Fampoux road, Dingwall Trench. What was unusual about this bombardment was that it came from artillery situated behind Germans lines at Monchy. The Germans fired these guns so as to have better impact on Allied trenches from that angle, which was nearly straight from the south. Pudding Trench was in a strategic location, situated atop a hill and coveted by the Germans: from this rise in ground (as with any, even slight, rise anywhere on the Western Front), troops in occupation could observe enemy movement at long distances. Standing today where Pudding Trench once ran, one can easily see Monchy— also on rising ground—and the surrounding plains. At the time Lewis was there, the absence of most trees and bushes allowed enemy movements to be easily observed. The use of airships also assisted in the observation, and a photo exists of the Germans keeping a manned balloon behind the trees at Bois du

Sart (IWM Q52920), near the lines at Monchy. Beyond its immediate strategic value, the Germans wanted this ground so they could move their own
troops unseen during what would become their last major offensive.

As previously related, the areas before Arras and Arras itself had been devastated by German bombardment from 1914 on. In March of 1918, when the
Germans attempted their last great offensive, they initiated a final intense
bombardment of the town and its environs, devastating what little remained
intact. Villages like Fampoux and Monchy were mere piles of broken stone and
brick.

Figure 8. The ruins of Fampoux (IWM Q7015).

Arras, indeed, had been an important place for the Germans, who entered the
town for three days in 1914 but were quickly forced out. They remained just
beyond its reaches, holding the land around the town and forming a salient—
placing the town, one might say, in a peninsula surrounded on three sides by
the enemy and consequently shelled from three directions. In the spring of
1915, a battle was fought to force the Germans back in order to provide relief
for the town. This advance by the French lasted from 9 May to 19 June, during which time the Germans had been pushed back only two to four kilometers. These days brought to both sides numerous casualties. From April to May
of 1917 another significant offensive ensued in which the Germans were
pushed back, with Vimy Ridge, Monchy, and other important villages taken

from them. Again, in the spring of 1918, Arras was a primary target for the Germans; the attack code name was MARS. German General Ludendorff, having been successful with his attack on the Somme (the 2nd Somme), attempted to "regain the initiative [. . . .] This new operation had Arras as its objective and began on March 28" (Tucker 164). Yet when he could not succeed against either Arras or Amiens, Ludendorff called off the offensive (5 April), only to renew it just south of Ypres along the Lys River from 9–21 April (Tucker 164–165). The "Battle of Arras" (as discussed in the major histories of the war) is the battle of April 1917, which occurred before Lewis was in France. This previous battle and 1918's MARS offensive have as a result been sometimes confused.

As Lewis remained in Fampoux through March 28, the action increased steadily into April. On 1 April, after a day during which the British forces used their advantage of "good observation both North and South of the river, and many targets were successfully fired on" (*WD*), the battalion moved into the new front line during the night with the companies, Lewis's listed first, arranged as follows:

"Light" Company from H.17.b.4.4. to 150 yards North of CAMEL AVENUE. (*WD*)

This location I have marked by arrows on the aerial photo of the trenches at Fampoux. The number/letter references are used as coordinates on trench maps only.[2] The other companies were situated as follows:

"A" Company from FAMPOUX Road to H.17.b.4.4.
"B" Company [Laurence Johnson's] South of FAMPOUX Road.
"C" Company in PUDDING and PORT trenches. (*WD*)

Rain fell on 2 April, again bringing muddy conditions to the trenches, but enemy shelling was below the new average. On 3 April, the weather improved, and while shelling generally continued to be light, two trenches—Stoke and Pudding—took more shelling, with the men in Pudding enduring it all day. Pudding, being the strategic line atop the hill, was filled with dugouts. A farmer who owns land in this region told me that tunnels from these dugouts extended down the hill to Fampoux, presumably linking some of these dugouts. One may observe on the trench map (National Archives (PRO) WO297/1839 that they occur about every fifteen to twenty feet. Dugouts were reinforced and offered some added protection from the shelling.

On 4 April, heavy shelling took place on the front line, and less enemy movement was observed south of the Scarpe; rain again fell in the evening. The 5th brought renewed action from 6:30 A.M. on when "hostile artillery commenced a heavy and systematic shelling of our trenches. Shelling began about 100 yards in front of STOKE Trench and gradually extended to PORT and PUDDING Trenches, and areas in the rear" (*WD*). Fampoux itself endured light shelling, but the Fampoux road was "heavily shelled with Heavies and Field Guns" (*WD*), shelling intended to prevent a quick retreat and to prohibit the arrival of any reinforcements to the area. While the shelling in some of these areas abated mid-morning, again Pudding and Port were shelled throughout the day along with Pepper and Camel, which retained significant damage. One man was killed and one wounded this day, and at night the battalion was relieved; they moved back from these lines into brigade reserve. In reserve "Light" Company occupied trenches west of battalion headquarters (at H.15.a.3.5)—the trenches just northeast of Athies below Cam Avenue. "B" Company was placed in the village of Athies; "A" Company was set in Cam Avenue; "C" Company moved into Cam Valley (*WD*).

After a day standing in reserve and a night spent working on Carolina Trench, the battalion was relieved the next day and moved away from the Fampoux area.

As has been shown not only of his time in Monchy but also of this time in Fampoux, Lewis had seen a significant amount of action. Yet Lewis wrote in his autobiography that men who had seen longer and worse combat than he had been in had already presented much about their experiences; he himself did not see the need to say much more (*SBJ* 195). Here, I believe, Lewis was again posing. His words might be seen as suitable deference toward men who performed incredible feats of arms or who were in for the duration of the war and who endured service in particularly active sectors. Or his words may be put down to self-deprecation. In either case one point remains: the words are not true. Even at this point in his war he had lost friends. He had endured raids, shelling, gas, mud, sleepless nights, the sight and the stench of corpses, bombs (falling whilst attempting a risky visit to the latrine). He experienced the daily conditions of the trenches, trench fever, hours spent making and installing wire, a collapsed dugout in which some of his battalion were buried, direct hits in his line. He endured, in short, every aspect of war that soldiers at the Front endured. There was nothing more of the war to behold—unless it meant being wounded.

NOTES

1.   Walter Hooper, in *Letters of C. S. Lewis: Revised and Enlarged Edition*, remarks in an editorial comment that "Jack was discharged from the hospital on 28 February. He rejoined his battalion at Fampoux" (77).

2. For instructions on reading these coordinates, see the text at the bottom of the trench map IWM map 36aSE (Map 3 on p. 121), which provides a brief description. Majendie also discusses how these coordinates are read.

WORKS CITED

Junger, Ernst. *The Storm of Steel*. New York: Fertig, 1996.
Stallworthy, John. *Wilfred Owen: A Biography*. Oxford: Oxford UP, 1977.
Tucker, Spencer C. *The Great War 1914–18*. Bloomington: Indiana UP, 1998.
Waugh, Evelyn. *A Little Learning*. Boston: Little, Brown, 1964.

CHAPTER *9*

The Power Who Slays

THE LUDENDORFF OFFENSIVE, THE LAST GERMAN PUSH, occurring in the spring of 1918, was to be a "series of attacks designed to push the British army back on the Channel, isolating it from the French Army"; once accomplished it would allow the Germans to turn on the British (Tucker 160). And once the British were overwhelmed, the French would surrender. The initial attack, called Michael, ran from 21 March to 5 April and saw the Germans troops well supplied in overwhelming numbers move against the juncture of British and French units on the Front. Where it began for the British, it was called the Second Battle of the Somme. After his O.T.C. training, Paddy Moore became a second lieutenant assigned to the 2nd Rifle Battalion. His battalion was in the Somme area when the German push began. The attack was set from La Fère to Arras, and on the second day communication was broken between the French on the south of the line and the British on the north (Tucker 162). The Germans began to push the British back early on, with the village of Baupaume being captured on 24 and Albert on 26 March, but the British also inflicted heavy casualties on the German troops who were moving over open ground. Paddy Moore's battalion, as his battalion's war diary shows, moved on 23 March towards the front and were advancing to the village of Pargny, "coming under heavy shell fire, while crossing the high ground above the river" where they "took over line of river from N[orth] of PARGNY bridge to

S[outh] of" Fontaine les Pargny (WO95/1731). One company succeeded in rushing the bridge and penetrating into the enemy line but were pushed back immediately with casualties to and some prisoners taken from the enemy; two machine guns were also captured. Of their own men, five officers were killed with "60 other ranks killed and wounded" (WO95/1731). The next day was critical for Moore's battalion: the Germans bombed their position on the river bank just after dawn and succeeded in crossing the river on the right and left of the line: "Situation became very precarious and withdrawal was ordered. This was effected in good order, but with very heavy casualties, Battalion taking up line of sunken road 500 yards E[east] of" the village of Morchain (WO95/1731). They remained there for only about an hour after which they retreated another 300 yards to the northeast outskirts of Morchain. The men held this position until about 4:00 P.M. and then were ordered to withdraw.

By the time of this withdrawal Paddy Moore was dead. He was first listed as missing—perhaps in the action at the bridge head. A letter written by Mrs. Moore indicates that he was captured but managed to escape and return to his unit. She laments that he had escaped (*LP* VI.44), which would have allowed him to remain relatively safe and behind lines. This information of his escape from the Germans is not reported in his military record nor in his battalion's diary. According to indications given by Mrs. Moore to Paddy's school and printed in his school's magazine in May, he had been listed as missing on 24 March and was presumed dead, as all other senior ranks and the majority of the other ranks of his company were also casualties (*CL* 369–370). In the same materials, Moore is praised for his fight against the German advance.

The battalion diary lists for 24 March that Moore was among the "wounded and missing" (WO95/1731). Mrs. Moore would not receive confirmation that her son was dead until 5 September, until which time she knew only what the diary indicates, that he was wounded and missing. Before September she had attempted to discover what had happened to him, apparently pressing the War Office to locate a witness who had been last to see Paddy. News that came back from two witnesses conflicted on the point slightly but left no doubt that Paddy was dead. The first witness, Rifleman R. V. Lilley, reported to the War Office on 8 February 1919 that "On 23rd March in the village of Bethencourt on the canal bank I saw Moore's body lying in front of a dug-out. I recognised him. The ground was not held, the body was left" and described Moore as "5' 6" fair, no Moustache, near 30" (WO339/97704). The War Office, in reporting this news to Mrs. Moore concedes that "the date is not correct" but nonetheless seems to confirm his death (WO339/97704). Another report, however, from Rifleman J. Howe in "A" Company, provides a different story:

I saw Mr. Moore get killed near Nestle about March 24. It was about 4 or 5 A.M. while we were retiring [retreating]. About an hour earlier we got word that the enemy was getting round us and we commenced to retire. When Mr. Moore got killed we were coming rapidly down a road which the enemy had covered with M[achine] G[un]. I was about 3 yards behind Mr. Moore when I saw him fall with a wound in the leg. I stopped and bound up the wound. While I was binding up his leg, he got another bullet right through his head, which killed him instantly. The enemy were very close and we could do nothing byt [sic] leave the body. I had known Lt. Moore 3 months and am quite sure of him. Mr. Moore was in A Co. and his initials were E. F. C. (WO339/97704)

This news would not reach Mrs. Moore and Lewis until the following year. One point in this account is suspicious: the certainty of the bullet which killed Moore. Compare it to this relatively well-known passage in which a soldier on leave visits the mother of a friend who has in actuality suffered an excruciating death:

This quaking, sobbing woman who shakes me and cries out on me: "Why are you living then, when he is dead?"—who drowns me in tears and calls out: "What are you there for at all, child, when you—"—who drops into a chair and wails: "Did you see him? Did you see him then? How did he die?"

I tell her he was shot through the heart and died instantaneously. She looks at me, she doubts me: "You lie. I know better. I have felt how terribly he died. I have heard his voice at night, I have felt his anguish—tell the truth, I want to know it, I must know it." (Remarque 182–183)

The well-known passage brings Paul, the protagonist of *All Quiet on the Western Front*, to confront more than this woman who pleads with him to tell her the truth: "I cannot bear the uncertainty. Tell me how it was and even though it will be terrible, it will be far better than what I have to think if you don't" (183). Paul "will never tell her," for "when a man has seen so many dead he cannot understand any longer why there should be so much anguish over a single individual. So I say rather impatiently: 'He died immediately. He felt absolutely nothing at all. His face was quite calm" (Remarque 183). But when the dead man's mother makes him swear an oath—"by everything that is sacred to you"—this disillusioned soldier finds it absurd: "Good God, what is there that is sacred to me?" (Remarque 184). But the woman presses further: "Are you willing never to come back yourself, if it isn't true?" to which he can only reply in the affirmative and observe "I would swear to anything [. . . .] I have to tell her how it happened so I invent a story and I almost believe it myself" (Remarque 184).

Even a bullet in the head does not always bring death. Bullets similar to those used in WWI struck American President Kennedy in 1963; one recalls

the widely publicized details of the damage and his lingering. In years of reading about the trauma of war and the fate of soldiers, perhaps the worst death
I have read about came from just such a single bullet to the head:

> Pratt was hopeless. His head was shattered. Splatterings of brain lay in a pool under
> him, but he refused to die. Old Corporal Welch looked after him, held his body and
> arms as they writhed and fought feebly as he lay. It was over two hours before he died,
> hours of July sunshine in a crowded place where perhaps a dozen men sat with the smell
> of blood while all the time above the soothing of the corporal came a gurgling and
> moaning from his lips, now high and liquid, now low and dry—a death rattle fit for
> the most blood thirsty novelist. (Winter 109)

Ernst Junger knew what a single bullet could do: "the volunteer, Motullo, was
killed by a shot through the head. Though his brain fell over his face to his chin,
his mind was still clear when we took him to the nearest dugout" (231).
Another man crouched against the trench wall, shot through the forehead,
bleeding as if blood "poured out of a bucket. The snorting death-rattles
sounded at longer intervals and at last ceased" (Junger 273–274).

These incomprehensible events create a dilemma similar to that which
Joseph Conrad's character Marlow faced in meeting Kurtz's intended in *Heart
of Darkness*: the witness to appalling misery is at a loss on how to explain to
another person the horrible event. Marlow could not tell the woman that
Kurtz's last words were not her name but were instead "The horror! The horror!" The precedent in The Great War was to tell family something softer than
the reality. Whereas Vera Brittain learned one tale of her brother's death, that
"he had reportedly been shot through the head by a sniper and had died instantaneously" (Bishop and Bostridge 399), Brittain herself sought and received
3 reports, one from a private, "the most direct and vivid" (439) who was with
him during the attack in which he was killed:

> Shortly after the trench was regained Capt. Brittain who was keeping a sharp look out
> on the enemy was shot through the Head by an enemy sniper, he only lived a few min-
> utes. (440)

Lewis knew very well what shapes death at the front could take—knew that
Moore likely died in a way different from what the War Office reports presented, reports which Mrs. Moore, like many mothers in that day, would apparently accept unquestioningly.

Moore is buried at Pargny British Cemetery, which was "made after the
Armistice, by concentrations from the surrounding battlefields; the majority
of the burials are those of officers and men [. . .] whose resistance at the
Somme crossings on the 24th March, 1918, materially helped to delay the

German advance" ("Ernest").1 His enlistment number was 186223 (PRO WO338/14).

Figure 9. Paddy Moore's grave marker, near Pargny. (Photo: author)

Moore was not alone among Lewis's friends to fall. Alexander Gordon Sutton, 2nd lieutenant in the 2nd Rifle Brigade ("Alexander"), was one of the five men with Lewis in O.T.C. at Oxford, and joined the men in going to Mrs. Moore's house; he died on 2 January 1918. Sutton's father, Lewis would later recall, survived his wife, but all 5 of his sons had been killed in the war (*CL* 417). Liz Tait, who possesses records pertaining to the Sutton family, wrote that "5 [brothers] served and four were lost. Leonard Noel Sutton survived and is buried in the family grave. He escaped death when the ship he was in was torpedoed."

[Photo by Walton Adams.
THE LATE SECOND LIEUTENANT A. G. SUTTON,
RIFLE BRIGADE.

Second Lieutenant A. G. Sutton was killed in action on Jan.
2nd, 1918, aged 19. He was the youngest son of Mr. Leonard
Sutton, Hillside, Reading. He was educated at St. Andrew's,
Southborough, and Repton. He was trained at Oxford Officers'
Cadet Battalion in the summer of 1917, received his commission in
October, and went abroad to join his Battalion on December 2nd.
This is the third son Mr. Sutton has lost in the war.

Figure 10. Alexander Gordon Sutton in O.T.C. uniform.

Figure 11. Alexander Gordon Sutton's grave in Belgium. (Courtesy, Tait)

Thomas Kerrison Davey, another of the five friends in O.T.C., was in the 6th Rifle Brigade, attached to the 1st Rifle Brigade. His father received the usual telegrams from the War Office:

> Regret 2nd Lieut. T K Davey Rifle Brigade reported March Thirtieth general Hospital Dannes Carriers with gunshot wound left arm & chest dangerously ill. Visit not possible. (TNA(PRO)WO339/79376)

This was followed by another:

> Deeply regret 2nd Lieut T K Davey Rifle Brigade died of wounds March thirtyfirst [sic]. The Army Council Express sympathy. (TNA(PRO)WO339/79376)

He died at the 20th General Hospital and is buried at Etaples in a cemetery containing 10,769 graves; the town had been filled with mobile military hospitals during the war. Davey's stone has at the bottom the first two sentences of the Lord's Prayer. He was 19. In his effects sent home were some items telling of his injuries: he carried a pistol on a lanyard, as Lewis would have done. His comb is listed as broken as is the wrist strap to his watch. He likely kept his comb in the left pocket of his tunic, and the bullet penetrating his left wrist and arm must have passed into his chest, as the first telegram indicated. He carried letters and a photo, tobacco pouch, pipe, a metal cigarette case, a whistle (used by the army to initiate attacks) (TNA(PRO)WO339/79376).

Here it may be said that Martin Somerville—not merely another friend of Lewis's from O.T.C. who went with the men to Mrs. Moore's house while they were all in Oxford, but the man whom Lewis wrote was his main companion during those days (*CL* 317)—died of wounds in September in Palestine. Sutton's obituary provides information about his interests in life and in this region of fighting:

> His military training after he left Eton enlarged his horizon and developed his character, and his letters showed the widening circle of his interests. The last one, which came from "somewhere in Palestine" just before his death, is full of observation and wise comments upon the novel experiences of his eventful journey eastwards and of scenes in Malta, Egypt, Jaffre, and other places, and having begun with a cry for a letter, [ends] with "all good wishes to the House." Had he lived and taken up the life's work to which all his tastes drew him, he would have been ordained. But if he had had to choose the place and occasion of his death, he would have grasped at the chance of dying in Palestine in the cause of right, taking his share in the fighting that seems likely to prove the most important operation in the liberation of the Holy Land. The Crusading spirit would have moved him to that selection. He leaves behind him the memory of a blameless life and of ability that would have taken him far. ("In Memoriam")

Somerville had been at Eton "from September 1912 to Easter 1917. His father, Annesley Ashworth Somerville, was on the staff [of Eton . . .] from 1885–1922, and went on to become MP for Windsor" (Hatfield). Martin suffered a "gunshot wound to the groin" from which he "died at no.26 Casualty Clearing Station, Palestine" (TNA(PRO)WO339/98419) and is buried at the Ramla (formerly Ramleh) War Cemetery in Israel, twelve kilometers southeast of Jaffra ("Martin").

The list of his effects communicates something of the man; among these is his revolver in holster, "6 books, 1 Prayer book, 1 Rosary [. . .] (TNA(PRO) WO339/98419). The telegram that his father received at Eton, a document received literally by millions of families during the war, is by necessity terse, but in being so must have been a very cold communiqué to arrive at one's house:

> Deeply regret inform you that 2/Lieut M A Somerville Rifle Brigade died of wounds twentyfirst September The Army Council express Sympathy Kindly wire Casualties

520/5 War Office full name address relationship next of kin of this officer (TNA(PRO)
WO339/98419)

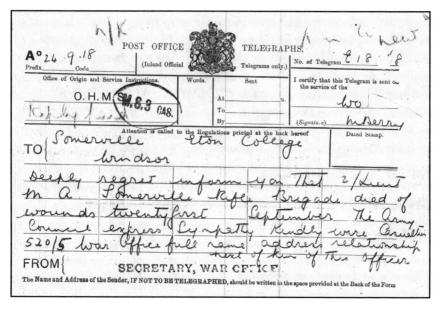

Figure 12. War Office telegram regarding Martin Somerville's death. (TNA(PRO)WO339/
98419)

At the beginning of April in the midst of the German advance, Lewis was
occupied with concerns about his own fate and would not learn the fate of his
friends until later. Among the rising action all along the north of the Front was
another area the allies were failing to hold: Lewis's battalion marched north
to counter the massive advance of Germans between Bethune and Armentiers.
His battalion was a part of the British force moved from the Arras area to
replace the faltering Portuguese troops: "This division was of poor quality and
had been held in the line longer than normal. The Portuguese broke immediately and left a six-mile wide gap in the line" (Tucker 165–166). The British
troops themselves were forced back 15 to 20 miles in area. German losses in
their advance were about 109,000 men. The Allies lost 146,000, two thirds
of them British (Tucker 165). As with the dead and wounded in the Somme
area, the German advance moved at such speed that, as with Moore's corpse,
the dead were often left where they lay, only months later to be gathered and
buried. Warnie, writing home to his father in July of 1916, reported how he
had surveyed the devastation of ground passed through when the British
advanced—"the abomination of desolation":

in a strip of ground perhaps 3 miles broad, there is no living thing—not a blade of grass,
not a tree, not a building which stands more than three feet high: one cannot walk over
it without difficulty, for there are no two square yards which do not contain a shell hole:
and all round are men who look as if they were asleep [. . . .] (*LP* V.109–110)

Jack's battalion was moved north as follows: from the area near Athies, they
were relieved from the trenches on the night of 7th and 8th April and marched
to St. Laurent Blangy, "where it embussed and [. . .] conveyed to "Y" hutments, North of the Arras—St. Pol Road, [near] Duisans" (*WD*), with two men
wounded during the relief. The day of the 8th, the battalion cleaned up and
made repairs to and replaced damaged gear. On the afternoon of the 9th, the
Germans shelled the "Y" hutments, a camp, with "high velocity guns," which
brought the battalion to move to the village of Hermaville, a shift not completed until that night and the early morning hours of the 10th. Duties of cleaning and refitting were continued the next day, at which time the battalion also
received a draft of 162 men and 3 officers. On the 11th, however, orders arrived
that the battalion should be prepared to march from Hermaville for Bruay at
3-and-one-half hours' notice. At 8:00 A.M. next day they marched from
Hermaville for an embussing point near Duisans. Embussing at 1:00 P.M., they
moved through Houdain and Bruay and debussed at 6:00 P.M. along the road
from Lillers to Busnes. At 7:00 P.M. they marched from this point to Gonneham
and on to Bellerive, and were then assigned places in the line along the La
Bassee canal: "C" company were in the line from Douce Creme Farm to the
foot bridge (no longer in existence, but at Q.31.a.8.2 on map 36ASE).
Johnson's company, "B," was placed from that same footbridge to Point Levis
at Q.32.c.6.8. Lewis's company, "Light," was placed in support in Mount
Bernenchon, and "A" was further back in reserve in Bellerive. Battalion headquarters was located at V.5.b.5.8 (*WD*).

The area was not merely unusual in appearance. What Warnie had described
in his 1916 letter was the usual aspect of the front, a vast area devoid of vegetation and, of course, civilians—a moonscape of death and the junk of war.
But the Mount Bernenchon area was lush and relatively pristine. Majendie
describes it thus:

> The next day was quiet: it was evident that the German advance was at a standstill for
> the time being, and that the enemy's infantry had got well ahead of his guns. The sur-
> roundings were completely novel: the countryside was green and untouched by war:
> the farms were standing and were full of furniture, food and live stock.
>
> This change from the dismal landscape of previous trench positions was very
> marked and very welcome in most ways. The tragedy of the situation, however, was
> vividly brought to mind by the streams of refugees, who had been met on the march
> forward, fleeing before the Germans.

> The only trenches that existed were on the South bank of the Canal: these had been constructed long before by the French, but proved of great value.
>
> Neither side knew with any certainty the dispositions of the other, though during the day our patrols established the fact that the enemy were holding the village of Riez du Vinage. (73–74)

These aspects made the area very odd, not least since the war had continued for three years, but the battalion would be further amazed:

> This day presented some unusual sights: the British front line ran along the South bank of the Canal, but in spite of this the tow-path was alive with French civilians on bicycles and even in carts, busily intent on rescuing their most cherished possessions from their deserted homes.
>
> The German guns were presumably moving forward to their new positions, and this unusual movement in the front line drew no hostile shelling.
>
> Before steps were taken to stop it, quite a number of French civilians crossed the Canal and proceeded to their homes in no man's land. The fate of these in most cases is not known, but unfortunately many lost their lives or were wounded in the subsequent operations. (Majendie 74)

On the 13th, the battalion continued to have a relatively quiet time; "enemy artillery was only moderately active," but towards evening Bernenchon was shelled and a group of buildings set ablaze (*WD*). Patrols were sent out, determining that Riez was held by the Germans but "apparently not in strength" (*WD*). During the night of the 13th and the morning of the 14th, "the Right Company [Lewis's "Light" company] established a series of posts from FOOT-BRIDGE to road fork at Q.36.0.2" (*WD*).

The ensuing action by the British, performed during the German's standstill and for the purpose of securing bridges over the canal, meant taking the village of Riez. As seen on the maps (and as still exists), the area east of Riez was marked by a large wood, the Bois de Pacaut in which the Germans were entrenched. That small forest would prove to be a great obstacle to the taking of Riez. On 14 April the commanding officers met at brigade headquarters where a plan was determined: the taking of Riez was to begin immediately.

The objective for the operation was to amass the battalions working with the Somerset Light Infantry: the 1st Hampshire Regiment would move forward on the left, but to the rear, joining up with the 61st Division in the village of Carvin. Action would begin at 6:30 P.M. the night of the 14th. The Somersets would move by individual companies, each holding an area south of the canal and cross the bridges to the north side of the canal—by no more than one or two men at a time so as not to raise enemy suspicion—and establish themselves in the houses and along the roads leading to Riez. All companies were to be in place for the advance by 6:00 P.M. when a barrage of heavy

British cannon would begin to shell Riez. No movement of massed companies would take place before 6:00 P.M. to avoid being caught in their own barrage. At 6:30 P.M. a barrage from British 18-pounders would fall on the west edge of Riez and begin to creep through the village at 6:40. At 6:30 the massed companies were to begin their move into Riez, following the moving barrage, a normal procedure in an attack—and one that often went wrong during the war when movement between artillery and the advancing infantry were not coordinated. If uncoordinated, the maneuver could produce numerous casualties of friendly fire.

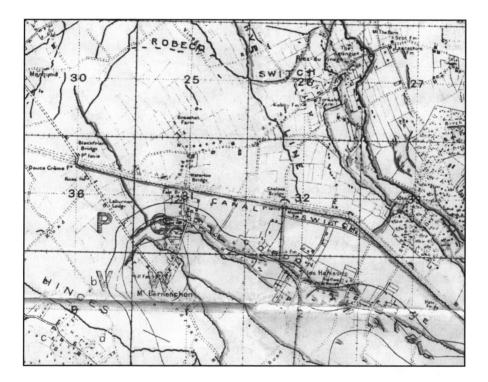

Map 3. Bernenchon Riez trench map, IWM Map 36aSE, showing the lines in the Mount Bernenchon area as they were up to 22 August 1918. The canal where the footbridge crosses it is at the center of quadrant 31, Riez in quadrant 26, and the Bois de Pacaut in quadrant 33. (Reproduced from the 1917 Ordnance Survey)

Assembly areas before the attack were as follows: Lewis's "Light" company was to occupy "the houses just North of the Canal in Q32a60" (*WD*). Johnson's "B" company was to assemble in the houses "along the Riez road, held by the advanced posts, and houses on the North bank of the Canal close to the footbridge, at Q31a82" (*WD*). The advanced posts in the houses north of the canal had been established by Lewis's company, and one sees that the two companies were mixed in their assembly. The left end of Lewis's company and the right end of Johnson's company would be mixed together during the course of the ensuing advance.

A word should be said about the condition of the canal during the war and its appearance today. One of the farm houses, standing today on the north side of the canal, along the "rue de la Passerelle" (or the "footbridge road"), is owned by Mr. Jean Caudron, who provided very helpful information about the area as it was during the war—and how it stands today. The canal was widened after the war. The footbridge that crossed it at rue de la Passerelle was not replaced. The trench that ran along the south side of the canal is, therefore, gone, although an overflow ditch exists today beside a walking path that runs along the canal. When Mr. Caudron purchased the farmhouse, he was told by its previous owners that during the First World War it was partially destroyed by British shells that accidentally fell on it. Majendie's history corroborates his story: "Shortly before zero [when advance on Riez began] some heavy shells fell North of the Canal at Q31, and caused several casualties" (76). Not, that is, enemy shells. As McGreevy notes, "Everyone endured this threat" of shells "from their opponents, but few liked to think that these artillery shells were actually their own falling short, as often occurred" (59). One notes Majendie's reticence on just whose shells fell on the farm. They were some of the heavy shells intended to "soften" German troops in Riez and preceded the 6:30 P.M. 18-pounder barrage, which would begin the advance. Part of Lewis's and Johnson's men would have been massed around what is now Mr. Caudron's farmhouse on the north side of the canal.

From the fork in the road at Q26c20, "B" company would stand south of the road along a 300 yard line facing southeast ("C" company similarly assembled but to the north of the road), and "Light" company, with its right on the drawbridge in Q32, would extend "300 yards along the road to Riez"; "A" company faced northeast "with its center on the road about Q31b58" (Majendie 76). By 6:00 P.M., all companies were relatively in place north of the canal and assembled for the attack which, in the end, was carried out by Lewis's battalion alone without aid from the other battalions. Majendie relates that their action "proved the value of the Wanquentin training" (76). Nevertheless, things had not begun as planned: the battalion faced half-right— facing, that is, the Bois de Pacaut—and would finish the advance with an "objective [. . .] almost semi-circular in shape" encompassing the village of Riez and standing north on the left and east on the right (Majendie 76). At zero hour, the battalion was still "some distance short of the line from which it had been decided that the attack should be launched: in consequence the

Figure 13. The Rue de la Passerelle, looking away from Riez toward a farm around which Lewis and his men gathered before the attack. After being wounded, Lewis would have been carried back along this road on a stretcher. (Photo: author)

leading troops were unable to get close up to the barrage" (Majendie 76). While remaining at a reasonably safe distance behind a barrage, it was yet important that the infantry follow closely on the fire support that a barrage offered ahead of them; it forced the enemy to cower in their trenches and dugouts as the infantry moved up.

"At 6:30 P.M., when the creeping barrage started, German machine guns opened fire from Riez and the Bois de Pacaut. Owing to the accuracy of this fire the advance was temporarily held up about Q31b89" until Captain L. A. Osborne of "A" company moved through the advancing troops with two of his own platoons (Majendie 77). The other companies moved up, with "A" company reaching the village first; "Light Company in the meantime on the right had also come under heavy machine gun fire from the Bois de Pacaut, and the two left platoons were checked. The other two platoons continued to advance by section rushes" (Majendie 77). Lewis's platoon, on the left of "Light" company, but set against the right of Johnson's platoons, would have been those men advancing in section rushes. The German machine gun fire from the wood was silenced by British artillery and machine gun, and "Light Company took up its allotted position" at which point "some Germans ran out and surrendered" (Majendie 77). Lewis wrote comically in his autobiography about how he "captured" over half-a-hundred prisoners, which meant they merely surrendered to him (*SBJ* 197). This event would have been remarkable, which is why he mentions it, during a very serious undertaking, for even as these men surrendered, "determined fighting [. . .] took place in the village, chiefly in the Southern half [where Lewis was located] and a good number of Germans were killed" (Majendie 77). A company of Germans with six machine guns also counter-attacked from the east outskirts of the village to the north end of the Bois de Pacaut, resulting in an estimated 40% casualties among the Germans (the others either running away or surrendering) and in the capture of the six machine guns (Majendie 77). By 7:15 P.M. the entire objective had been attained, the village captured, and Lewis's company was situated along a line on the right, "holding from the Canal to Riez, facing the Western side of the Bois de Pacaut" (Majendie 78). Their left flank would have been at the houses at Q26.d.4.4. in Riez, against the right of John's company at the houses at roughly the same point, but one mark north and east.

At dawn on 15 April, a party of Germans, "estimated at least 200 strong" approached by twos and threes via shell holes, and more movement was seen at the north end of the wood; they came under heavy fire and "German stretcher bearers were busy for the remainder of the day" (Majendie 78). Later on the 15th, orders were issued that the right platoon of "Light" company, situated just north of the canal and facing the west side of the Bois de Pacaut, would assist the Duke of Wellington's Regiment who stood on "Light" company's right, in attacking the wood, both units forming up together at the edge of the wood. As a platoon reached a point where they were level with the next platoon, they would merge platoons and increase their strength while attacking. The advance did not transpire as planned: the Dukes halted under heavy artillery fire that caused serious casualties. "Light" company, unaware of the Dukes' situation, advanced; the two right platoons carried out their orders and moved towards the wood despite having no support on their own right; remarkably, they entered the wood at about Q33a83. Meeting fierce resistance, as could be expected, they could not hold their place in the wood and fell back to dig in with the Dukes. Both "Light" and the Dukes suffered about 50% casualties in the maneuver (Majendie 79).

As with any attack, a barrage of heavy shells upon the Germans would precede the initial attack, and men would follow a creeping barrage of lighter shells. On the 15th, as Majendie relates, "the companies and battalions were a good deal mixed" and part of that day was spent in reorganizing the units (79). The battalion diary condenses daily reports at this point, which would have been quite busy: the entry for 14 April actually reports the action for 14, 15, and the night of 16/17 April, resuming distinct daily entries only on 17 April. As Lewis was reported wounded on 15 April, a number of recorded moments indicate when he might have been wounded. It is probable that during the initial, pre-attack barrage by British guns, a shell fell short and hit its own lines, toward the left end of "Light" company where it met with "B" company near the village. Lewis would have been standing at the extreme left of his men with his sergeant, Harry Ayres. Both men would have been standing with Laurence Johnson, who was on the extreme right of his "B" company.

Ayres, Lewis presumed, was killed by the shell that hit himself (*SBJ* 196). The sergeant has no known grave, an indication he was either hit directly or that his body was lost as the Germans overran the area. A number of graves for unknown British soldiers are in the churchyard at Mount Bernenchon; it may be that Ayres is buried in one of them. His name appears in the Loos Memorial at the village of Loos-en-Gohelle ("Harry"). Ayres was 32.

Laurence Johnson died of his wounds and is buried at Pernes British Cemetery. He was 20. At the bottom of his stone is written "The rest is silence" (Hamlet's last words). The effects he carried when he died and were subsequently sent home tell a little about him: "Metal Cigarette Case, Silver Flask (L.B.J.), Leather Tobacco Pouch, Wrist Watch & Guard, Safety Pin, Crucifix and chain, Pocket Knife, 1 Wrist Identity disc, Nail Clippers, 2 Stars, Cheque Book, Record of Services, Personal letters" (PRO WO 339/83074). The stars are signal flares for emergency use to call for help. The safety pin had a special use: inside each uniform was a pouch sewn together containing bandages. Medics sometimes had difficulty opening this sewn pouch. Some men tore open their own pouch before entering battle and kept it closed with a safety pin; it was thus more quickly accessed by medics if need arose.

Lewis wrote in his autobiography that his capturing a group of German soldiers was a story that did not deserve to be related; neither did the story of his wounding, nor did his envisioning a VAD nurse as a Greek goddess (*SBJ* 197). Yet he, indeed, says much, not only in his autobiography but through his early poetry about his wounding—and no less about the trauma of his whole war experience. He indicates two important things about his being wounded. When his mind cleared and he realized what had happened, he believed himself dead. But then he regarded himself at a mental distance, an objective perspective as, simply, a man who was ceasing to be (*SBJ* 197).

As he did about the war before it affected him personally, he said he began to philosophize about the event—or so he does in his autobiography, how it seemed to him that there were separate selves that existed within him

(*SBJ* 197–198). So he indicates in his autobiography. On the other hand, in his poem *Dymer*, the event is not philosophically attended at all but is distinct in its immediacy of recollection: there was a sound, a flash, and he fell face-first in a garden (*Dymer* 74).

If Lewis was on the left flank of his company, next to Johnson, who stood on his own company's right flank, they would have stood behind the houses, where gardens are today, along the road just inside the south-central and east edge of Riez. He writes in *Dymer* with no indication of philosophizing:

> When next he found himself no house was there,
> No garden and great trees. Beside a lane
> In grass he lay. Now first he was aware
> That, all one side, his body glowed with pain:
> [. . . . .]
> Without a pause
> It clung like a great beast with fastened claws;
> [. . . .]
> That for a time he could not frame a thought
> Nor know himself for self, nor pain for pain,
> [. . . .]
> Within, the thundering pain. That quiet hour
> Heeded it not. It throbbed, it raged with power
> Fit to convulse the heavens: and at his side
> The soft peace drenched the meadows far and wide. (*Dymer* 76–77)

These lines are significant, as are many others which will be explored, in revealing Lewis's trauma from not merely his wounds but from the whole of his war experience.

I do not propose a literary analysis of Lewis's poetry; it is the traumatic face of his war, hidden behind the public expression of his experiences, that his early poetry, such as in the above lines, leaves exposed.

NOTE

1. The Commonwealth War Graves Commission has, on its web site, listed Moore's first names incorrectly as "Ernest Frank Courtenay Moore," which should be Edward Francis Courtenay Moore. Thus the reference in the works cited to "Ernest."

WORKS CITED

"Alexander Gordon Sutton." *Commonwealth War Graves Commission.* <http://yard.ccta.gov.uk/cwgc/register.ns/wwwcreaateservicedetails?openagent&439488>. 14 March 1999

Bishop, Alan, and Mark Bostridge, eds. *Letters from a Lost Generation: First World War Letters of Vera Brittain and Four Friends.* London: Abacus, 1999.

Brittain, Vera. *Testament of Youth.* London: Penguin, 1994.

Caudron, Jean. Personal interview. Mount Bernenchon, France, 2 May 2002.

"Ernest Frank Courtenay Moore MC." *Commonwealth War Graves Commission.* <http://yard. ccta.gov.uk/cwgc/register.ns/wwwcreaateservicedetails?openagent&2281700>. 14 March 1999.

"Harry Charles Ayres." *Commonwealth War Graves Commission.* <http://yard.ccta.gov.uk/cwgc/register.nsf/wwwcreateservicedetails?openagent&726885>. 14 March 1999.

Hatfield, P. College Archivist, Eton College Library. Personal letter, 6 June 2002.

"In Memoriam." *The Eton College Chronicle* 3 October 1918 (n.p.)

Junger, Ernst. *The Storm of Steel.* New York: Fertig, 1996.

Majendie, V. B. H. *A History of the 1st Battalion: The Somerset Light Infantry (Prince Albert's), July 1st, 1916, to the End of the War.* Taunton, England: Goodman, 1921.

"Martin Ashworth Somerville." *Commonwealth War Graves Commission.* <http://yard. ccta.gov. uk/cwgc/register.ns/wwwcreaateservicedetails?openagent&653342>. 14 March 1999.

Remarque, Erich Maria. *All Quiet on the Western Front.* Boston: Little, Brown, 1929.

Tait, Liz. E-mail to author. 20 August 2002.

Tucker, Spencer C. *The Great War 1914–18.* Bloomington: Indiana UP, 1998.

Winter, Denis. *Death's Men: Soldiers of the Great War.* London: Penguin, 1979.

CHAPTER 10

The Angel of Pain

UPON BEING WOUNDED, AS WARNIE RELATED AFTER talking with Jack (*LP* V., 309), Lewis crawled back from the place where he fell and was found by a stretcher bearer. Hansen explains the usual sequence of events thereafter:

> Typically, a wounded soldier was taken by his comrades directly to a first-aid station set up in the trenches. From there he would be carried by stretcher-bearers (*brancardiers*) through a communication trench leading back to the nearest *poste de secours*. Ideally, the *postes* would be located less than a mile from the first-line trenches in some type of bombproof structure, such as a specially timbered cave or reinforced farmhouse cellar. (xv–xvi)

Stretcher bearers, despite their best efforts, could not help but give many a wounded man an excruciating ride over shell-marked ground—and likely something worse while under fire—to the aid station where a doctor would be waiting. Ernst Junger described the ride of one man who "got a bullet from somewhere through the chest [. . . ;] when he was being carried back he had a leg broken on one of the many occasions when his bearers had to take cover from the shell-fire. He died at the dressing station" (102). Aid stations, being close the line, were targets for the enemy, and Siegfried Sassoon tells of one aid post hit; its doctor was buried but dug out. The rest of its occupants were killed.

Lewis's carriers would have borne him down the Rue de la Passerelle and back across the footbridge, a feature the Germans certainly kept under some amount of fire to prevent the British from bringing up further reserves. The plans for the attack in the War Diary indicate that the battalion's aid post was set in Les Harisoirs, just across the canal from Bois de Pacaut and east of Mount Bernenchon at W.2.a.8.2; the aid post appears to have been in farm buildings (IWM 36aSE). In this post "physicians cleaned and dressed the wounds, immobilized fractures, or in the most severe cases, performed emergency amputations" (Hansen xvi). Once at the aid station, medical personnel would have cut Lewis's clothes off and dressed his wounds in preparation for his journey to the clearing station. He laments to his father this violation of his uniform (*CL* 368), but it may not have been the medics who desecrated his trousers. A platoon commander whom Ernst Junger discovered had been hit by a shell and, as was common, "fragments of his uniform and clothing, torn from his body the force of the explosion [. . . were] hanging above him on the splintered remnant of a thorn hedge" (294). In various accounts from the war, clothes are torn or shredded without the skin being touched. It is likely, given Lewis's proximity to the blast—evidenced by his wounds—his uniform had been a mass of small holes and various-sized tears before it was completely removed by medical staff.

Ambulance drivers, by the end of the war, picked up the wounded at the aid station (Hansen xvi)—a dangerous prospect as aid stations were less than a mile from the front line, easily observable, and thus easily shelled. The map of the area shows a railway line (now gone) that passed the location of the aid post, and a pill box built during the war stands today not far from where the aid station was; its ceiling is reinforced with train rails embedded in the layers of concrete. However, I presume the train would not have been operating so close to the front lines. Lewis was probably placed in an ambulance—perhaps a Ford or a Fiat, but there were other makes of vehicles operating on the front. Fiats could carry loads of wounded up hills; some drivers complained that Fords loaded with wounded could not make steep hills with their belt-driven transmission and were generally reserved for flatter ground as in the area surrounding Bernenchon. There are accounts, however, where Fords were used in the mountains on the Italian front—at least one of these vehicles was without brakes and was stopped from rolling off a mountain with its female driver by French soldiers who had standing nearby. Lewis would have been driven over shell-shot roads for a long and painful ride to a casualty clearing station. As Sassoon told of his ride when he was shot through the shoulder blade: "For an hour and a half we bumped and swayed along ruined roads till we came to the Casualty Clearing Station [. . .] and all I got that night was a cup of Bovril and an anti-tetanus injection" (170). Junger recalled that "near me in the jolt-ing ambulance lay a man with an abdominal wound who implored his com-rades to shoot him with the orderly's revolver" (29); wounded once again later in the war, Junger this time encountered an ambulance driver who "without paying any heed to the cries of the occupants, went at full speed over the paved road, for it was being shelled, and neither shell-holes nor other obstructions could stop him" (106).

Hansen explained that the ambulances working the front-line aid stations "brought wounded men [. . .] back to evacuation hospitals, which could usu-ally be reached by car in about forty-five minutes" (xv). Between the hospital and the Front was a clearing station from which the wounded were moved to a train for various hospitals; Lewis would have been transported by train to a hospital on the coast. Sassoon recalled "strange and terrible" memories of the train which bore him to hospital: men with excruciating wounds and not least "a cargo of men in whose minds the horrors they had escaped from were still vitalized and violent" (170). Lewis probably arrived in Etaples late at night on the 15th or in the early morning of the 16th April. He was placed in the Number 6 British Red Cross Hospital, which had been moved to Etaples from Paris-Plage in July of 1915 (Baker); also known as the Liverpool Merchants Mobile Hospital (*CL* 366), it was one of many hospitals set up as a series of temporary huts (*CL* 375). As the Commonwealth War Graves Commission explains, during the war the area around Etaples saw a concentration not only of hospitals but of reinforcement camps:

> it was remote from attack, except from aircraft, and accessible by railway from both the northern or the southern battlefields. In 1917, 100,000 troops were camped among the sand dunes and the hospitals, which included eleven general, one stationary, four Red Cross hospitals, and a convalescent depot, could deal with 22,000 wounded or sick. ("Thomas Kerrison Davey")

After being wounded, Lewis sent his first note to his father on 16 April, written in an unknown hand—certainly that of a nurse—indicating that he was "slightly wounded" (*CL* 365). The handwriting may have been that of nurse whom Lewis said was to him the representation of the goddess Artemis (*SBJ* 197). Perhaps it was his father's idea, or perhaps he heard from elsewhere, but Albert communicated to Warnie that Jack was severely wounded. The telegram Albert received indicated merely that Jack had been wounded (*LP* V.308). Even if one were slightly wounded, penicillin did not exist, and the soil at most places in the Front was full of rusted metal and strewn with the corpses of men and horses; even slight wounds would fester, become infected, and could easily turn gangrenous. Thus an anti-tetanus shot was by regular practice administered to the wounded upon their arrival at dressing stations. But Lewis was, indeed, severely wounded; the first letter was written for Albert's comfort in the normal tenor of Jack's communication with his father. His medical record as well as Albert's and Jack's letters to the War Office, written to obtain the Wound Gratuity owed to Lewis, all employ the terms "severely wounded" (TNA (PRO) WO339/105408). The wounds, as listed in a medical board report contained in Lewis's military record, were described thus: "He was struck by shell fragments" (not shrapnel) "which caused 3 wounds." The first was a wound to the left chest, just behind his shoulder which was followed by complications and found to have fractured "4th left rib." This wound, it seems, was caused by the two shell fragments that remained in his chest. These were removed years later: "Lewis had been troubled by some shrapnel he had been carrying since the last war, and in August 1944 he had it removed" (Hooper 39)[1] The second wound was to the left wrist and "quite superficial," with the third wound inflicting his left leg just above and behind the knee (PRO WO339/105408). In a second note to his father, on 17 April, he provided by his own hand his address at the hospital in Etaples and mentioned that his left arm was indisposed (CL 367). On 4 May he offered his father further explanation about his wounds. Jack was annoyed that Albert received news from military officials that his wounds included both arms and his face—this latter, he explained, was due to debris that caught his eye during the blast; it was abrasive but did not cause a wound per se. Jack then explained his wounds to Albert in a attempt to relieve his father's fears (CL 367), description which minimizes but approximates what his medical record indicates.

Before he wrote this letter Warnie had visited Jack in the hospital. On 24 April Warnie was at Doullens and, having borrowed a motorcycle, drove up to Etaples to see his brother, writing a report to Albert:

> I don't know who was responsible for the phrase "severely wounded," but it gave me a desperately bad fright. As a matter of fact you will be glad to hear that [Jack] is not much the worse, and is in better spirits than I have seen him for a long time. He was in great fettle and we had a long [talk. . . .] A shell burst close to where he was standing, killing a Sergeant, and luckily for "It" [Jack] he only stopped three bits: one in the cheek and two in the hands: he then crawled back and was picked up by a stretcher bearer. (LP V.309)

He was not quite as well as Warnie reported, as Jack explained to his father in his next letter. The fragment that went in beneath his arm penetrated near to his heart, and Jack had been told the doctors would leave it there to no ill effect (CL 368).

Exacerbating the trauma of being wounded, he had also learned news of Paddy Moore: "My friend Mrs. Moore is in great trouble—Paddy has been missing for over a month and is almost certainly dead" (*CL* 369). Why is it not Paddy in trouble but Mrs. Moore? Paddy's fate he has decided already. On the other hand, Mrs. Moore and Paddy's sister Maureen are now without a male support in an age when a single woman would encounter difficulty supporting herself and a child. He believed Paddy was the first of his friends to have been killed. In this he was mistaken. Jack, in Etaples, had not yet heard the fate of another friend from Keble, Thomas Davey, who had died on 31 March; his body lay buried not far to the south, at Le Treport, where in February Jack had recuperated from trench fever.

Lewis resumed writing to Arthur in May and, among the talk of literature, makes a lengthy explanation as to why he talked of literature and of personal issues but not of the war. Arthur must have prodded Lewis on the point. In answer, Lewis asserts that his letters to Arthur from Kirkpatrick's and from the university were full of discussion on topics the two shared in common; the Army, on the other hand, had nothing stimulating about it. Lewis, however, promises that upon his return, he will tell Arthur about it all—but only if Arthur asks (*CL* 370–371). The letter smacks of the mode of avoidance that typified Lewis's approach to war.

Yet if Arthur read Jack's next letters carefully, he would find that his friend was, indeed, telling him much about what he was in the midst of suffering and that it could not be so lightly dismissed. In the next letter is an implicit and a natural fear among those who have already been wounded. As he was waiting to ship across from France to England, German aircraft bombed the area and brought all movement to a halt: "you feel so helpless in bed, knowing you can't walk or anything even if you get out of it" (*CL* 372). This expressed fear appears to be an indication of the trauma he has experienced, a fear of being subject once more to the same terrors already experienced—in this case compounded by the inability to flee danger. Further, Jack has already established plans upon arriving in England, implicit in his next request to Arthur: Can you "come and see me in hospital in England for a few days? It would [. . .] give you an opportunity to meet Mrs Moore" (*CL* 372). His father would know nothing of the arrangement.

As to the delay he met in shipping back to England, it was not uncommon for hospitals to be targets of shelling. In at least one case the attacking aircraft had been shot down. Warnie wrote to Albert on 7 June, once Jack was safely back in England, how fine it was that Jack was securely away from France and angrily repeated a story of some Germans who, as with Jack's hospital in Etaples, dropped shells on a medical emplacement—hospitals in which the Germans themselves were cared for after being wounded in their capture (*CL* 379).

In Jack's military record, the "Arrival Report" has the "Date of Embarkation for England" marked as 22 May (TNA (PRO) WO339/105408). The date he actually arrived remains a question, but on 25 May, he telegrams his father the address of his next hospital, which was Endsleigh Palace Hospital in London (*CL 373*). This building survives today, virtually unchanged on the outside from its wartime appearance, at 25 Gordon Street. It is today the University College Student Union. It had been the Endsleigh Palace Hotel and was acquired by the war department in 1915 as an exceptionally spacious hospital for officers ("New Hospital").

It had two operating theatres on the top floor. It is located near Euston station; at the time of the war, the Euston Hotel stood immediately before the station, and across the street were gardens encompassing the entire square; this

Figure 14. Endsleigh Palace Hotel, 25 Gordon Street, was converted to "Endsleigh Palace Hospital" during the war. It is today the Student Union of University College, London.
(Photo: author)

garden no longer exists today. That land was purchased by the Friends Society, who built a meeting house upon the site. The Euston Hotel also no longer exists. Maureen Moore—later in life Lady Dunbar—was Paddy's sister. When asked in interview about Lewis's wounds and this hospital, she recalled that

> [Jack] had shrapnel quite near his heart all his life. But they [did not remove it] because it was so near his heart. And he then came back and was in a hospital at Endsleigh Palace, in London. And we went up there and I talked to him, visited him. It had a very pleasant garden and I remember sitting, watching Jack there in convalescent uniform. And then there was the talk that he would go back in to the war again, but he had a small wound on, I think his left wrist which wouldn't heal up and that really saved him being sent back again. (Ref.)

The uniform she described was all blue; convalescent cases were made to wear these, which were loathed by many returning wounded.

Lewis writes warmly of this time in the Endsleigh hospital, telling Arthur that he was happily adjusted by a window in what—after dugouts and barracks—seemed a luxurious place, and more: London was full of booksellers. He had a window from which he could view the setting sun, and looking over the station to the Hampstead Heath, he was met with a passion for the past (*CL* 375).

Yet he adds more on his other interests, things that lie behind Lady Dunbar's visits to the hospital:

> Of course, you can easily understand what other and greater reasons there are for me to be happy. There are still two pieces of shrapnel in my chest, but [. . .] no discomfort: <Mrs. Moore and> I are always hoping that it *will* start to give some trouble and thus secure me a longer illness. (This is quite like the Malvern days again, isn't it)? (*CL* 373–374)

Mrs. Moore, whose name was expurgated by Arthur in this letter (hence the pointed brackets, where they have been restored), was in London at least by 29 May, when this was written; the reasons for him to be happy were well understood by Arthur but remain unclear to many Lewis readers.

I believe that Lewis and Janie Moore had had sexual relations before he went to France, a situation that seems to have continued after his return to England and his recovery from the worst of the wounds. Such a relationship—whatever one thinks of Lewis after his conversion and of the Christian writer he eventually became—was not an unknown event nor a surprising one. It is easily understood if one considers carefully these two persons and the context of their lives. Lewis, eighteen, an atheist, just off to war, highly romantic, with an interest in eroticism one might have suspected in an older, more experienced person, clearly fancies Janie Moore. She is clearly taken with him in return. Even though he later found Laurence Johnson's morality appealing, Jack did not mark his own behavior as decidedly changed by an adoption of Johnson's values. Jack's emotional situation was significant: he had lost his mother as a child. Janie, with the nurturing sense of one who "just lived my life for my son" (qtd in Wilson 59) would not have been blind to this emotional need in Jack, and if he found initially a mother figure in her, he also quickly grew to love her romantically. The person from whom Jack expected comfort, Albert, had failed him, and the consequent estrangement increased even in Jack's times of greatest need. In the midst of the separation from Albert, a sexual relationship with Janie Moore also carries an element of defiance as well as the taboo which Jack spoke about in his letters to Arthur, while at Oxford, and later in his poem *Dymer*. Green and Hooper minimize this possibility:

> His affection for Mrs Moore—his infatuation, as it seemed to his friends and even to his brother who knew him more intimately than any of them—may have started with that incomprehensible passion which attractive middle-aged women seem occasionally able to inspire in susceptible youths: but it very soon turned from the desire for a mistress into the creation of a mother-substitute [. . . .] (56)

Yet one other important influence, stemming from unique conditions in wartime, must also be admitted to the discussion of this relationship. It was not uncommon (J. Winter says it was a theme found "time and time again" in wartime art) for women to provide the soldier's comfort—giving a pleasant time in bed to a soldier who was about to go to the Front—or as one postcard has it, "an exquisite hour which I will always remember" (J. Winter 189). An element of this tendency is evident in the "furious love affair" Lewis's roommate had with a nurse during the time he was recovering from pyrexia at the hospital in Le Treport. Hemingway presents just such a scenario in *Farewell to Arms*. These young men were being sent into deplorable conditions for one purpose: to kill—a job that, in the sense of Gertrude Stein's "Lost Generation," annihilated the war generation metaphorically, in terms of their values as well as literally—and yet they might never know the love of a woman before dying in the midst of that youth. Mrs. Moore was attractive, still in her 40s, sexually awake, and without a husband. Lewis wrote explicit letters to Arthur treating his relationship with Mrs. Moore before he went to France, and he evokes that same sense of the relationship by his remark in the above letter regarding the "other and greater reasons there are for me to be happy." The presence of a sexual element, quite simply, is the only content that Arthur expunged from any letter; in this case he does so with Janie's name in this and other letters just as he crosses out explicit reference to sexual issues—masturbation, flagellation, and homosexuality among them—in the letters Jack wrote to him.

Figure 15. One of many such postcards, this one French, expressing a role women were often expected to play for soldiers. It reads "In the Trench of Love" and "A counter attack."

In the literature of the war, social acceptance of such relationships is also treated. R. H. Mottram's *The Spanish Farm* (1924) is set in Flanders during WWI. The young female protagonist, Madeleine, is left to hold a tattered world together for the men in her life. At one point she ponders her sexual relations with one British soldier, not as justification but as explanation:

> In all those years of loss and waste it occurred to her naturally to build and replace what she could, and all the love and care she could not give to the children she might not bear, she gave to this grown-up child, who needed it, and took it willingly enough, once he ceased to think. (139)

> Later, when the war has ended, she reconsiders the relationship, which has in the meantime shifted from its earlier intimacy: "Nor was her feeling unreasonable. The only thing she and [the soldier] had in common, was the War" (256). It is Mrs. Moore and Jack's wartime relationship, whatever it became in later years.

Remarque's *All Quiet on the Western Front* also treats just such a relationship. Paul, Remarque's protagonist, meets a woman who is a symbol of such relationships for soldiers, relationships having nothing to do with prostitution: "The little brunette strokes my hair and says what all the French women say: "*La guerre—grand malheur—pauvres garcons—*" (The war—great evil—poor boys);

> I hold her arm tightly and press my lips into the palm of her hand. Her fingers close round my face. Close above me are her bewildering eyes, the soft brown of her skin and her red lips. Her mouth speaks words I do not understand. Nor do I fully understand her eyes; they seem to say more than we anticipated when we came here. [. . .] But I—I am lost in remoteness, in weakness, and in a passion to which I yield myself trustingly. My desires are strangely compounded of yearning and misery. I feel giddy [. . .] and let myself drop into the unknown, come what may [. . . .] and I let it all fall from me, war and terror and grossness, in order to awaken young and happy [. . . .] (Remarque 153–154)

Throughout his time in France, Lewis's letters to Arthur continually echo the theme of regaining the pre-war days when he, like Remarque's protagonist and millions of other young men before that war, had also been young and happy: "You, who have never lost that life, cannot understand the longing with which I look back to it" (*CL* 378).

In Mottram's *Spanish Farm* once more we find a parallel moment: when the stark realization of the world after war "seemed to gather and descend upon her," Madeleine asks aloud, "'What will become of it all?'" [. . . .] It, the undefined, being the old happy easy life of pre-war. A great sob broke from her, and at its sound in that lonely place of memories, she pulled herself together, put away her things, and looked up [. . .] throwing in vain a little mould of forgetfulness on the face of recollection that, buried, yet refused to die" (206–207). For Lewis it was as the narrator in Mottram's novel further explains:

> It was not so much that he wanted her, as that he wanted to be cared for. The moment had been preparing during the whole of his year's service in France. The dangers he had faced, rough out-of-door life, the fasting and feasting, his guardian's death, and his own growing perception of the inevitable fate before him; the nervous overstrain and shock, the convalescence and rest—all culminated in that instant with the fatal appropriateness called Providence. (Mottram, *Sixty-Four* 274)

I have already pointed out that when Odysseus returned to Penelope, husband and wife talked (but only after conjugal union), and then renewed the old life, that existed before the war at Troy. Yet Odysseus tells her absolutely nothing of the horrors he has seen in that war. He tells her about monsters and nymphs, yes, but nothing about the war. Similarly, Remarque's protagonist, mere days before he meets the young French woman, has looked upon war's worst vestiges, even as Lewis had experienced them at Fampoux and in the attack on Riez:

> We see men living with their skulls blown open; we see soldiers run with their two feet cut off, they stagger on their splintered stumps into the next shell-hole; a lance corporal crawls a mile and half on his hands dragging his smashed knee after him; another goes to the dressing-station and over his clasped hands bulge his intestines; we see men without mouths, without jaws, without faces; we find one man who had held the artery of his arm in his teeth for two hours in order not to bleed to death. The sun goes down, night comes, the shells whine, life is at an end. (Remarque *All Quiet* 135)[2]

There were also friends who were lost, and with their deaths came the guilt of having survived them. Paul, like Odysseus, can discuss such memories with no one; no conversation with another character contains these descriptions. Paul's memories are, instead, contrasted against recollections of what life was before the war and what life is in current society. One observes the same recollections and their requisite contrasts in Siegfried Sassoon's memories. Memories of war and lingering trauma seem, for some soldiers, to be escaped in large part within a sexual relationship if not within a few sexual moments (and we are here reminded not only of Paul's relationship with the French woman but of Odysseus's relationship with the nymph, which is not typified by love: love is not in Odysseus' calculations). This is not to say that Lewis did not find escape in his books, a suspension of his immediate sufferings and, not least, the trauma which would emerge, producing physiological manifestations. But— one may assume—contact with a woman did far more to help some soldiers escape the indescribable horrors of war than did books.

Erich Remarque expressed such things very simply in a remarkable book that appeared after *All Quiet* and traced the persistent effects of the war upon veterans returning home, *The Road Back* (1930). In explaining what a woman meant to a young soldier returning home, he writes, "after the war he was lost, because he went always in fear of himself and of his memories, and looked for something whereby to steady himself. And this girl was that to him" (321). One recalls that Septimus Warren Smith, in *Mrs. Dalloway*, likewise married Rezia for one purpose: to regain his ability to feel, to appease the lingering trauma. For a returned soldier, whose memories are full of the war, a woman is invested with immense importance, especially during quietly shared moments between war's clamoring destruction:

> Who knows but that in a few days he may be hanging on the barbed wire, with torn limbs, bellowing, thirsting, perishing?—Yet one more swig of this heavy wine, yet one more breath, one glimpse more into the insubstantial world of moving color, dreams, women, inflaming whispers, words, under whose spell the blood becomes like a black fountain; under whose touch the years of filth and madness and hopelessness resolve and change to sweet singing eddies of memory and hope. To-morrow death will rush in again with his guns, hand grenades, flame throwers, blood and annihilation, but today, this soft skin, fragrant and calling as life itself. What intoxicating shadows upon the shoulders, what soft arms!—It crackles and flashes and bursts and pours down, the sky burns.—Why tomorrow it may all be over—bloody war! that taught us to recognize only the moment and to have it. (Remarque *The Road Back* 264–265)

As far as anyone at this time knew, Jack would heal physically before the war was over, which would mean a return to battle. He had only the moments of recuperation; Janie Moore was continually with him in those moments.

In a letter of March 1919 to the War Office, Albert, a solicitor, sought to secure Jack's wound gratuity, about which the War Office had said, "in view of the nature of your wounds you are not entitled" (TNA (PRO): WO339/105408). The War Office was not interested in reconsidering the matter until, apparently, Albert's letter arrived. The letter reads, in part, as follows:

I do know something of the "Nature of the Wounds" and also of cases in which gra-
tuities and pensions have recently been granted to Officers.
(1) My Son, as he informed you, was "severely wounded" on the 15th April 1918.
[. . .]
(3) a piece of the Shell which wounded him is still in his left lung and will remain there
     for the rest of his life.
(4) He is incapable of taking any violent exercise.
(5) As a result of Shock he suffers from a distressing weakness which need not be
     described here in detail. (PRO WO339/105408)

The fifth point is the issue. It is evident that Jack was suffering symptoms of
Post Traumatic Stress Disorder, known at the time as "shell shock," and its
manifestations were often physiological. The nature of the manifestation can
be but guesswork, but it is directly due to "shock." Roger Green and Walter
Hooper speak to the nature of his wounds, that Lewis "over twenty years later"
had "the piece of shrapnel [. . .] removed from his chest" and "a further result
of his experiences at the front seems to have been a 'distressing weakness' of
the bladder from which he suffered for the rest of his life" (60). "Distressing
weakness" is a quote from Albert's letter; the assumption that the weakness
resided in the bladder belongs either to Green or to Hooper, but the word
"bladder" does not exist in Lewis's military medical record, nor does it occur
in later evaluations by the medical board. How is one to explain Albert's
reluctance to describe it in his letter? If it were simply a matter of a weakness
in the bladder, the point hardly seems so sensitive that it could not be named
even in 1919 in a letter to the War Office; yet neither will Jack name it in a letter to his father written 23 February 1919 in which he describes his condition
(*LP* VI.92). When Warnie compiled the Lewis family records, he included some
of Jack's statements concerning mental symptoms of the shock, which included recurring dreams. Jack hoped they would disappear in time. But Warren
omitted a section of a letter in which Jack described the physiological manifestations (*LP* VI.69). Jack, Albert, and Warnie were no prudes; Jack's letters
to Arthur, while private, still address intensely private topics Jack felt he could
mention to Arthur.

Whatever physiological manifestation or weakness emerged, I do not
believe it changed the sexual nature of Jack's relationship with Janie Moore.
Many readers will bristle at this suggestion, made also by A. N. Wilson, and
not surprisingly as many have taken on a role of guardians of Lewis's reputa-
tion. I must assert again that such a relationship would not in the least be aston-
ishing. Their relationship, as it was at this time, must be put down to one central
thing: an immediate and mutual need for comfort in the midst of immense
heartbreak, of uncertainty for the future, and of trauma. And what is to pre-

vent it in the young Lewis? Traditional morality? As Paul in Remarque's novel observed, "Good God, what is sacred to me?—such things change pretty quickly with us" (Remarque 184). Jack himself writes around this time quite positively of Arthur's homosexuality:

> Congratulations old man. I am delighted that you have had the moral courage to form your own opinions <independently,> in defiance of the old taboos. I am not sure I agree with you: but, as you hint in your letter, <this penchant is a sort of mystery only to be fully understood by those who are made that way—and my views on it can be at best but emotion.> (*CL* 371)

In the same letter Jack explains his morals at the time—in an oft-quoted and well-worn passage usually taken for its philosophical import, not for what it reveals about the severe disillusion Lewis felt after the war. He envisioned a world divided between the spiritual and the material, the material being replete with carnality and the elements of war that would destroy the spiritual element, that little spark of being existing within but dominated by the physical (*CL* 371).

It is a philosophy that reveals a desire to escape the physical world for the horrors it has precipitated on him, those of the war; he has been writing poems, which would be collected in his first book, *Spirits in Bondage*. In reading the poems, one notes a growing tension in his mind, a hostility with which he regards the physical world set against a fondness for the mythical world he found in literature. But here it is primary to assert that although he claims that he is developing more "monastic" views regarding carnality, his views are not at all monastic, as he has just praised Arthur's self-adjustment *toward* the taboo. At this time, Lewis believed in no deity and certainly not in one who would damn him for following the interests of the flesh (*CL* 379). Further, Jack recommends an adjustment to Arthur's pursuit of homosexual interests in a passage Arthur attempted to erase (*CL* 384). Lewis advises not that Arthur should drop his interests, but that he be discriminate, not chasing after every love interest he happens across.

Don W. King, in reviewing A. N. Wilson's biography of Lewis, finds Wilson's Freudian slant obtrusive despite the strong evidence, including Lewis's relationships with Moore (mother/wife figure) and Albert (father/rival figure) as well as a comment from Lewis, who failed to receive, even after being wounded, a visit from his father: Lewis observes the absence of word from Albert and asks if he hasn't done himself in (King). I see little of Freud here: it was not uncommon for the war generation (and the generation which followed) to hold severe animosity towards the elder generation. Part of the war paradigm, or the "myth of the war" as defined by Paul Fussell and Samuel Hynes among others, is that on-going "war" between the generations—between those who fought the war and their parents who, by way of their traditional values, created and sustained the war and thus marked as suspect and hostile the same values they wanted their children to use in rebuilding the shattered world. Evelyn Waugh, perhaps the chief spokesperson for this generational war—whose crowd of Bright Young Things, for instance, rebelled lavishly against the traditional values—drew sketches of the Seven Deadly Sins, among which was "that grim act parricide" (Carpenter, photo section between 180–181). Certainly Lewis's new morality and his relationship with Mrs. Moore have not only a Freudian aspect but reflect some measure of Lewis's resentment towards his father as a part of his generation's resentment of the world their elders created. Jack's relationship with Mrs. Moore is a departure marked by its animosity towards Albert, animosity that would increase before subsiding. Eric Remarque would write in tones, perhaps similar to those Jack seemed to adopt with Albert, that

> I still see that this is my father, but also I can see he is just a kindly, somewhat older man, rather cautious and pedantic, whose views have no longer any meaning for me. (261)

It must be conceded, beyond all the debate about the nature of his relationship with Janie Moore and his animosity toward Albert that, at this time, Lewis held nothing sacred beyond the comfort of Janie Moore and the secure and romantic world he found in literature. These were, simply, the summation of his life. His morality would not prohibit him from a sexual relationship with her, which he clearly wanted. And Janie Moore had no one but Jack and a dependent child, Maureen. She thus followed Jack whereever he was sent—first to London, where she could stay with her sister, Edith Askins, who worked in the War Office.

In his next letter to Arthur, Jack addresses topics of literary issues and philosophical ponderings. Another letter to his father on 12 June shows Lewis is up from his bed and wandering about London to the book shops but also mentions that he will go to Surrey to visit Kirkpatrick (*CL* 380). He has made a very mild suggestion that Albert might visit him.

No real pursuit instance of Albert visiting London actually follows, of course, and in his next letter, the reason seems to be not Albert's illness, but his company. He tells Arthur that he has gone to the theatre to see *The Valkyrie* and was not alone in attending it (*CL* 381). It is obvious that Jack has gone with Mrs. Moore. The point of significance is this timely conjunction between his romantic ideals and Mrs. Moore. From his early days he saw the beauty of

Rackham's illustrations of the *Ring* and Wagner's work as an embodiment of his romantic sense. Still relishing that romantic sense as late as 1927, he wrote in his diary about translating the *Edda*,

> It is an exciting experience, when I remember my first passion for things Norse under the initiation of Longfellow [. . .] at about the age of nine: and its return much stronger when I was about 13, when the high priests were M. Arnold, Wagner's music, and the Arthur Rackham *Ring*. [. . . .] The old authentic thrill came back to me once or twice this morning [. . . .] (*AMR* 448)

The connection is not some detached, philosophical event in his mind. One of Rackham's illustrations, that which depicts Siegfried at the moment he discovers Fear, evokes the romance coupled with the erotic sense Lewis must have felt both at the time of puberty, when he first saw it, as well as what he felt, at this time, sitting with Janie Moore in the theatre. The senses are coupled, as for Wagner's hero, with the fear he met in war: there stands the hero with sword in hand, looking upon the enchanted and enchanting maiden, her breasts exposed.

A parallel epiphane is easy to observe in Joyce's *Portrait of the Artist as a Young Man*, the moment when Stephen, who has just performed intellectual battle with a priest, stands upon the beach gazing at the young woman in the surf whose skirts the sea breezes have blown up round her legs. As Lewis sat with Janie Moore in the Drury Lane theatre, listening to the music, recalling his romantic youth and sitting with this person he loved, one can easily see the significance of not only this conjunction between his romantic pre-war ideals and Janie Moore, but also the inevitable collision that had occurred between his earlier romantic assumptions and the shattering realities of war.

There is contrast in how Jack presents his relationship with Mrs. Moore to Arthur on the one hand and to Albert on the other hand. In the letter to Arthur written the day after he visited Kirkpatrick, Jack also wrote that he had not gone alone, which clearly indicated to Arthur that Mrs. Moore had accompanied Jack to the village; concerning the same event, he wrote to Albert merely that he had gone to visit his old tutor (*CL* 384). Likewise, he tells Albert of going to the theatre to see opera but does not mention that Mrs. Moore also attended; instead Jack retains a distance towards her in casting his letters to Albert, which he does not do in his letters to Arthur. To his father he says that she is merely in London visiting Edith Askins, her sister; he and Mrs. Moore have seen one another frequently, he admits, but gives the reasons as her need since losing Paddy and also asserts a sense of what he owes to her for her kindnesses (*CL* 387).

Figure 16. Arthur Rackham's illustration from *Der Ring des Nibelungen*: Siegfried meeting Fear, with this caption on the protective sheet: "Magical rapture/Pierces my heart;/Fixed is my gaze/Burning with terror;/I reel, my heart faints and fails!" (© Courtesy of the Arthur Rackman Estate/Bridgeman Art Library)

Against Albert's hopes, Jack softly avoids the possibility of going home to convalesce but provides a gentle explanation and excuses; while he asserts he is homesick, which may well be, he is nonetheless not interested in returning home; he would rather have Albert visit him in London (*CL* 387).

When Jack does choose a place to convalesce, it is no surprise that he stays in England. On 29 August, he writes again to his father that it is a great mischance that he could not return to Ireland to recouperate, so he went instead to Bristol to be near Janie Moore but also mentions to Albert Perret, who was previously with Lewis in France and had been wounded before Jack. He also claims that he will be kept confined in the military hospital in Bristol (*CL* 387). Yet we must doubt that Jack is disappointed, and his insistence that he will be kept confined we must take as a security device so that Albert would not visit him and interrupt his time with Mrs. Moore (*CL* 388).

As he did during his time in Le Treport, Jack begins to muse upon his fate. In a letter to Albert, he wrote that "I could sit down and cry over the whole business: and yet of course we have both much to be thankful for [. . . .] If I had not been wounded when I was, I should have gone through a terrible time" (*CL* 388). His unit suffered severe casualties in the weeks following Jack's wounding. Beyond reflection on his own survival are thoughts for those who did not: he had learned that almost all the men he knew in his unit were dead; he remembers Laurence Johnson at some length and can't believe he is dead; he is clearly, in this letter, heavily beset by grief for all that has occurred (*CL* 388). Not these thoughts alone trouble him; the wound in his leg also continued to give him difficulty, which he mentions while still in London—the bandage slipping while he was crossing a street in London (*CL* 387)—and again when he has been moved to Bristol.

What Lewis finds to divert himself is important. Beginning from the time Lewis was in O.T.C. in Oxford through the time he was in France, he was writing a book of poetry, the work that eventually became *Spirits in Bondage*. When settled in Bristol, Jack tells Arthur that that he is making a clear copy of his poems for a publisher (*CL* 389).

These poems chronicle the traumatic events he encountered and their immediate effects upon him. His later poem, *Dymer*, is Lewis in the midst of working through trauma's lingering effects. They both reveal the collapse of his collective assumptions, an event which is the center of human trauma, as will be discussed in detail later. For the moment, he experiences something shared among other soldiers, something beyond his resentment for Albert or his love for Mrs. Moore: Lewis seems to feel a keen reluctance to re-enter Albert's world, that world which the war changed very little.

On 10 August, Albert is exasperated at having virtually no word from Jack and wonders what he is doing; Albert expresses his frustration to Warnie, who in France can offer little assistance (*LP* VI.20). Jack's new address was Ashton Court, Clifton, Bristol (*LP* VI.20). Albert's and Warnie's suspicions rose and were directed towards Mrs. Moore. One of Warnie's subalterns arranged that his wife in Bristol should attempt to discover something of Mrs. Moore and what Jack was doing with her. Warnie also writes to Albert that another woman offered him a similar arrangement, which Warnie declined (*LP* VI.20). Albert attempted to get Jack home by forwarding him application for the Ulster Volunteer Force, which Jack excuses himself from submitting on the same basis as a wheel that makes no noise will be ignored. Jack reasons that he may be given extra time to recuperate if he keeps out of the medical board's line of vision; he paints for Albert the picture of a return to the lines (*CL* 391).

It was the right tack if he hoped to quell Albert's activity by predicting the thing Albert wanted least. Yet Jack excuses himself further from attempting to move to Ireland and once more asserts that he would prefer Albert come to visit him and become acquainted with Janie Moore (*CL* 391); he explores possibilities of them having time together both in Bristol after Jack is free of convalescence and on duty in a period of home service in England (*CL* 392). Of course, none of these plans transpire, and Jack writes in September that he will not gain a period of service in Ireland; he is nearly back in full repair (*CL* 395–396). Through this time, Jack continually appeases but puts off his father despite promises and expressions of affection.

Despite the usual talk of books in his letters to Arthur, Jack ends abruptly, in a moment revealing his deeper feelings: "Oh don't you sometimes feel that everything is dead? I feel, and apparently you feel, a sort of impossibility in getting on solidly with any serious book in the way we used to do" (*CL* 395). To me this indicates Jack's growing realization that the secure citadel of his assumptions has failed him. Many a soldier returned feeling thus, as for instance occurs in Erich Remarque's works, which are filled with examples of a dissociation between a former soldier and his former life, his former society, his former work. Some of those soldiers recover while others wallow and sink beneath their disorientation. Such a feeling is also a mark of Vera Brittain's experience when she returned to her studies at Oxford once the war ended.

Despite the good news that Jack's poems were accepted by Heinemann's, he reports the bad news that confirmed his fears for Paddy Moore. The letters that described Paddy being killed had arrived from the War Office. Jack also felt keenly his luck in missing the remaining weeks of that German advance (*CL* 400).

Upon hearing the news of Paddy, Albert himself wrote to Mrs. Moore, offering sympathy for her loss and thanks her for her care of Jack (*CL* 402). Near this time, Jack also informed his father that Martin Somerville has also been killed (*CL* 402). Thus all the men at Oxford who were in O.T.C. with Lewis had died: Davey, Moore, Sutton, and Somerville. Another man that Lewis assumed had died, Denis Howard de Pass, went into the 12th Rifle Brigade, was captured on 1 April 1918, and survived the war (*CL* 402). Apparently Lewis was not close to de Pass and seems not to have sought further information about him after the war.

Lewis, was passed by a examining board for further convalescence in a camp on the Salisbury Plain, Perham Downs Camp, and wrote to Arthur that he had not been away on leave but was with Janie Moore (*CL* 403); she had also followed Jack to the camp, securing rooms nearby (*CL* 404). This was in late October, and with rumors of the war's end circulating, everyone it seems to have been thinking back to what the war had meant. Janie Moore, writing to Albert, remarks that her dreams for Paddy, as so many parents could say, were lost in the battlefields of France (*LP* VI.44–45). One point that rankles Jack is the Germans' propensity for naming trenches (e.g., the "Siegfried Line") after Wagnerian heroes (*CL* 405–406). He might be speaking as well of his pre-war assumptions and the shattering effects the war had upon them. But mostly Jack was thinking repeatedly of the friends he has lost and how he could possibly keep out of France.

Siegfried Sassoon recalled that "I had an uncomfortable habit of remembering, when I woke up in the morning, that the War was still going on and waiting for me to go back to it" (117), a habit many men in Lewis's position shared at the time. But as the rumors of the war's end increased, on 10 November (the day before the armistice) he wrote to his father, that a day's time would end their worries and possibly bring an end to his personal involvement in the war (*CL* 415). The next day brought peace: "It is almost incredible that the war is over, isn't it—not to have that 'going back' hanging over my head all the time. This time last year I was in the trenches, & now [. . .]" (*CL* 419). From the time he wrote this to Arthur, he had but another twenty-odd days left in active service, albeit he had a fear that, having once served, he would be at the beck of the military forever after (*CL* 420). At this time, however, he began to ponder arrangements for re-entering Oxford. Once again he was moved; the entire command depot shifted to Eastbourne. On 24 December, however, Jack was demobilized. He did not inform his father, but reached home on 27 December, and Warnie, at home in Ireland and on leave since 23 December, records the event in his diary:

A red letter day. We were sitting in the study about 11 o'clock this morning when we saw a cab coming up the avenue. It was Jacks! He has been demobilized thank God. Needless to say there were great doings [. . . .]

It was as if the evil dream of four years had passed away and we were still in the year 1913. In the evening there was bubbly for dinner in honor of the event. The first time I have ever had champagne at home. Had the usual long conversation with Jacks after going to bed. (*LP* VI.79)

Warren, on Jack's birthday of November of 1918, had still been in France and wrote to Albert, with the sense of disbelief that probably everyone in Europe was feeling,

Now that it is all over, I don't mind admitting that the thing [war] was a nightmare to me the whole time he [Jack] was out here. I couldn't get him out of my mind and I used to wake up in the middle of the night wondering if he was still alive or not. But thank God it is all finished now. Can you believe it is really over? I cannot. (*LP* VI.73)

Perhaps it was not, in some sense, over. In *Mrs. Dalloway*, appearing as late as 1925, Virginia Woolf writes,

For it was the middle of June. The War was over, except for some one like Mrs. Foxcroft at the Embassy last night eating her heart out because that nice boy was killed and now the old Manor House must go to a cousin; or Lady Bexborough who opened a bazaar, they said, with the telegram in her hand, John, her favorite, killed; but it was over; thank Heaven—over. (3)

"Except for. . . ." Woolf's novel traces not only a day in Clarissa Dalloway's life, but the last day of a soldier's life, that of Septimus Warren Smith, for whom the war was most decidedly not over. Similarly, it was not over for Jack despite a very short time remaining in the army and wrangling with the War Office over the wound gratuity, which he was eventually awarded and the sum later increased (TNA (PRO) WO339/105408). Mrs. Moore also wrangled with the War Office—it was over Paddy's effects.

About these external matters, let me just provide a few notes which shed light on Moore's relationship with her son and with her estranged husband. It is imponderable, the thousands, perhaps millions, of young men who died in that war without having written a will. As the men were of legal age and most often dying intestate, the War Office would not relinquish to the family any pay due to the dead (indicated in their pay books) or their effects until it could be proven that the family had a legal right to the estate. It was not usually a complicated matter to prove but often required an attorney. Mrs. Moore's case was complicated by the fact that the Europe was decidedly patrilinial, and Paddy's father vied to receive his effects, which included a little pay but, more importantly, the posthumously awarded Military Cross. The letters from both parents to the War Office exist in Paddy's military record. While understandable in a period of grief, Janie Moore's letters to the War Office ramble with panic and desperation that nevertheless bring one to see the woman Warnie described harshly as devouring Jack's time in later life, even driving him to a nervous breakdown. Indeed, after reading her letters, one suspects that she is the woman Jack drew in *The Great Divorce* who demands repeatedly to see her son—to possess him, that is, and take him away from his higher good, which she is not allowed to do.

Warren indicated in his memoir that Mrs. Moore was wholly self-concerned; the letters in Paddy's military file and her letter to Albert, previously mentioned, spoke not of Paddy himself but precisely how the war had thwarted *her* dreams for Paddy (*LP* VI.44–45). One cannot grudge her grief; that is other than possessiveness. Mr. Moore, as her letters to the War Office also indicate, sent Janie from Ireland to live in England with the children and provided her with £120 a year; she also had £100 a year of her own. Mr. Moore remained in Ireland and, as Janie's account has it, had not seen Paddy since 1913. Mr. Moore's handwriting proved for me entirely undecipherable, and thus I can provide nothing of his comments on the matter of his son.

Warnie observed "Mrs. Moore's extreme unsuitability as a companion" for Jack, that "she was a woman of very limited mind, and notably domineering and possessive by temperament. She cut down to a minimum his visits to his father, interfered constantly with his work, and imposed a heavy burden of minor domestic tasks" on him; "her conversation was chiefly about herself" (Lewis 12). Jack, as is commonly known today, set up house with Mrs. Moore and Maureen, and lived thus for the rest of Janie Moore's life, but as Warren explained, early on Jack's arrangement with the Moores was concealed from Albert, who was sending Jack money; Jack as a student had hardly the resources to manage a family of his own (Lewis 12). Warnie, however, remarks that "I dwell on this rather unhappy business with some regret, but it was one of the central and determining circumstances in Jack's life. He hinted at it, darkly, in *Surprised by Joy*, and it is reflected with painful clarity in various passages in his books" (Lewis 13). That allusion is this:

> I returned to Oxford—"demobbed"—in January 1919. But before I say anything of my life there I must warn the reader that one huge and complex episode will be omitted. I have no choice about this reticence. All I can or need say is that my earlier hostility to the emotions was very fully and variously avenged. (*SBJ* 198)

Establishing house with Moore was, I believe, but a small part of this dark allusion. The emotions were not solely those having to do with love, though in large part the allusion includes his love for Mrs. Moore. But further: his feelings of love were inextricably mixed with his war experience, a war which in Lewis's psyche was far from over. The war would rage on for years within him as it did within tens of thousands of other soldiers.

The past's presence in every present moment becomes a central feature of Modernism for no insignificant reason and is a main theme in *Mrs. Dalloway* and other works like T. S. Eliot's *Waste Land*—works exemplary in their prophetic vision that individuals and society would not easily escape (although they might deny) the war's darker influences; its shadow stretches far into the century for both society and the individual. The military little understood trauma; it did not teach a soldier returning home how to cope with war's psychological residues. As Erich Remarque wrote, postwar society did not teach returning men "what life is. You should have taught us to live again!" (328). The military taught one how to ignore lethal panic in the midst of battle, what soldiers called a moment of getting one's "balls up" or "the wind up." It did not teach one how to forget those lessons. And in 1921, Lewis records in his diary a poignant moment of his war history:

> **Sunday 18 June:** I woke up late this morning in such a state of misery and depression as I never remember to have had. There was no apparent reason. Really rather ridiculous—found myself in tears, for the first time for many a long day, while dressing. I concealed this well as I could and it passed off after breakfast. I suppose it is some sort of pathological reaction by which I pay for not having had conscious wind up or exhaustion during schools.
>
> Wrote a few stanzas of "Dymer" in the morning [. . . .] (*AMR* 51)

It was not because of schools. If, as Warren said, Jack's relationship with Mrs. Moore is "reflected with painful clarity in various passages in his books," so much more do passages of his books clearly reflect his war, how it shattered his early assumptions about life, the world, and himself. Remarque's protagonist recalls a moment when he lay in a field as the war's fierce haunting began—at long last—to subside, and "My face is wet; and only then do I discover that I am weeping, incontinently weeping, as if all that were now over, gone for ever—" (310). Remarque's character is in joy at this moment of the war's remove because the war's haunting has subsided. Lewis wept, I believe, because he had repressed the trauma of his war. The shaping of that trauma is at the center of not only Lewis's first book, *Spirits in Bondage*, which is a collection of war poetry published while he was still in military service. His first attempts to exorcise war's trauma from himself—to recall it and to face it—are the central aspect of his long poem *Dymer*, which he was writing the very morning he wept, that morning after war.

NOTES

1. Shrapnel was a round ball of lead which would not have been allowed to remain in the body. Shell fragments are part of the hard, steel casing of a shell. The confusion of terms may be due in part to Lewis, who used both "shrapnel" and "fragment" at different times in describing his wounds.
2. Discussion has continued on how much battle Remarque experienced in the war; it matters little to the veracity of the novel as I use it, for if such descriptions are not found there, they may be found in parallels elsewhere—in fiction and non-fiction.

WORKS CITED

Baker, Chris. "The Stationary and General Hospitals of 1914–1918." *The Long, Long Trail.* 26 May 2003. <http://www.1914–1918.net/hospitals.htm> 2003.

Carpenter, Humphrey. *The Brideshead Generation: Evelyn Waugh and His Friends.* New York: Houghton Mifflin, 1990.

"Demythologizing C. S. Lewis." *World* 5 (May 19, 1990): 14–15.

Green, Roger Lancelyn and Walter Hooper. *C.S. Lewis: A Biography.* New York: Harcourt, 1974.

Hansen, Arlen J. *Gentlemen Volunteers: The Story of American Ambulance Drivers in the Great War August 1914–September 1918.* New York: Arcade, 1996.

Hooper, Walter, ed. *C. S. Lewis: A Companion & Guide.* San Francisco: Harper, 1998.

Junger, Ernst. *The Storm of Steel.* New York: Fertig, 1996.

King, Don W. "Demythologizing C. S. Lewis." Rev. of *C. S. Lewis: A Biography* by A. N. Wilson. 26 May 2003. http://www.montreat.edu/dking/lewis/Wilsonreview.htm 1990.

Lewis, W. H. Memoir. *C. S. Lewis Letters.* Ed. W. H. Lewis. New York: Harcourt, 1966.

Mottram, R. H. *Sixty-Four, Ninety-Four! The Spanish Farm Trilogy.* London: Penguin, 1979.

———. *The Spanish Farm.* London: Penguin, 1936.

"New Hospital for Officers." *The Daily Graphic.* 26 July 1915: 10.

Remarque, Erich Maria. *All Quiet on the Western Front.* Boston: Little, Brown, 1958.

———. *The Road Back.* Trans. A. W. Wheen. New York: Fawcett, 1931.

"Thomas Kerrison Davey." *Commonwealth War Graves Commision.* <http://yard.ccta.gov.uk/cwgc/register.ns/wwwcreaateservicedetails?openagent&500454>. 14 March 1999.

Wilson, A. N. *C. S. Lewis: A Biography.* New York: Norton, 1990.

Winter, J. M. *The Experience of World War I.* New York: Oxford UP, 1995.

Woolf, Virginia. *Mrs. Dalloway.* New York: Knopf, 1993.

CHAPTER 11

Embedded fragments

THE LETTERS, DIARY, AND POETRY LEWIS WROTE through the years after he was wounded all show distinct signs of a continuing trauma. Its exact nature and its subsequent manifestations are difficult to estimate, not least because both he and his brother attempted to conceal them at the point Warren placed an ellipsis in the *Lewis Papers*. At that point, it will be recalled, Jack discussed the symptoms of that stress. The omission was an act most certainly performed at Jack's recommendation. Jack further minimized his suffering decades later when he wrote his autobiography. Only by understanding the nature of war trauma generally—its causes, effects, duration, and treatments—and by building a deep context from these things may we examine Lewis's early poetry and understand its statements on war. Obviously, Lewis as "a case" cannot be diagnosed at this distance in time, and I have not the proper training to "diagnose" anyone. However, we may examine parallels to Lewis's experiences and examine them in light of what was known during the war and what is known today about Post Traumatic Stress Disorder, or PTSD. If we cannot rely completely on his letters and reported conversations as evidence of his trauma, we may yet consider medical literature and case studies as well as statements from other WWI veterans. All of these types of works reveal close parallels to Lewis's experiences, and these I will explore.

One study in particular serves to illustrate the unique nature of World War I and its effects on people:

> Before 1914, it seemed to most of us that civilization with its drains, and its banks, and
> its social amenities by which to prevent friction of the emotions, and its policemen and
> law courts to stop even the suggestion of physical clash, had stilted in us any possibil-
> ity of living in an environment of danger and destruction, of dirt and foul odors. In
> the vast majority, the power of the human animal to exist in quite novel and abominable
> surroundings has been amply vindicated; but in a certain number the adaptation has
> been less complete, and be it noticed, these people have been most often those who
> found even the normal life of peace time a hard and tempestuous affair. (Kennedy 17)

The above was written not, as one might expect, in a study of the war's effect
on society, but in a medical paper on "The Nature of Nervousness in Soldiers,"
written by neurologist Foster Kennedy of the Royal Army Medical Corps. It
was presented before the American Neurological Association in May of 1918
while Lewis lay in hospital in France. Kennedy began by establishing an important context:

> For eighteen months the term "shell shock" has been employed in medical literature
> and, colloquially also, in the British Army to cover all cases of nervous instability
> occurring in the course of war. Under this heading have been massed cases of amne-
> sia, anergic stupor, sleeplessness, nightmare, mutism, functional blindness, tremors,
> palsies, and further, neuroses, occurring not only under fighting strain but also in indi-
> viduals who, failing in self confidence, suffer doubts and apprehensions while still
> waiting for transport overseas. (Kennedy 17)

What today is called PTSD was a phenomenon just beginning to be understood at the time Kennedy was writing, and while it is recognized now, the disorder still holds some mystery for doctors. In continuing work on PTSD,
exemplary cases and consequent studies such as Kennedy's that date from the
First World War remain standard features in discussions of the phenomenon
today. Not only are actual cases from the war considered in current medical literature, but some medical scholars today cite descriptive passages from fictional works such as Remarque's *All Quiet on the Western Front* (Van der Hart et
al. 13) to illuminate events which are considered to lead to PTSD. These
authors presume a greater level of biographical accuracy in Remarque's work
than can be readily confirmed from information on Remarque's life and military record; nevertheless, their practice speaks to their informed perceptions
in noting instances where fictional works can provide accurate representations
of the events that gave rise to traumatic shock as well as noting accurate representations of consequent symptoms.

A number of important things emerge about the early awareness of PTSD.
First, the original descriptor, "shell shock," was soon determined to be misleading. The disorder was originally thought to be caused by the wave of compression created by a shell as it exploded: "High-velocity shells producing sonic

and pressure shock waves within 50–100 yards of impact were used. Caught in this range of impact, a man would exhibit a period of 'shock'" (Neill 149). It was believed that the compression wave caused physiological damage to the brain and nervous system, not an unreasonable assumption. Descriptions of force in an explosive event could be persuasive as provided by D. Forsyth in 1915 in *Lancet*:

> But by far the intensest [sic] strain is shellfire, especially by high explosives. The detonation, the flash, the heat of the explosion, the air concussion, the upheaval of the ground, and the acrid suffocating fumes combine in producing a violent assault on practically all of the senses simultaneously. The effect is often immediately intensified by the shrieks and groans and the sight of the dead and injured. This mental shock is the greatest in those who are most wrought at the moment of the explosion. (qtd. in Neill 149)

Beyond the initial shock, many soldiers were buried by the earth raised by explosions, as in the following case:

> . . . a young officer who was sent home from France on account of a wound received just as he was extricating himself from a mass of earth in which he had been buried. When he reached hospital in England he was nervous and suffered from disturbed sleep and loss of appetite. (Rivers 3)

Another case is that of

> an officer, whose burial as the result of a shell explosion had been followed by symptoms pointing to some degree of cerebral concussion. In spite of severe headache, vomiting, and disorder of micturition, he remained on duty for more than two months. He then collapsed altogether after a very trying experience, in which he had gone out to seek a fellow officer and had found his body blown into pieces, with head and limbs lying separated from the trunk. (Rivers 4)

Frederick Mott, in 1916, had first proffered the theory of physiological shock, believing that "there were undetected neurological injuries which were caused by shell shock," an event leaving "injury to what he called the 'intercalery neurons'" (Neill 149). In the second example, above, the symptoms of cerebral concussion seemed to validate the theory that physical neurological damage had occurred. When brains of soldiers who had supposedly died from concussive shock were dissected, signs of hemorrhage in critical areas of the brain were revealed to exist (Kennedy 18). However, this explanation of physical shock became increasingly suspect when symptoms of PTSD were also observed in a large number of soldiers experiencing diverse traumatic events, including those who merely witnessed or heard about another person's death or injury. Further, soldiers who suffered trauma were also objects of suspicion to many military authorities, including medical authorities.

To such authorities the symptoms of PTSD were often assumed to be a soldier's means of shirking his duty, a sign of cowardice, leading to many a man's death before a firing squad. Denis Winter quotes from the *British Medical Journal* of November 1914 in which Dr. Albert Wilson asserted "I do not think that the psychologists will get many cases" from the war. Yet that year "1,906 cases of behaviour disorder without physical cause were admitted to hospital" with the number growing to 20,327 the following year, "9 per cent of battle casualties" (Winter 129). In 1929, ten years after the war, about 65,000 soldiers were in still "in mental hospitals for 'shell shock'"—a conservative estimate (Winter 252). While some men were shot for cowardice, other solutions involved "extremely cruel" cures, "especially in Germany, Austria, and France" (Van der Hart et al. 20). On the assumption of malingering, Lynn Macdonald writes that

> both in the line and out of it, there was an all-too-ready acceptance of the fallacy that "nerves" was an excuse for "funkiness" or even cowardice. If it were not, why should one man break down and become a nervous casualty while a comrade who had had the same experience in the same circumstances remained apparently unaffected? It was assumed that the answer was to be found in the calibre of the man. (231)

Malingering was a tenacious assumption, adhered to by some military doctors even as late as 1918 and is the view which Kennedy, that year, still felt a need to defend against in asserting the reality of the disorder:

> Let me not be misunderstood: A conscious assumption of symptoms by soldiers in my experience—and in this I am completely supported by all other medical officers—is exceedingly rare; it is not rare for a man to go sick for a few hours to obtain a temporary alleviation of his lot, but very seldom does one meet a man malingering with a view to discharge from the service. (17)

Even when wider recognition of deeper psychical causes was becoming the norm, treatments remained extremely diverse. Mott, who turned from the theory of physiological shock to "fairly non-specific psychological causes," promoted a treatment that was equally non-specific but which essentially prescribed repression:

> Be cheerful and look cheerful is the note that should be sounded to these functional cases. Sympathy should be displaced, although it should be shown to all these fellows who have a fixed idea of never recovering; it is not their fault, it is a real thing to them and no one could be more grateful than those cases of functional nervous disability for those cheery words. (qtd. in Neill 149)

Neill also pointed to assumptions of the time, suspicions of "hereditary taint" and "organic deficits or tendencies" in patients that the conditions of war simply exposed; such assumptions had carried over from "turn-of-the-century neurologists" (149). Doctors holding such theories, laden with the melioristic assumptions of the nineteenth century, are illustrated well by two authors: Rudyard Kipling and Virginia Woolf.

Kipling, in his story "The Phantom Rickshaw," draws a picture of Jack Pansay, a man suffers recurrent meetings with one Mrs. Wessington, riding in her rickshaw being pulled by two servants. The problem is that Mrs. Wessington, the woman whom Pansay jilted after persuading her to leave her husband and enjoy a brief, shipboard affair, has died after reaching India. Not only she but also the servants who pulled her rickshaw have died of fever; the rickshaw itself was burned. Pansay nevertheless continues to see her in the rickshaw as the two servants pull it along; she stops in the road before Pansay and pleads for his forgiveness and to be friends again. The doctor in Kipling's tale, Heatherlegh, takes Pansay's case despite his certainty that Pansay is a cad; it's the novelty of the case that interests him. Dr. Heatherlegh's philosophy is simple: "Eyes, Pansay—all Eyes, Brain, and Stomach. And the greatest of these is Stomach. You've too much conceited Brain, too little Stomach, and thoroughly unhealthy Eyes. Get your Stomach straight and the rest follows. And all that's French for a liver pill" (Kipling 39). It is appropriate that he articulates his materialist philosophy in a parody of I Corinthians 13: "faith, hope, and love, and the greatest of these is love." Yet Heatherlegh's philosophy takes him only a short distance in understanding Pansay's case. The rickshaw appears just as both men near a point where the road they travel passes beneath an "overhanging shale cliff" (Kipling 39). Spying the rickshaw before him, Pansay stops dead in the road. At the moment that Heatherlegh—who cannot see the specter—urges Pansay to move forward, the shale gives way in a massive slide and buries the road: "Man, if we'd gone forward we should have been ten feet deep in our graves by now" says Heatherlegh, who inadvertently begins a quotation from *Hamlet* (I.5)—"There are more things in heaven and earth"—but cannot finish the line ("than are dreamt of in your philosophy").

Another literary example of doctors holding to the old ideology comes from one who understood both mental illness and the doctors of her day. In *Mrs. Dalloway*, Virginia Woolf casts one doctor in particular, Holmes, as retaining a view similar to Heatherlegh's. Holmes is called upon to tend Septimus Warren Smith, who suffers beneath symptoms of PTSD. In the war Smith had "developed manliness; he was promoted; he drew the attention, indeed the affection of his officer, Evans by name" (Woolf 86). Then, "when Evans was killed, just before the Armistice, in Italy, Septimus, far from showing any emotion or recognising that here was the end of a friendship, congratulated himself upon feeling very little and very reasonably. The War had taught

him. [. . . .] The last shells missed him. He watched them explode with indifference" (86). Later, from beneath his repression of the shock, the effects
emerge severely: sleeplessness, multi-sensory hallucinations, and irritability,
among other things, and Holmes is consulted. His diagnosis of Smith's condition is parallel to Heatherlegh's estimation of Pansay's, and more. It is akin
to Mott's optimistic view of 1916, "be cheerful and look cheerful": "Dr.
Holmes [. . . .] brushed it all aside—headaches, sleeplessness, fears, dreams—
nerve symptoms and nothing more, he said. If Dr. Holmes found himself even
half a pound below eleven stone six, he asked his wife for another plate of por-
ridge at breakfast" (Woolf 91). Further, "he continued, health is largely a matter in our own control. Throw yourself into outside interests; take up some
hobby [. . . ,] for did he not owe his own excellent health . . . to the fact that
he could always switch off from his patients on to old furniture?" (Woolf 91).
"Though this be madness, yet there is method in it," as was observed of
Hamlet, and just so wisdom resides not in Holmes but ironically in the traumatized Smith: "When the damned fool came again, Septimus refused to see
him" (91). To escape Holmes, however, Smith throws himself not into a
hobby but out of a window to his death.

I don't believe it an accident—E. M. Forster being one of the Bloomsbury
group—that a line of thinking similar to Holmes's appears in *Room with a View*,
the point at which Lucy Honeychurch comments to Mr. Emerson on his son,
young George's, brooding over a "knot, a tangle, a blemish in the eternal
smoothness," in essence "a young man melancholy because the universe
wouldn't fit, because life was a tangle or a wind" (31). Lucy advises, "your son
wants employment. Has he no particular hobby? Why, I myself have worries,
but I can generally forget them at the piano; and collecting stamps did no end
of good for my brother" (Forster 31). The Emersons, in this sense, stand for
those who oppose a philosophy (which Lucy parrots) that is blindly optimistic about its power to move civilization forward, blind in its belief that it
is sufficient appeasement for all disconsolate moments; yet it lacks the foresight
necessary to avoid pushing itself into a world war, lacks any means of coping
with its individual or collective trauma when its basic assumptions are violated. The Emersons are those of whom the WWI surgeon and French poet
Georges Duhamel spoke: "like clever children [they] realize that the modern
world would not know how to live or die without the meticulous discipline of
the sciences" (213). Duhamel continued, "I have seen the monstrous steriliz-
er on its throne. I tell you, of a truth, civilization is not to be found there any
more than in the shining forceps of the surgeon. Civilization is not in this terrible trumpery; and if it is not in the heart of man, then it exists nowhere"
(216).

The medical field, fortunately, looked more deeply into both the experiences of soldiers' trauma with its often-delayed and tenaciously persistent effects as well as into possible means of alleviation. The causes and treatments they discovered had to do not only with the physical moment of trauma and not only with the reexperiencing of it but also, directly, with traumatized persons' views of life, their assumptions about the world and humankind. They discovered that people's early environments and experiences contributed to the development of their views and assumptions as will be discussed in greater detail momentarily.

That young George Emerson, in Forster's *Room with a View*, could not satisfactorily make sense of the universe shows that some persons—at least Forster—suspected the deep connection between the human psyche and one's assumptions about the cosmos, and suspected no less how an event might affect a person if a radical disparity were exposed between real events on the one hand and the person's collective assumptions on the other hand. Doctors since the war have developed a larger awareness of trauma's effects on people whose assumptions have been shattered, but it was the pervasive impact and the unique nature of the First World War that brought about conditions in which these things became known.

Yet it is the very uniqueness of the war that gives rise to lingering critical questions regarding trauma. One primary question is why humankind should be brought to see a unique collection of symptoms in military men so late in the history of the world, so late in the history of warfare. Lewis's coping mechanism, that which he developed in his youth, involved his viewing things from a detached, literary standpoint; the mechanism is seen early in his war experience when he makes an attempt to interpret his war as something found in Homer. That mechanism was—as were other, varied coping mechanisms soldiers relied upon—singularly inept in confronting a war that was radically unique and unprecedented in history. Further, the recorded traumatic symptoms soldiers developed in this war seem as unique among humans as the war itself was among wars. Kennedy described the "conditions under which the present war are being fought [as] the rudest and largest experiment in biologic adaptation to which the human race has been exposed" (17). This is a point emphasized in medical studies as late as the year 2000:

> the years of World War I [. . .] were a time of immense suffering, not only among warring soldiers, but also among civilians in the various countries at war and in surrounding countries to which displaced people fled. In addition to the suffering of the countless refugees from the war zones, there was increasing hunger and shortage of all kinds of essential commodities throughout many countries [. . .], along with exten-

sive environmental damage and the total destruction of civil infrastructures. (Van der Hart et al. 4)

Central among Lewis's experiences are those stemming from the unique nature of this war, so often described, and which Lewis himself remarked—the surrealistically posed corpses, among them. Van der Hart and his colleagues note the

> constant stress of seeing fellow soldiers being killed or wounded, of the stench and sight of unburied decomposing bodies, of hearing unheeded screams for help from the wounded trapped in no-man's land, and of helplessly watching the wounded drown in mud without the possibility of being rescued [. . . .] Finally, fear was an ever-present experience. (4)

The new technological innovations of this warfare were alone sufficient to create horrors previously unimagined in the human mind even if the American Civil War brought those who knew war to suspect the possibility of them. One feature well understood by doctors now was strikingly disturbing to soldiers in the Great War—the peculiar immobility, where millions "were killed or maimed simply sitting in their trenches, not in actual face-to-face combat" (Neill 149). These characteristics of war stand in grave contrast to a the largely mobile wars experienced by soldiers of both the preceding wars and in wars thereafter.

Another important consideration is both how PTSD has been understood and debated by today's doctors and how today's judgments are applied to cases long-since "serviceable"—cases either concluded by the death of the person traumatized or by a resolution of their trauma. Once again I want to emphasize that cases from WWI are still central in today's discussions of PTSD. In the diagnostic manual (DSM-IV) published by the American Psychiatric Association, the "essential feature" of PTSD is described as

> the development of characteristic symptoms following exposure to an extreme traumatic stressor involving direct personal experience of an event that involves actual or threatened death or serious injury, or other threat to one's physical integrity; or witnessing an event that involves death, injury, or a threat to the physical integrity of another person; or learning about unexpected of violent death, serious harm, or threat of death or injury experienced by a family member or other close associate. (*Diagnostic* 424)

Among an adult person's responses, the disorder "must involve intense fear, helplessness, or horror," with characteristic symptoms including "persistent reexperiencing of the traumatic event [. . .], persistent avoidance of stimuli associated with the trauma [. . . ,] numbing of general responsiveness" and "persistent symptoms of increased arousal" (*Diagnostic* 424). Other noted symptoms are "irritability, anger, nightmares, low libido, and decreased functioning" (Daie and Witztum 244). Such symptoms as these are by no means limited to those who have been in military combat. Victims of crime, auto accident, rape, or natural catastrophes can develop symptoms of PTSD. Even learning that "one's child has a life-threatening disease" can produce the disorder, but it "may be especially severe or long lasting when the stressor is of human design"; further, it "may increase as the intensity of and physical proximity to the stressor increase" (*Diagnostic* 424). One may presume social distance (a close friend, not a stranger, dying) as an intensifying factor of traumatic events as well as the physical distance (proximity to an exploding shell). For an accurate diagnosis to be applied, a "full symptom picture must be present for more than 1 month" (*Diagnostic* 424).

Reexperiencing the event in some degree is a common result of trauma; persons typically experience "recurrent and intrusive recollections of the event [. . .] or recurrent distressing dreams during which the event is replayed" (*Diagnostic* 424). Rarely does the re-experiencing of the traumatic event become so severe as to produce a dissociative state—a state when personalities of an individual become unassociated, one aspect of the personality identifying with the traumatic event, while another aspect of the personality cannot recall or allow awareness of the event (Van der Hart et al. 6). When occurring, it is a condition that may "last from a few seconds to several hours, or even days, during which components of the event are relived and the person behaves as though experiencing the event at that moment" (*Diagnostic* 424). Re-experiences of a traumatic event may be triggered by relatively parallel events, situations "that resemble or symbolize an aspect of the traumatic event (e.g., anniversaries of the traumatic event; cold, snowy weather or uniformed guards for survivors of death camps in cold climates; hot, humid weather for combat veterans of the South Pacific; entering any elevator for a woman who was raped in an elevator)" (*Diagnostic* 424). While not all traumatized persons suffer severely dissociative symptoms, it is not surprising that "stimuli associated with the trauma are persistently avoided" and that "the person makes deliberate efforts to avoid thoughts, feeling, or conversations about the traumatic event [. . .] and to avoid activities, situations, or people who arouse recollections of it" (*Diagnostic* 424–425).

Another feature of PTSD understood today is what seems sometimes to be a remarkable delay in the appearance of symptoms; while they "usually begin within the first 3 months after the trauma [. . .] *there may be a delay of months, or even years, before symptoms appear*" (*Diagnostic* 426, emphasis mine). At the moment of the traumatic event, however (and if not then, at least within a month), the acute form of the disorder produces "characteristic anxiety, dissociative, and other symptoms," at least three of which appear: "a subjective sense of numbing, detachment, or absence of emotional responsiveness; a reduction in awareness of his or her surroundings; derealization; depersonalization; or dissociative amnesia" (*Diagnostic* 429). Individuals suffering from Acute Stress Disorder can

> have a decrease in emotional responsiveness, often finding it difficult or impossible to experience pleasure in previously enjoyable activities, and frequently feel guilty about pursuing usual life tasks. They may experience difficulty concentrating, feel detached from their bodies, experience the world as unreal or dreamlike, or have increasing difficulty recalling specific details of the traumatic event. (*Diagnostic* 429)

Paul Fussell noted dissociative symptoms, without naming them as such: detachment from the body experienced by soldiers and the tendency of soldiers to view themselves as acting in a play (195–196). Further, he quotes a major who described the sense of unreality soldiers sometimes felt: "a queer new feeling these last few days intensified last night. A sort of feeling of unreality, as if I were acting on a stage" (Fussell 192). Another soldier, Carrington, "testifies to the division of the psyche into something like actor, on the one hand, and spectator, on the other, especially during the moments of heightened anxiety when one is 'beside oneself'" (qtd. in Fussell 192). In yet another account, a captain describes a view of himself having been wounded this way:

> The curious thing was that he was not here; he was somewhere else. On a high place, . . . looking down at this solitary figure picking its way between the shell holes. He thought: that's young Captain Jim Hilton, that little figure. I wonder if he'll make it. . . . He was an observer, not a participant. It was always like that in war though he had not realized it before. You were never you. The part of you was somewhere else. (qtd. in Fussell 192–193)

Dissociation did not have to take place only when one had been wounded but could take place when one was undergoing bombardment:

> We had nothing to do but sit and listen for the roar of the 5.9's, lasting for five seconds each, perhaps twice a minute. One would be talking aimlessly of some unimportant thing when the warning would begin. The speaker's voice would check for an infinitesimal fraction of a second; then he would finish his sentence with a studied normality marvellously [sic] true to life. (qtd. in Fussell 192)

These words provides the reality missing from Lewis's minimalist description that the Germans kept his unit docile by continuous if relatively light shelling (*SBJ* 195).

The dissociation affects also what would be assumed to be natural emotions. Septimus Warren Smith congratulates himself on feeling very little at the death of his friend Evans. The perception in soldiers is that at such moments, they are intact and coping well with, for them, unprecedented, horrific experiences. It continues into their later experiences, as in a case of a soldier in hospital, which Denis Winter relates:

> All the men in the ward with the exception of myself are bad cases. They have been here some days and I have watched them with the eye of a man who observes but cannot feel—I can feel no more . . . there is now a routine as each case in the ward is dealt with. I see how nervous they become, those whom nurses must prepare for the surgeon's visit. They have a horror of the pain which daily they have to endure [. . . .] (199)

It is precisely the same response Septimus Warren Smith articulated to himself in Woolf's *Mrs. Dalloway*: "he could not feel" (86). Ernst Junger writes that, in looking at a new recruit and "along the channel of his thoughts I had a shock when I realized for the first time how callous the war had made me. One got to regarding men as mere matter" (294). While it may be a matter of degrees, the reaction shows a dissociation from what we would call "normal" feelings.

In some cases of trauma, conversion reactions—also called conversion symptoms—appear. They are symptoms which are still popularly and inaccurately regarded as the primary identifying symptom of "shell shock" (Gaffney). The symptoms involve "voluntary motor or sensory functioning and are thus referred to as 'pseudoneurological'" (*Diagnostic* 452). Various medical films made during the war show veterans walking as if palsied, or with severe ticks, blindness, deafness, or paralysis. Other motor symptoms include anything from "impaired coordination or balance" to "a sensation of a lump in the throat, and urinary retention" while sensory "symptoms or deficits" can include things like "loss of touch or pain sensation, double vision, blindness, deafness, and hallucinations" as well as "seizures or convulsions" (*Diagnostic* 452). Such symptoms are illogical when they are true conversions of the trauma into a physiological manifestation; they may mimic inconsistently a motor or sensory impairment, but if actual conversion symptoms arise directly out of a psychological trauma, they tend to "follow the individual's conceptualization of a condition" (*Diagnostic* 453). But insofar as conversion disorders may be psychologically manifested, inconsistencies often appear in them which do not readily appear in strictly physiological disorders. For instance, a conversion disorder may appear in the patient having a "paralyzed" arm; yet, if the arm is raised above the head and released, the arm "will briefly retain its position, then fall to the side" instead of hitting the patient's head (*Diagnostic* 453). In a case of true paralysis, the arm would fall immediately and hit the patient's head.

Another example: if a patient's conversion symptoms appear as seizures, the individual convulsions will differ from one another, and abnormal brain activity "will not be evident on an EEG" (*Diagnostic* 453).

A few cases from medical studies will help to illustrate such symptoms common in PTSD cases. In one case, a soldier who had been wounded developed

> in addition to the symptoms of anxiety-hysteria . . . , a twitch of the lower jaw. This was rather slowly depressed and the mouth opened with a sigh as if about to yawn or take a deep breath [. . . .] An officer to whom this man was most attached . . . was killed alongside him in the trenches; the patient had seen his officer gasping for breath in the death agony. To use his own words, he "had never seen such sights before." (Van der Hart et al. 13)

One film in the Imperial War Museum shows a WWI veteran who developed a tic after he had bayoneted an enemy in the mouth. The involuntary movement resembled the event: the solider quickly opened his mouth widely, while moving his head backwards as if being stabbed in his own mouth; this involuntary action repeated every few seconds.

In another, more extreme case, a captain of 20 years was admitted to hospital; he would sit up in bed, "muttering continuously, moving his head and body from side to side, stretching out first one hand and then the other as if pushing away some hateful object, alternating this movement by that of passing his hand across the forehead. There seemed to be a perseveration of the gestures of horror" (Van der Hart et al. 14). These actions, or "motor symptoms" appeared when the man was apparently suffering hallucinations. If, however, he was engaged in talk, "he would answer questions rationally and the movements would become quieter, although his utterances remained jerky and hesitant" (Van der Hart et al. 14–15). Doctors discovered that when a shell exploded near this captain, "he had not lost consciousness"; rather, he "received a terrible emotional shock" when "a piece of exploded shell had knocked off the head of a brother officer while he was talking to him, scattering blood and brains over his face," an event which left the captain a year later without "emotional stability" (Van der Hart et al. 15). The man was eventually declared permanently unfit for military duty.

This man's re-experience of the event and the perseveration in his gesture of horror are complicated matters, but the dissociation of his personalities, or the "somatoform symptoms" (he stopped re-experiencing the event when distracted by talk, at which point he appeared rational), is considerably more complex still. It is a reaction, essentially, wherein a person has not (in today's popular terms) mentally "owned" the event, has not confronted it and discovered a way to accept the event as a fact of the world but instead has relegated it to another region, or to a different aspect, of personality. The area of personality to which it is delivered "recalls" it and can, in moments, re-experience it, causing the victim to even act on that memory outwardly and involuntarily. This is an important aspect of the symptoms, as seen in this case in which a soldier developed a tic of the fingers:

> The leading symptom was a peculiar rotary motion of the forefinger and thumb [. . .]. The symptom was eliminated by direct suggestion; but reappeared immediately after a fearful dream which the patient could not recollect. [. . .]. In hypnosis the dream was at once recovered, namely, a Russian soldier throwing himself upon the patient. He then recollected that he had seen this Russian appear upon the parapet of the trench as he was adjusting, by screwing action of finger and thumb, the time-fuse of a hand-grenade, and that in the next moment he was "knocked out" by an explosion. (Van der Hart et al. 19)

In such cases the event causes a soldier to develop a tic from traumatic events unremembered in waking moments. In sleep, however, he may shout commands or fire an invisible weapon and show intense fear. He will recall nothing of the events that eventually cause him to awake in a profuse sweat.

Symptoms seem not to go away of their own accord and cannot be repressed without ill effect. This is illustrated in one remarkable case: a certain officer could clearly remember his traumatic event. He had gone out to find an officer friend and discovered the friend's dismembered corpse. Rivers relates the symptoms this officer developed:

> From that time he had been haunted at night by the vision of his dead and mutilated friend. When he slept he had nightmares in which his friend appeared, sometimes as he had seen him mangled on the field, sometimes in the still more terrifying aspect of one whose limbs and features had been eaten away by leprosy. The mutilated or leprous officer of the dream would come nearer and nearer until the patient suddenly awoke pouring sweat and in a state of utmost terror. He dreaded to go to sleep, and spent each day looking forward in painful anticipation of the night. He had been advised to keep all thoughts of war from his mind, but the experience which recurred so often at night was so insistent that he could not keep it wholly from his thoughts, much as he tried to do so. Nevertheless, there is no question but that he was striving by day to dispel memories only to bring them upon him with redoubled force and horror when he slept. (Rivers 4)

Repression made symptoms increase in this case.

In the diagnostic manual, an important aspect is given as to the nature of conversion reaction: "The more medically naive the person, the more implausible are the presenting symptoms. More sophisticated persons tend to have more subtle symptoms and deficits that may closely resemble neurological or other general medical conditions" (*Diagnostic* 452–453). This remark implies a link, mentioned earlier, between the victim of trauma and that person's understanding of life—the person's paradigm or collective assumptions about life—and a further link is noted to personal history:

> There is some evidence that social supports, family history, childhood experiences, personality variables, and preexisting mental disorders may influence the development of Posttraumatic Stress Disorder. This disorder can develop in individuals without any predisposing conditions, particularly if the stressor is especially extreme. (*Diagnostic* 426–427)

Such is the conclusion of one study, "The Aftermath of Victimization: Rebuilding Shattered Assumptions," in which the author writes that "Much of the psychological trauma produced by victimizing events derives from the shattering of very basic assumptions that victims have held about the operation of the world" (Janoff-Bulman 17). This theory centers upon the assumption that we have all developed "a theory of reality that brings order into what otherwise would be a chaotic world of experience" (qtd. in Janoff-Bulman 17). Citing various studies on this matter, Janoff-Bulman shows that a broad awareness has developed of the importance of an individual's collection of assumptions about reality, variously called world models, paradigms, structures of meaning; the assumptions "are learned and confirmed by the experience of many years" and "provide the framework within which to conduct 'normal' (i.e., day to day) living" (17–18). Three basic assumptions are these: we are "personally invulnerable;" the world is "meaningful and comprehensible"; we may view ourselves "in a positive light" (Janoff-Bulman 18). The assumptions are "implicit, rather than explicit" and are on the whole "relatively inaccessible to introspection" (Janoff-Bulman 18). A traumatic event challenges these assumptions, and victims suffer a "loss of equilibrium. The world is suddenly out of whack. Things no longer work the way they used to" (qtd. in Janoff-Bulman 18). The results may appear in a traumatized person developing symptoms of PTSD as we have seen, but centrally the sufferer's "perceptions are now marked by threat, danger, insecurity, and self-questioning" (Janoff-Bulman 18). Such senses are inherent in Lewis's remark to Arthur, already quoted, "You, who have never lost that life, cannot understand the longing with which I look back to it" (*CL* 378) and the account of intense fears when his hospital in France was bombed (*CL* 372).

Janoff-Bulman also points to an important statement that appears commonly in soldiers' accounts of the war: "a victim feels a sense of 'helplessness against overpowering forces . . . and apprehension that anything may now happen to him [. . . .]'" (19). Further, the study asserts that victims may no longer "perceive themselves as safe and secure in a benign environment. They have experienced a malevolent world" (20). Siegfried Sassoon struggled with these precise lines of thought in moments during the war, recollections unusual for their open introspection:

> [. . .] my thoughts were powerless against unhappiness so huge. I couldn't alter European history, or order the artillery to stop firing. I could stare at the War as I stared at the sultry sky, longing for life and freedom and vaguely altruistic about my fellow-victims [. . . .] and altogether, I concluded, Armageddon was too immense for my solitary understanding. (82–83)

An expression of horror is something Sassoon defended as an appropriate response:

> At the risk of being thought squeamish or even unsoldierly, I still maintain that an ordinary human being has a right to be momentarily horrified by a mangled body seen on an afternoon walk, although people with sound common sense can always refute me by saying that life is full of gruesome sights and violent catastrophes. (147)

Yet in a later moment, his thoughts reveal a comparative numbness upon seeing the hands of a corpse sticking up from the earth, one hand seeming to indict heaven, a gesture that Sassoon gradually came to see, upon passing the place repeatedly, as a petition to God:

> Such sights must be taken for granted, I thought, as I gasped and slithered and stumbled with my disconsolate crew. Floating on the surface of the flooded trench was the mask of a human face which had detached itself from the skull. (157)

It is just that: detachment from the whole being, but face of emotion taken off the foundation of thought. Janoff-Bulman's understanding applies here: "victims are apt to find themselves at a loss to explain why they were victimized" (21). Sassoon's mental laugh provides the context for many soldiers' reactions, one that also comes from the German soldier Friedrich Durrenmatt:

> And indeed, things happen without anyone in particular being responsible for them. Everything is dragged along and everyone gets caught somewhere in the sweep of events. We are all collectively guilty, collectively bogged down in the sins of out fathers and of our forefathers. . . . That is our misfortune, but not our guilt. . . . Comedy alone is suitable for us. (qtd. in Fussell 204).

This comedy—dark, cynical, brooding over cruel ironies—is that which scholars have not only defined as the Great War soldiers' mode of recollection but have also placed at the center of the 20th century's mode of recollection—at least in the West. Fussell asserted that "the Great War was more ironic than any before or since. It was a hideous embarrassment to the prevailing Meliorist myth which had dominated the public consciousness for a century" (8). It was, as Lytton Strachey asserted broodingly "the abridgement of hope," and if joy remained, "it is joy that is long since dead; and if there are smiles, they are sardonical" (qtd. in Fussell 3). Fussell goes so far as to write that irony "embodies the contemporary equivalent of the experience offered [. . . .] I am saying that there seems to be one dominating form of modern understanding; that it is essentially ironic; and that it originates largely in the application of mind and memory to the events of the Great War" (35). I disagree. Irony may be a means of recall; it may even be an initial means of coping for some as well as an extended means of recollecting a traumatic event, but through examination of studies of PTSD, one comes to suspect that psychologically it is not a means of coming to terms with a traumatic event nor of rebuilding one's shattered assumptions about the world. This is not to say such irony is not understandable—and it certainly is durable as an initial panacea. As T. S. Eliot wrote, "human kind cannot bear very much reality," and the war's most basic aspect was its precipitation of realities so traumatic that they could not easily be borne by the human psyche. Years after the war Lewis would write *Pilgrim's Regress*, in which he described the things which destroyed the old paradigm for the citizens of Eschropolis. They explain to Pilgrim, "we lost our ideals when there was a war in this country"; others add, as in a chant, "it was the mud and the blood" (*Regress* 54). Stephane Audoin-Rouzeau and Annette Becker have illustrated that the collective violence (to Lewis, the "blood") of the Great War was unprecedented in history. Other soldiers, among the many Ernst Junger, point to the mud, literally the trauma of living in mud, as simply depleting of hope and bringing one to utter despair. Some men who in battle at Passchendaele fell into the mud and survived drowning were found to have gone mad.

We arrive, then, at a point where we must ask, what is the means of coping, of eventual resolution—if such may be attained—to such violation of not only one's person in being wounded and cast into the dire conditions of the Front, but to one's psyche by means of violating one's collective assumptions about the cosmos? The victim of trauma must discover a means by which to integrate the traumatic experience into his or her belief system, must adjust his or her paradigm to explain a new perception of the world's realities. Even if victims will not perceive the world as "wholly benevolent, or themselves as entirely invulnerable," still they must shift their assumptions or construct new assumptions; at the center of those assumptions are the ideas that the world is "not wholly malevolent" and that they themselves are "not uniquely vulnerable to misfortune" (Janoff-Bulman 22). Meanwhile, repetition (often intrusive recollections) of the event in the memory can occur until "the new information is integrated" and "stored in active memory" which is when "the information becomes part of 'long-term models and inner schemata'" (Janoff-Bulman 23). Traumatic events, and victims' means of coping with them, cause individuals to "eventually change inner models" (Janoff-Bulman 23).

Whereas early in the war medical personnel believed that an organic or genetic fault made some men more susceptible to the traumatic event, vulnerability does not reside simply in a person's assumptions but in the nature of how those assumptions are held by the individual:

> To the extent that particular assumptions are held with extreme confidence and have not been challenged, they are more likely to be utterly shattered, with devastating results for the victim. [. . .] cultural truisms (i.e. beliefs so widely accepted that people are unpracticed in defending them) are "highly vulnerable to influence" because people have no counterarguments to use in resisting persuasive messages. (Janoff-Bulman 23)

The persuasive messages—the traumatic events—call into question the individual's assumption(s). Thus, an individual who believes that "the world is a truly benevolent place" but has never encountered an event contradicting that view is an individual whose "assumption will be easily destroyed by the experience of victimization, and the process of rebuilding is apt to be a difficult one" (Janoff-Bulman 23).

This is not to say that Lewis's assumptions before he entered the war were singularly naive; his mother's death, as various biographers have noted, and as Lewis himself remarked in his autobiography, taught him that the world was uncertain and that terrors were a distinct possibility. Nevertheless, his tenacity in preferring, in expecting, in constructing an idyllic, literary world was an action revealing his implicit assumptions, assumptions largely unquestioned when he entered the war. His time at Kirk's and at Oxford just before his entrance to the war seemed to reinforce to the young Lewis that his dreams for life and the future would be realized; the war loomed, dark and immense, against that dream. He is not unusual in this. Prior to the war his suppositions, like those of millions of young men at that time, were largely unquestioned and untested, and whatever else Lewis became in later years, he was a teenager when he arrived at the Front and as such was what Fussell saw as yet another measure of his society's vulnerable innocence (Fussell 23). Whereas Lewis, like other men his age, had heard the distinct rumblings of war for some years before arriving at the Front themselves, they still retained their idylls of a secure world replete with its collective assumptions. Lewis's time at Kirk's and the following, brief time at Oxford was essentially Lewis's ideal world, the world of his literature. However in those years before entering military service, the nightmares of being wounded give evidence to the "persuasive messages" his world was increasingly receiving—messages of horror in contrast to the expectations of scholarship and walks in a quiet, English countryside with the dreaming spires of Oxford on the horizon. As we have seen, the shattering messages he received before entering the war had come from the news of wounded friends, from newspapers, from empty rooms at Oxford, and from Warnie, home on leave. As with millions of other people in Europe then, his collective assumptions were being shattered with unimaginable and historically unparalleled events, and his assumptions encompassed the societal, the cultural, and the theological—they involved everything from the nature of God to the nature of humankind. They also included oneself.

Coping strategies vary, of course and are as varied perhaps as individuals. Some strategies common to trauma victims are these. The victim may redefine the event, an action which is more likely to scceed if prior assumptions about the world can be retained through the tramatic event. In examining the event, victims may, for instance, view their circumstances in light of worse events that others have suffered, view them as less severe due to a "favorable attribute"; view them as ultimately delivering a benefit (Janoff-Bulman 25). Another strategy is to discover meaning in the traumatic event, so it may be viewed as "serving a purpose" which will allow the victim to "reestablish a belief in an orderly, comprehensible world" (Janoff-Bulman 25–26). One sees Lewis's struggle to reach this point in the letter to his father written after the armistice: "I am the only survivor [. . . .] One cannot help wondering why." (*CL* 416–417).

Victims may also change in their behaviors (change employment, residence, or some other feature of life over which the victim can assert control); they may also turn to others for emotional support, and victims may seek professional help when family or friends fail them (Janoff-Bulman 27–28). This is particularly important: "Victims need to know that social supports are unconditionally available; if they are unavailable or negative in tone, the victim may find this more distressing than the initial victimizing experience" (Janoff-Bulman 28).

Last, victims commonly show a tendency toward self-blame, a category under which I would place survivor guilt. Survivor guilt does not mean that the survivor had something to do with the events causing others to suffer. Studies disagree on whether self-blame was a sign of good or bad coping; one study has proposed that there are two types of self-blame, with negative "attributions to one's enduring personality characteristics" being "maladaptive" (Janoff-Bulman 29). A person who self-blames is one who "focuses on the past and the question of deservedness" instead of on the "avoidability of misfortune" (Janoff-Bulman 29), and the "incomprehensibility of victimization is largely reflected in the question 'why me'" (Janoff-Bulman 30).

Military doctors during the Great War had observed all these—and other—reactions and symptoms but had not at that time understood well the nature of them. The more forward-looking doctors worked with soldiers by talking with them, which moved victims from repression of the event into discussion of their recollections, and by creating new contexts for those events. One case, previously described, illustrates this: the officer went out to find his fellow officer and had discovered that his friend had been blown into pieces. This officer, it will be recalled, was told not to think about the war. Yet the more he repressed the thoughts of the event, the worse his dreams became until he was in severe dread of sleeping (Rivers 4). The doctor who took this case sought to provide a new context for considering the event: "The aspect to which I drew his attention was that the mangled state of the body of his friend was conclusive evidence that he had been killed outright and had been spared the long and lingering illness and suffering which is too often the fate of those who sustain mortal wounds" (Rivers 4). In viewing the event in this context, the officer "brightened at once and said that this aspect of the case had never occurred to him, nor had it been suggested by any of those to whom he had previously related his story" (Rivers 4). The officer ceased to dream for some nights, after which

> he dreamt that he went out into No Man's Land to seek his friend and saw his mangled body just as in the other dreams, but without the horror which had always previously been present. He knelt beside his friend to save for the relatives any objects of value which were upon the body, a pious task he had fulfilled in the actual scene, and as he was taking off the Sam Browne belt he woke with none of the horror and terror of the past, but weeping gently, feeling only sadness for the loss of a friend. (Rivers 4)

In Woolf's *Mrs. Dalloway*, a remarkable parallel exists to this case. Septimus Warren Smith had repressed the events of his officer Evans's death, but, in noticing he had ceased to feel anything at all, married the young Italian woman, Rezia, in hopes of restoring his ability to feel. His condition only grew worse. Yet in their last moments together, Septimus and Rezia share the intimate jokes and laughter of a married couple, and Septimus comes back to himself. It is the connection with Rezia which helps him, but equally so his courageous attempts to look at things as they are. His last looks at real things during the war—among which was the mutilation of his close friend Evans—were too horrible to recall; in repressing them, he moved into delusional and surrealistic visions that disallowed a simple appraisal of real, everyday objects. In his last moments,

> He began, very cautiously, to open his eyes, to see whether a gramophone was really there. But real things—real things were too exciting. He must be cautious. He would

> not go mad. First he looked at the fashion papers on the lower shelf, then, gradually
> at the gramophone with the green trumpet. Nothing could be more exact. And so,
> gathering courage, he looked at the sideboard; the plate of bananas; the engraving of
> Queen Victoria and the Prince Consort; at the mantelpiece, with the jar of roses. None
> of these things moved. All were still; all were real. (142)

During the war, all of the everyday objects Septimus had looked at objective-
ly were, as the final shells fell in the war, flying about explosively. In peacetime
in London, in the park, he had seen the trees moving, as children were running and playing, and he heard them screaming; he watched a plane wheel over-
head. Septimus could not see *things* in their reality in peacetime, for he has seen
similar things in war's other, horrible reality. Such was the case with Evans when
Septimus saw him killed. We are given to understand this in the next moment
in which he risks everything to look at his wife, whom he fears might have been
subjected to the severe realities he had seen in war:

> he shaded his eyes so that the might see only a little of her face at a time, first the chin,
> then the nose, then the forehead, in case it were deformed, or had some terrible mark
> on it. But no, there she was, perfectly natural [. . . .] (Woolf 142)

But it is not *things*, physical objects and phenomena, alone he has seen in
war: it is also the violation of his paradigm, which centered for Septimus on
the traditional: Shakespeare, his highest symbol of England, and Miss Isabel
Pole, his ideal English woman. The "things" he saw in war served primarily to
violate his assumptions about life and the world.

The passage is a very important moment in Woolf's writing, and no less
important among statements to the British public of 1925 as to what veterans
were suffering when, as the novel says at its beginning "the War was over, except
for some one like [. . .]" (5). Her descriptions of Septimus's ills are implicit,
not explicit, as if even Woolf's articulation of Septimus's ills must be suppressed
in her post-war society. They are veiled, yet one must be willing to look closely at these realities (Woolf seems to be saying) if people are to be at all understood; one must go beyond the point where Septimus's doctors would not go.
Notably, it is Septimus's connection and communication with his wife that
brings him the immense courage to once more face realities as they are. Much
has been written about the "talking cure," a concept from WWI that has been
explored even in film in *Regeneration*. The question is, when and how does
Lewis talk about his war, in what context is his articulation of trauma?

Having looked at the record of Lewis's war experience, one must also closely examine the traumatic effects they precipitated. I have examined through parallel events and through studies both the actualities of his service and the various
aspects of trauma the soldiers generally suffer. What remains to be examined

is something Lewis once said of communication: we must understand what people are unable to say.

WORKS CITED

Daie, Netzer, and Eliezer Witztum. "A Case of Posttraumatic Stress Disorder Masked by Pseudoseizures in a Jewish Iranian Immigrant in Israel." *Journal of Nervous and Mental Disease.* 182, no. 4. April, 1994. 244–245.

Diagnostic and Statistical Manual of Mental Disorders-IV. 4th Edition. Washington, D.C.: American Psychiatric Association, 1994.

Duhamel, Georges. "Civilization." *The Penguin Book of First World War Prose.* John Glover and Jon Silkin, eds. London: Penguin, 1990. 210–216.

Forster, E. M. *A Room with a View.* New York: Vintage, 1989.

Fussell, Paul. *The Great War and Modern Memory.* New York: Oxford UP, 1975.

Gaffney, J. M., Dr. Personal interview. 12 December 2001.

Janoff-Bulman, Ronnie. "The Aftermath of Victimization: Rebuilding Shattered Assumptions." *Trauma and Its Wake.* Vol. 1. C. R. Figley, ed. New York: Brunner, 1985.

Junger, Ernst. *The Storm of Steel.* New York: Fertig, 1996.

Kennedy, Foster. "The Nature of Nervousness in Soldiers." *Journal of the American Medical Association.* 1918:71 (July 6): 17–21.

Kipling, Rudyard. "The Phantom Rickshaw." *The Man Who Would Be King and Other Stories.* New York: Oxford UP, 1991. 26–48.

Macdonald, Lynn. *The Roses of No Man's Land.* London: Penguin, 1993.

Neill, John R. "How Psychiatric Symptoms Varied in World War I and II." *Military Medicine.* 158 (March) 1993. 149–151.

Remarque, Erich Maria. *The Road Back.* Trans. A. W. Wheen. New York: Fawcett, 1931.

Rivers, W. H. R. "An Address on The Repression of War Experience." *The Repression of War Experience.* University of Kansas. 12 September 2002. <http://raven.cc.ukans.edu/~kansite/ww_one/comment/rivers.htm>

Van der Hart, Onno, Annemieke van Dijke, Maarten van Son, and Kathy Steele. "Somatoform Dissociation in Traumatized World War I Combat Soldiers: A Neglected Clinical Heritage." 30 November 2001. <http://www.trauma-pages.com/vdhart 2000.htm>.

Winter, Denis. *Death's Men: Soldiers of the Great War.* London: Penguin, 1979.

Woolf, Virginia. *Mrs. Dalloway.* San Francisco: Harcourt, 1990.

CHAPTER 12

Reluctant Confessions

IN WRITING A STATEMENT, ALREADY PROVIDED, THAT his time in war was "cut off from the rest of my experience" and even "unimportant" (*SBJ* 196), Lewis echoed Septimus Warren Smith in his detachment from feeling. Septimus, "far from showing any emotion or recognizing that here was the end of a friendship, congratulated himself upon feeling very little and very reasonably" at the death of Evans (Woolf 86). Yet Lewis's sentiment would have been reasonable in 1918. Successful repression appeared to some medical personnel at that time to be a sign that one had begun to deal with a traumatic event. Lewis's statement also seems, like Septimus's, to carry the congratulatory tone for the detachment he still felt even as late as 1955 when he wrote *Surprised by Joy*. That book shows, I believe, that Lewis did not understand or at least could not communicate the lasting effects of the war on his feelings (or his lack of feeling). This is not to say that he lied. The problem resides in the nature of the beast with which he contended; as for many veterans, perhaps Lewis did not deliberately wish to distract others when he postured but rather wished to redirect his own thoughts, which is a mode of repression. Nevertheless, I believe that, as for other soldiers, his war was too painful to examine in the relentless ways he examined academic and religious issues. The war did not fit into the ruthless logic that Lewis was known to wield. Yet for all the avoidance of his war, its effects upon him emerged, albeit implicitly.

Lewis comes closest to confronting his war when he does *not* examine the import of what he is saying in relation to his reactions to it—as when he writes of the moment he was wounded: the "proposition 'Here is a man dying' stood before my mind as dry, as factual, as unemotional as something in a textbook. It was not even interesting" (197). In that statement exists what seems (to those of us who have not seen combat) an odd numbness, an odd detachment, which is why it stands out; we see that he does not feel what we would assume is "normal" about the event. And his remark comes decades after the war. As Lewis wrote to his father from Eastbourne in December of 1918, when considering how he might be released from the military, he mentions metaphorically that he could still perceive his uniform's fittings under his scholar's dress (*CL* 422). Indeed, many years beyond the war it remained the same: the war experiences show beneath the scholar's work. "We are soldiers still without having been aware of it" wrote Remarque near the end of *The Road Back* (292). But Lewis's reaction is not odd at all. His reactions are quite usual for those who have been through combat, who have seen friends die, and who have been themselves wounded.

Paul Fussell's observations of dissociative symptoms in soldiers, provided above, include one point which he describes without using the medical terms: a sense of detachment from the body, the tendency of soldiers to view themselves as acting in a play (195–196). Fussell quoted a number of soldiers in illustrating this sense, including one major who described the sense of unreality soldiers sometimes felt, and a soldier, Carrington, who "testifies to the division of the psyche into something like actor, on the one hand, and spectator, on the other, especially during the moments of heightened anxiety when one is 'beside oneself'" (192). The more poignant example contained this statement, which a wounded soldier thought of himself, in the third-person, just when he was wounded: "You were never you. The part of you was somewhere else" (qtd in Fussell 193). Joanna Bourke quotes this soldier's remarkable account:

> body and soul seemed to be entirely divorced, even to the extent that I felt that I no longer inhabited my body. My shell at the bidding of purely automatic forces, over which I had no control, ran hither and thither collecting men, hacking its way through the scrub with a rifle, and directed the fire of my platoon and in short struggled with all the duties which I had been taught to perform. But my mind was a distinct and separate entity. I seemed to hover at some height above my own body and to observe its doings and the doings of others with a sort of detached interest. (231)

Lewis's experience is similar, at least as he re-examines it in 1955, seeing the event merely as a philosophical equation—Kant's division between separate selves—and Lewis is convinced that there were separate selves mildly linked together within him (197–198). This account shows the same literary detachment from reality as does his remark that his war is that which Homer depicted. The details of violence Lewis would convey openly in *Dymer*, a poem to be treated later. It is enough to say here that detachment from the these experiences is one central effect of the trauma he suffered and something Lewis shared with traumatized soldiers. Other parallels exist.

Although no literal "shell shock" is recognized to exist (a shock producing physical damage to the brain and nervous system), Lewis was of course close to the exploding shell, an event coming only at the end of a series of traumatizing events—the continual shelling of the trenches at Fampoux among them. We remark the pain he suffered from his wounds described in lines from *Dymer* (*Dymer* 76–77).

Ernst Junger, describing his own experience without the poetry, has similar third-person associations to self and pain:

> I had not gone twenty steps when the flash of a shrapnel blinded me as I struggled up out of a shell-hole. It burst not ten paces in front of me at a height of three meters. I felt two dull blows against my chest and shoulder. My rifle flew from my hands of its own accord and I fell backwards into the shell-hole. I should still hear remotely Ehlers shouting as he went by, "It's finished him. [. . .]" When I woke from a long fainting fit all was still. I tried to stand up, but I felt a sharp pain in my right shoulder that increased with every movement. My breath was short and gasping. The lung could not get enough air. "Hit through lung and shoulder," I thought [. . .]. (187)

Shell fragments hit Lewis in his left side from slightly behind, as he wrote to his father, and he could lie on his right side only after some weeks (*CL* 368). A physician who recently looked over Lewis's medical records—a mass of jottings, many undecipherable and employing medical terminology of the day—remarked that

> Lewis was probably struck from behind and received a penetrating injury to the left side of his chest, resulting in a fractured 4th rib (and coughing up blood), but escaped with no significant loss of lung function. While he had good air entry in his lung (which would have excluded a collapsed lung), there was dullness on percussion (which would reflect evidence of fluid accumulation around the foreign body [. . .] lodged in the upper lobe of his left lung). The injuries to left leg and left wrist were superficial involving soft tissue damage only. (Green and Hooper 44 n.)

As Lewis recovered from his wounds, some effects disappeared while other, more significant effects appeared. The debris from the blast swelled his left eye, a temporary effect. He would have had, as any victim in close proximity to an explosion, many small cuts and bruises from the pulverizing debris launched as the shell exploded. In this modern war, doctors removed from victims not only shell fragments, shrapnel, stones, wood, and bits of one's uniform and equipment, but also the teeth and bones of other soldiers hit by the same explosion—a very commonplace but seldom discussed aspect of modern war as Aundoin-Rouzeau and Becker have explained (20). Philip Gibbs, whose *Realities of War* would document the dire condition of many survivors, mentions among more visible scars men "with chunks of steel in their lungs" (qtd. in McGreevy 222). Lewis took just such a fragment, which, as noted, was left inside him; any organic debris would have been removed.

There was also that weakness which Lewis would not name to his father in the letter of 23 February 1919 (*LP* VI.92). It will also be recalled that Albert, in attempting to assist Jack in securing his wound gratuity, wrote to the War Office that Jack "suffers from a distressing weakness which need not be described here in detail" (TNA (PRO) WO339/105408), and in the Lewis papers, it will also be recalled, Warren placed an ellipsis at the point which explains the weakness. What we do have is evidence of recurring nightmares and an ache in his head at certain times of the day (*CL* 417–418), both of which case studies describe as symptomatic. Also as we have seen, the dreams of those soldiers suffering PTSD often carry great significance: according to various trauma studies, dreams can indicate unresolved issues related to trauma, things beneath the surface that have not been integrated within one's collective assumptions. Lewis is quick to dismiss his aches and frightening dreams. As seemed proper at the time, he is optimistic and dismissive towards these symptoms; that is, he represses them. Yet despite his attempts at repression, the effects he would not mention (being repressed in writing even in letters to his father, in his father's letters to the War Office, and in the *Lewis Papers*) remained and were persistent. A part of the effects may have gained momentum or may have been signaled by his recurrent dreams, which were, I find, something few soldiers discussed in detail. Sassoon was one who did:

> More than once I wasn't sure whether I was awake or asleep [. . . .] Shapes of mutilated soldiers came crawling across the floor; the floor [. . .] littered with fragments of mangled flesh. Faces glared upward; hands clutched at neck or belly; a livid grinning face with bristly moustache peered at me above the edge of my bed; his hands clawed at the sheets. Some were like the dummy figures used to deceive snipers; others were alive and looked at me reproachfully as though envying me the warm safety of life which they'd longed for when they shivered in the gloomy dawn, waiting for the whistles to blow and the bombardment to lift [. . . .] One in battle equipment pulled himself painfully toward me and fumbled in his tunic for a letter; as he reached forward to give it to me his head lolled sideways and he collapsed; there was a hole in his jaw and the blood spread across his white face like ink spilt on blotting paper. (175–176)

One notes here the prominence of guilt for having survived, as Lewis also must have felt.

Guilt also for having killed seeped through soldiers' dreams, "ghostly shadows of things past, but strangely changed; memories that rise up again of grey, sightless faces, cries and accusations" (Remarque 232). In this case, Remarque gives one German soldier's recurrent nightmare, one that is still repeating itself years after the war. It reviews the moment a soldier killed an English enemy with a grenade:

> The crash of the explosion tears into the air, splinters twanging—a cry goes up, long-drawn, frantic with horror. [. . . .] The Englishman is lying clear in the open field; his two legs are blown off at the knees, the blood is pouring out; the bands of his puttees, far unrolled, trail out behind him like loose ribbons; he is lying on his belly; with his arms he paddles the grass; his mouth is wide open, shrieking.
>
> He heaves himself around and sees me. Then he props himself on his arms and rears his trunk like a seal; he shrieks at me and bleeds, bleeds.—The red face grows pale and sinks in, the gaze snaps, and eyes and mouth are at last no more than black caverns in a swiftly decaying countenance, that slowly inclines to the earth, sags and sinks into the dandelions. Finished! (249–250)

But in this dream, the enemy is not finished: the image rises, pursues him, despite repeated grenades thrown at the specter, who finally clutches and strangles the dreamer, dragging him to the edge of a pit. Joanna Bourke has discussed the guilt not only of survivors but that of killers. Soldiers have also a fear of retribution for having killed even in the context of war. "Sometimes," she writes quoting a veteran, "consciences circled guiltily around and around fears of retribution: 'no fox hole was deep enough to protect him from an avenging fate'" (222). Such is the essence of the nightmare Remarque presents; it is a dream circling, repeating itself darkly in the conscience of Remarque's protagonist as did Lewis's nightmare.

In the last chapter we saw what the suppression of such dreams could do to a soldier, and one can only guess the difficulty Lewis faced by revealing statements he made later in life. As WWII approached, Lewis delineated the horrors of his war experience to Dom Bede Griffiths and admitted that he thought perhaps ceasing to exist was an option better than experiencing another war due to not only the multi-faceted suffering he experienced in the war but also due to the nightmares derived from memory that, as for Remarque's German soldier, above, continued years beyond the experiences (*Letters* 320).

Memories as well as dreams, dreams from memories: these recurrent features and the knowledge of the barbaric sufferings war brings are a measure of his trauma. They are what he recalls as another storm of war gathered strength. Years before his letter to Griffiths, Lewis seemed to have established this same view. It was in 1923. Lewis was walking with his friend Neville Coghill, who believed he ought to fight if another war broke out but that a war for any cause other than the Crown would not be justified. Lewis disagreed, replying that "the only real issue was civilization against barbarism" (*Letters* 180–181).

By "civilization" Lewis would mean commonly agreed-upon assumptions that retain some order in society, but the war had effectively shattered such assumptions. At the center of his own assumptions is the belief that society is civilized, and it is hinged upon a common belief in ordering principles. That is just what Lewis would come to describe in *Mere Christianity*: "Human beings, after all, have some sense; they see that you cannot have real safety or happiness except in a society where everyone plays fair, and it is because they see this that they try to behave decently" (29). Such a society no longer existed though many would attempt to reassert it. I believe that the war's extreme barbarism (uncivilized acts) is its one feature that most violated soldiers' collective assumptions, and an issue that Audoin-Rouzeau and Becker have treated at length, quoting in one moment this testimony of a soldier:

> Not only did the war make us dead, impotent, or blind. In the midst of beautiful actions, of sacrifice and self-abnegation, it also awoke within us, sometimes to the point of paroxysm, ancient instincts of cruelty and barbarity. At the time, I . . . who have never punched anyone, who loathes disorder and brutality, took pleasure in killing. When we crawled towards the enemy during a raid, a grenade in our hand and a knife in our teeth, like cut-throats, we felt fear in our gut, and yet an ineluctable force urged us on. Taking the enemy by surprise in his trench, jumping on him, enjoying the terror of a man who doesn't believe in the devil yet suddenly sees him dive down to the ground! That barbarous, horrendous moment had a unique flavour for us, a morbid appeal; we were like those unfortunate drug addicts who know the magnitude of the risk but can't keep themselves from taking more poison. (42)

Such events, instilled in one the realization of humankind's—one's own—barbarity.

The whole of this new war served to violate everything that soldiers had believed in. Janoff-Bulman, in her thesis regarding trauma, explains not only an individual soldier's experience from the moment of trauma to the rebuilding of assumptions, but more, she also explains what happened to society generally; once the realities of war were conveyed to the population, society also staggered beneath the weight of war's realities. I began this book by discussing the seemingly secure world of H. G. Wells's Mr. Britling, a character who reels when his own son and his assumptions about the world are shattered by war. Nothing less occurred within society after September 11, 2001, which can stand as an illustration of what happens to a society generally whenever traumatic events occur. It is also stands as a primary event, like Lewis's war, of barbarity. Such violations of society's assumptions are what lie behind Thompson and Warner's observation (given in the introduction) that

> English culture had been as profoundly shattered by the experience as had Britain's economy or her international position. It seems likely that public life at all levels suffered [. . .] (85).

As seen in this statement, the use of the word *shattered* is important in describing both the micro and the macro phenomena, and I believe that society's collective trauma (revealed in as diverse ways in society and culture as revealed in a person) serves ironically only to compound the trauma in the individual. Such trauma would, I assume, further disorient the individual who looks beyond him or herself to rebuilt the paradigm. As Janoff-Bulman wrote,

> cultural truisms (i.e. beliefs so widely accepted that people are unpracticed in defending them) are "highly vulnerable to influence" [i.e. trauma] because people have no counterarguments to use in resisting persuasive messages. (23)

Modernist lament resided within early 20-century perceptions that those cultural truisms had been violated. As stated by one critic, R. Albert,

> Torment, suffering, fatigued daring, above all ugliness, sadness, a neurotic psychology . . . a total ignorance of joy. . . . It is exactly thus that [the] decadent art at the end of a civilization represents man: defeated, mutilated, degenerated. (qtd. in McGreevy 235–236)

This describes not simply much of art in 1923 Europe but also the assumptions of post-war society. That art was intended, like Otto Dix's art, to be disturbing, to de-center society in its adherence to unexamined pre-war assumptions. Such art must also have served to further disturb the already unstable paradigmatic equilibrium of many a surviving veteran. Such art was a way of taking off the blinkers and looking straight into the abyss. Eliot's *Waste Land* is a literary work that, to me, was intended to accomplish the same thing.

However these issues stand for an entire culture, Lewis himself seemed focused upon the events that shattered his own assumptions. Those events he chronicled in *Spirits in Bondage*, which he was writing throughout his war service. That book seems less influenced by whatever collective trauma his society was suffering. As he wrote in his autobiography, *Surprised by Joy*, a place remained in his collective assumptions for Joy, something about which, as R. Albert, quoted above, also noted: society was ignorant of joy. Part of both the shattering and the rebuilding of Lewis's assumptions was inextricably tied to his pursuit of Joy (as he defined it) and war's destruction of it. These things his poetry chronicles, but that issue must be held momentarily.

While still in hospital in France, events might have transpired to allow him to better contend with his trauma. Circumstances had done so for other soldiers. Lewis related that he had asked a nurse about the fate of his friends, Ayres and Johnson, but that she could tell him nothing about them. What more was or was not said to Lewis by his nurses we may now only guess. Other soldiers found great help in one VAD, Sister Henrietta Hall, who recorded this:

> We had a very nice man who came round trying to find the missing men. He was a lawyer in Bradford. That was his war work and he used to come every Sunday evening without fail to talk to the boys—those that could talk—trying to find out if they knew the missing men or knew what had happened to them, and very often he did find some of their comrades. The trouble was that it did tend to upset the boys a little bit. It took them back to those experiences just when they were beginning to forget them. All the same, I often used to think that it was a good thing for them to talk about it rather than bottle it up, because it always came out in some way and they used to have dreadful nightmares. It helped if they could talk and I always used to make a point of speaking to them. Even when we were busy I made time for it, because I thought that it was really necessary and a very important part of nursing them.
>
> I had an armchair in my office and I often used to say to a boy if he was upset, "Come and see me this morning, about half-past eleven, when I've finished the dressings. Come and talk to me for a little while and tell me your troubles." Often they were very upset about having to go back, especially when they'd been talking to the searcher about the action when they'd been hit, taking about a friend who'd been killed. It reminded them. But if they could get it off their chests, privately in my office, even have a bit of a cry, which they would have been ashamed to do in the ward, I used to think it made them feel a little bit better. (Macdonald 192–193)

No doubt Hall's provision of time for the men saved many of them lengthy bouts with traumatic memories and the persistent, intrusive thoughts that came through repression, as Rivers indicated: "A more frequent cause of failure of slight extent of improvement is met with in cases in which the repression has been allowed to continue for so long that it has become habit" (5). Hall provided the social support that Janoff-Bulman later indicated was important to many patients: she could "provide the victim with an opportunity to talk about the event and vent his or her emotions" and by doing so in a private place helped to "reduce the victim's self-perception of deviance" (28). As far as we know, Lewis had no access to a nurse like Henrietta Hall; given his reticence on the war, he may not have spoken to such a person had she been available. He had Mrs. Moore, who grieved for her son.

Janoff-Bulman explains that when victims do not find unconditional or suitable help from family or friends, they may move to another source who is more open and sympathetic. Lewis's relationship with his father had so deteriorated, Albert being not clearly sympathetic in action no matter what he felt towards his son, that Jack would not have found suitable help from him.

Their collaborative work to secure Jack's wound gratuity has a distinct ring of a lawyer writing for his client not for his son, which would not have been a prudent tone to take with the War Office. However, the photo of Albert and Jack in the garden of Little Lea, taken after the war, clearly displays the tension existing in the son toward the father. Albert's prying into Jack's affairs and finances exacerbated the division between them. He had sent money to Jack, who, to his father's chagrin, wrote checks to Mrs. Moore. Albert had looked into Jack's papers and discovered the fact, inflaming Jack's resentment to the point of an angry outburst for which he later apologized, but from which an estrangement was created that I believe did not heal completely by the time Albert died. From his father, Jack would not find either an ear of understanding or of sympathy for what he was suffering from the war, no matter how well-meaning Albert was towards his son.

Yet neither do I suppose that Lewis would have discussed his experiences deeply with Mrs. Moore. Whatever the nature of his relationship with Janie Moore, it is extremely doubtful that she could have provide an intelligent comfort such as Henrietta Hall provided for her soldiers, which opened a means for them to face their shattering experiences. Humphrey Carpenter relates that Lewis would instead have needed "a relief from Mrs Moore's illogical chatter" (15). Talk on the war in which Lewis took part would likely been between himself and Warren and other men at Oxford who returned from the war; generally veterans will speak of the war to one another but not to people who have never seen battle. On the other hand, I have heard veterans say that war's worst events are topics not discussed even between veterans. For Jack to speak thus with Mrs. Moore would have been, I believe, impossible. Discussions he had with other veterans are only generally indicated in, for instance as with the conversation Lewis mentioned in his diary of 1923. One evening he met Neville Coghill at his rooms in Exeter College where the two men and a number of others talked of tragedy and some time beyond that of memories of war (*AMR* 240). Other such conversations undoubtedly took place with Warren, who made the military his career. The brothers would have had talks about the war only when Warren was on leave from continued service, and, later, when Warren retired from the army to move in with Jack and Mrs. Moore. Such discussions also likely occurred with those in Lewis's literary circle, The Inklings. Veterans in that group included J. R. R. Tolkien, who served on the Somme in 1916, and Owen Barfield. I do not doubt that conversations among these men turned to the war on many occasions over their years of friendship. Yet even with these men who were both veterans and friends, Carpenter notes Lewis's "almost aggressive refusal to discuss deeply personal matters" (182). Did those deeply personal matters include his war?

Another person Lewis spoke with was Maureen Moore, Paddy's sister, still a girl and living with Mrs. Moore and Jack. It is highly unlikely that a conversation with the young Maureen went deeply into Lewis's trauma. But their talk held enough meaning for Lewis that he recorded in 1922 that Maureen and he talked after dining about the boys who were in the war with Jack, and Lewis includes himself as part of this topic (*AMR* 45).

Other reminders likely occurred, as did similar conversations: he wrote in his diary that Mrs. Moore reminded him one 15 April that he had been wounded that day four years earlier (*AMR* 20). Another time he met a friend with whom he recalled the odd arrangement of Lewis being under his command in O.T.C. (*AMR* 30). When Lewis went to bathe at Parson's Pleasure—an outdoor area where only men bathed, and in the nude, he found no scars from the war upon the men and felt that the men of his age were vanishing (*AMR* 39). This event occurred only four years after the war's end; plenty of men with scars were about and would be for decades, as with Lewis himself. Yet so many of his generation had passed on that he must have felt with others in that day that only a scarred remnant remained. One catches here a note of feeling old before one's time.

Another reminder of the war, but no conversation about it, came by way of an unexpected visit to the rooms at University College in which he first began his career. Upon attending a meeting of the literary society, the Martlets, he found the gathering of men in those rooms. It was the place he had been deposited, drunk, and where he awoke without knowing how he had arrived. Perhaps more significant is Lewis's observation, previously related, that Mrs. Moore "had been in this room" (*AMR* 125).

One other significant event has been recorded, occurring long after the Second World War, that renewed Lewis's memories from the war in an unpleasant way, and it seemed to have the same effect upon Warnie as it did upon Jack. Douglas Gresham, Lewis's stepson, had prepared to celebrate Guy Fawkes' night in a grand way, but

> somehow the lid of the large wooden chest containing the neatly stacked fireworks was left open, and a St. Catherine's wheel, breaking free of its restraint, hurled itself into the midst of the box. Seldom have I seen a more dramatic display; the simultaneous eruption of skyrockets, Roman candles, flying saucers, thunderclaps, untethered St. Catherine's wheels—a dozen or more of each, and others besides—hurling up into the air in all directions, provided a staggering sight. A few of the guests had to dive for cover, but that merely added to the fun [. . . .] and the "Guy," loaded with still more rockets and Vesuvius fountains, burnt with great gusto. (108)

It was only later that Lewis informed Douglas that his fireworks too disturbingly evoked the war for Jack's tastes to be enjoyable, a view in which

Figure 17. The view from Lewis's first rooms in University College, Oxford. (Photo: author)

Warnie concurred (108). In consequence, that was the last fling with the fireworks.

Whatever memories and discussions of the war arose in later years, evidence of the war's lingering effects appears most directly in Lewis's long poem, *Dymer*. But years before he began that work, while he was yet in hospital, Lewis was preparing his collection of poems, *Spirits in Bondage* for publication— poems that record not the effects of war, not the lingering trauma, but the actual, shattering events themselves.

WORKS CITED

Audoin-Rouzeau, Stephane, and Annette Becker. *14–18: Understanding the Great War*. Trans. Catherine Temerson. New York: Hill and Wang, 2002.

Bourke, Joanna. *An Intimate History of Killing: Face-to-Face Killing in Twentieth-Century Warfare*. London: Granta, 1999.

Carpenter, Humphrey. *The Inklings*. New York: Ballantine, 1978.

Fussell, Paul. *The Great War and Modern Memory*. Oxford: Oxford UP, 1975.

Green, Roger Lancelyn, and Walter Hooper. *C. S. Lewis*. London: HarperCollins, 2003.

Gresham, Douglas H. *Lenten Lands*. New York: Macmillan, 1988.

Janoff-Bulman, Ronnie. "The Aftermath of Victimization: Rebuilding Shattered Assumptions." *Trauma and Its Wake*. Vol. 1. C. R. Figley, ed. New York: Brunner, 1985.

Junger, Ernst. *The Storm of Steel*. New York: Fertig, 1996.

Lewis, C. S. *Letters of C. S. Lewis*. Ed. W. H. Lewis and Walter Hooper. New York: Harcourt, 1993.

Macdonald, Lynn. *The Roses of No Man's Land*. London: Penguin, 1993.

McGreevy, Linda F. *Bitter Witness: Otto Dix and the Great War*. New York: Peter Lang, 2001.

Remarque, Erich Maria. *The Road Back*. Trans. A. W. Wheen. New York: Fawcett, 1931.

Rivers, W. H. R. "An Address on The Repression of War Experience." *The Repression of War Experience*. University of Kansas. 12 September 2002. <http://raven.cc.ukans.edu/~kansite/ww_one/comment/rivers.htm>

Sassoon, Siegfried. *Memoirs of an Infantry Officer*. London: Faber, 1965.

Thompson, David, and Geoffrey Warner. *England in the Twentieth Century (1914–79)*. London: Penguin, 1991.

CHAPTER 13

The Beauty That Has Been

THE NEXT TWO CHAPTERS OFFER AN ANALYSIS of Lewis's two earliest publications, *Spirits in Bondage* and *Dymer*, in light of the context I have established around his war experience and relationships. Some introduction to these works is necessary.

As discussed at the beginning of this work, the extent of the war's influence upon Lewis may only be judged obliquely and with difficulty. Some of the difficulty arises in large part from his own posturing on the subject. It has been especially difficult to judge its influence upon his early poetry. Don King has pointed out, "The failure to see a connection between Lewis's wartime experience and [*Spirits in Bondage*] has occurred in part because we have accepted too quickly Lewis's statements in his autobiography, *Surprised by Joy*, where he suppresses the horrors of the battlefield" (454–455). But he does tell us much about his experiences. Both his literary tastes and the trauma of his war experiences, however, are intrinsically connected to his early poetry; they are inseparable from it. As Warren told us, Jack's writing is filled with references to Mrs. Moore; so too is it filled with references to war.

Yet the intense influence of the war upon Lewis has been minimized by Lewis scholars despite the evidence of intrinsic connections between his war experiences and his early poetic works and, ultimately, to his assumptions about life. Despite these connections, King remarks, "It is too much to say that

[*Spirits in Bondage*] is solely driven by Lewis's own battlefield experiences since we know more than half the poems are written before Lewis goes to France" ("Dualist" 463). In an attempt to establish a clear relation between the war and *Spirits in Bondage*, King puzzles over a common denominator between its poems, many of which do not address war or battle directly: "The most likely explanation is that [his] poems were influenced by the war because many were written while on the battlefield" (*Poet* 61). However, the issue is broader than the assumption behind this statement.

War poems need not contain images of the battlefield to be "war poetry." We may say as much for "war literature" collectively: it need not contain firsthand accounts of battle to be war literature. Vera Brittain's *Testament of Youth* is not an account of combat. Yet it is thoroughly war literature. Conversely, many individual poems by Edward Thomas, poems anthologized in collections of war poetry, contain nothing reminiscent of battlefields or the lingering of their horrors.

I would assert a new definition for war literature, a definition arising from Ronnie Janoff-Bulman's work: war literature records the shattering of assumptions and the consequent trauma that arises from war. It may also delineate the rebuilding of assumptions. This is the common denominator between all of Lewis's poems in *Spirits*. And such war literature, in this instance poetry, can occur in three forms (sometimes intermixed). First, it can be a record of specific, traumatic events—actual battlefield experiences, the events that shatter the collective assumptions of an individual. Second, war literature can also be a record of the lingering effects of trauma. Third, it may record the rebuilding of a paradigm that allows the victim to carry on in life, something that does not always occur with victims of trauma. In Lewis's case, his first book of poetry records the shattering of his assumptions about life, the cosmos, and himself, for that is the unique quality in war literature as I have defined it. But to limit war literature to works that are written upon, or even peripherally about, the field of battle is too simplistic.

This definition allows that war literature is a record of not merely an individual's experiences but also of a society's collective pre-war assumptions, its collective trauma, and its attempts to rebuild its assumptions. My example in this book of just such a work has been H. G. Wells' *Mr. Britling Sees It Through*, which examines by way of the national symbol, Mr. Britling, the trauma that war brought to British society on the home front. It examines a society before, during, and after the war. A large part of that work is spent illustrating the impact of war in contrast to its idyllic and blind pre-war assumptions.

A further difficulty for us in observing Lewis and his war poetry resides in the romantic notions Lewis retains as a young man at war, something that has colored interpretations of his early work. Romantic views of Lewis at war leave us with images of him that hanker after the soldierly idyll that Evelyn Waugh parodies in *Put Out More Flags*. Three women who are thinking of Basil Seal—the lightsomely caddish young man who has persistently refused to take responsibility for his life and actions (that is, to grow up)—his mother, sister, and mistress all entertain notions of him becoming a soldier in the Second World War. They associate Basil with the romantic images prevalent in their minds from the First War. One of the women

> saw him as Siegfried Sassoon, an infantry subaltern in a mud-bogged trench standing to dawn, his eyes on his wrist watch, waiting for zero hour; she saw him as Compton Mackenzie, spider in a web of Balkan intrigue, undermining a monarchy among olive trees and sculptured marble; she saw him as T. E. Lawrence and Rupert Brooke. (Waugh 17)

"Rupert Brooke," Waugh reiterates, "Old Bill, the Unknown Soldier—thus three fond women saw him, but Basil breakfasting late in Poppet Green's studio fell short and wide of all these ideals" (29). So too Lewis falls very short of the romantic notions of the 2nd lieutenant that his biographers have proffered to us. Recently one biographer extended this image of Lewis as a soldier, quoting this passage from an issue of *The Spectator* of November 1916:

> For those boys who hate the war, and suffer and endure with the smile that is sometimes so difficult, and long with a great longing for home and peace—some day some of them will look back on these days and will tell themselves that after all it was "Romance," the adventure which made their lives worth while. And they will long to feel once again the stirring of the old comradeship and love and loyalty, to dip their clasp-knives into the same pot of jam, and lie in the same dug-out, and work on the same bit of wire with the same machine gun striking terror into their hearts, and look into each other's eyes for the same courageous smile. For Romance, after all, is woven of the emotions, especially the elemental ones of love and loyalty and fear and pain [. . . .] But some day those who have not died will say: "Thank God I have lived! I have loved, and endured, and trembled, and trembling, dared. I have had my romance." (qtd. *CL* 251n–252n)

This quotation is prefaced with this interpretation: "The sentiments expressed by the young soldier [who wrote the above] are so like those Lewis was later to hold [. . . .]" (*CL* 251n). It is just that sentimentality, and these sentiments are not in the least like those which Lewis (or his brother, for that matter) would hold in recalling the war. In evidence of this stands the single moment of Douglas Gresham's Guy Fawkes celebrations that stirred up memories of war in both Lewis brothers.

Lewis's earliest poetry—*Spirits in Bondage* and *Dymer*—are, then, works driven centrally and directly by his wartime experiences: they are war literature. They record, as I have said with reference to Janoff-Bulman, the traumatic shattering of his assumptions. I do not say they are driven solely by Lewis's *actions* in war but by his wartime experiences, which begin much earlier than his official entry into the conflagration. It will be recalled that before Lewis ever entered officer training, he was troubled by nightmares of being wounded. At Kirkpatrick's he had seen flashes from bombs falling on London. He had seen the wounded; he had known of men who did not return from war. After arriving at Oxford, he walked through the rooms in University College belonging to a man he did not know and wondered if that man would return; Lewis certainly pondered his own fate—whether he himself would return. All of this occurred before his own active participation in the war; the nature and the facts of the war as observed on his home front was, for the adolescent Lewis, already affecting his assumptions about the world as did his mother's death when he was a child. Beginning before and continuing throughout the war, the events, the consequences, and the lingering effects of the war's shattering of his assumptions not only appear in but, indeed, are at the very center of his early poetry. It is what drives that poetry.

It is quite easy to see war poetry more narrowly than I have here defined it. In part, the poetry of Siegfried Sassoon, Wilfred Owen, and others who enlarge the horrors and aftermath of battle contribute to that narrow perspective. We can easily be led to assume that such is war poetry proper. Thus, perhaps, King and Hooper assume that war poetry (King goes on to cite such work from Sassoon and Owen) must be "morose" (King 454) or laden with "bullets, corpses, and barbed-wire" (Hooper xxxvi), or, again as King wrote, must describe literal "battlefield experiences."

Yet a definition of war poetry confining it to subjects of battle is far removed from what we observe in war poets and neglects very important distinctions set forth by Paul Fussell, for instance: prominent in war poetry is sky study as well as both memories and dreams of an ideal homeland among numerous other things. Further, beyond war poetry's political statements, beyond asserting the actualities of war in order to correct the home front's sanitized notions of war (in which bullets and blood must be described), beyond a lament and, as J. M. Winter has said, a memorial for the soldiers' lost youth (both the physical absence of a generation of young men but also the lost-ness of those who survived), it is also a part of a *"literature of separation"*—that "men in uniform formed what they called a race apart" (229). Among the many works that illustrate this distinction are Erich Remarque's *The Road Back*, but so also poetry that marks the separation between those who have been in battle and those who have not. Thus that observation attributed to Sassoon: "A man who endured the war at its worst was everlastingly differentiated from everyone—except his fellow soldiers."

War poetry may also record the memory of a place and time where, before the experience of war, one's assumptions were comparatively untested and certainly not violated. Such times and their places are often remembered as ideal, often believed to be better than they were, as many memoirs show and as various historians have noted. Yet beneath all these purposes, as I have said, war poetry describes collective and personal assumptions violated by war's traumatic events. It describes directly and indirectly the shattering experiences themselves, the overwhelming sights, sounds, smells, and terrors of war. As the shattering experiences occur, war poetry also records the longing to escape war, the soldiers' dreams of those ideal placcs and times beyond war's reach. War poetry recalls also the invasive memories, images, and dreams of the traumatic events, and sometimes present the poet's attempts to discover what has happened to pre-war assumptions held by the world and humankind.

I think that, most important to its nature, war literature also presents a record of a writer's attempts to rebuild shattered assumptions. This is war literature at its root. This is Lewis's war poetry. His work includes descriptions of the traumatic events of war, but such events and descriptions are the means by which he illustrates this central concern of war literature: paradigmatic rupture.

Spirits in Bondage was Lewis's first book, and even before it was published, one of its poems, "Death in Battle," appeared in an issue of *Reville*. It is interesting that Lewis's first publication is as a war poet, and in recognizing this fact, we recall Paul Fussell's remark about Lewis: that he was "a representative young man from the period" (40). If we may observe in these poems the destruction of Lewis's youthful assumptions about the world and life, it is an observation possible only because he wrote its poems just prior to and continuing through the months of his war service. Despite differences in their respective purposes for and tastes in poetry, one observes in both Siegfried Sassoon's and Lewis's poetry the struggle to comprehend and to articulate what has happened in the midst of war. And these articulations of war are propped against the seemingly idyllic England they left behind. While Sassoon examines the grimness of the Front and the home front for returning soldiers, Lewis scans the front, looking at war's devastation of nature, of both earthly and human nature, and more—the nature of a god that could allow such devastation to occur.

Lewis invested in this collection all his dreams for his future. In his youth and even after the war, Lewis hoped that he would become a poet. While still in officer training at Keble college, he had written to Arthur Greeves that during the four weeks' leave he was to have before heading for France, he would collect his poetry and find a publisher for it; if he should die, he would have his brief period of fame (*LP* V. 219).

It is a romantic imagining of himself as Rupert Brooke, with an awareness that young poets actually die in war. Warren Lewis noted that "In the two years intervening between Easter 1915 and Easter 1917, [Jack] wrote fifty-two poems which he copied carefully into an old [. . .] notebook" (*LP* IV.306). Readers who are interested in the publication details of *Spirits in Bondage* may refer to the preface to the volume and to the *C. S. Lewis Companion*. Analysis of their literary aspects may be found in other works and in Don King's book *C. S. Lewis, Poet*. My interest is with neither of these features but with the record they make of Lewis's war.

To this end, it is important that the poems are especially laden, as many others have pointed out but which is readily evident in reading the work, with the youthful and romantic enthusiasm for myth Lewis showed from a young age. As I have shown, Lewis's romantic tastes in literature were for, as he wrote to Arthur Greeves, more traditional works of literature which he felt granted stability in the midst of rapidly changing tastes (*CL* 342). For Lewis, these works were in large part Germanic myths and, in prose fiction, novels touching English country life, albeit occasionally imbued with fantasy. There were also the poems of Homer, Milton, and such. But the myths predominated. These tastes, he confesses in *Surprised by Joy*, formed a paradigm that he abandoned as being an idyll he had set up in his pre-war years (*SBJ* 166–167), but he could only abandon that paradigm in later life.

If his early poetry is dressed in myth, being tied to his early romantic propensities and the secure world they offered him, it is also tied to his society's tendencies to mythologize the war and its heroes like Rupert Brooke; seeing them through myth softened the fact that they did not return from war. Whatever his society's propensities, Lewis himself traced his zest for myth as arising from "a period of ecstasy. It consisted chiefly of moments when you were too happy to speak, when the gods and heroes rioted through your head" (*SBJ* 118); it was his youth's chief security and happiness. Far from being, philosophically, a "frustrated dualist" (King 454), Lewis is, in his first collection of poems, making an implicit record of how that happiness completely shattered, and he is seen to be confused at various levels—as regards the violent nature of human beings and the cosmos in which they seem to be trapped. Not least is he confused in his own clashing views about God (Hooper xviii). If his poems are mythical, myth is only the body, the physique, of that poetry. That is its outer dress, not what it *is*.

If war is seen as the quest of the warrior, then war poetry reveals a modern hero, as Frank Kermode said of one post-war character from Waugh, a victim-hero caught amid "chance collisions, absurd but sometimes fatal sequences of incident, in a small world where it is useless to seek a rational or just concatenation of events, or an account of human relations dictated by probability or decency" (xii).

However, that his are poems describing his war, Jack himself could not, I believe, see clearly nor articulate. It is seen in his *ad hominem* reaction to another war poet and his poems. Jack mentions in October 1918 that he saw a book that Heinemann published, Sassoon's *Counter-Attack*, which is now a standard of First World War poetry. Lewis saw Siegfried Sassoon, as "a horrid man" (*CL* 403). Sassoon is for Lewis a horrid man for two reasons. The first has solely to do with Sassoon's frank description of the war, which for Lewis evoked memories he wished to evade but which continually troubled him in his recurring dreams (*CL* 417–418). Sassoon's poetry had, in part, this purpose:

> What *was* this camouflage War which was manufactured by the press to aid the imaginations of people who had never seen the real thing? Many of them probably said that the papers gave them a sane and vigorous view of the overwhelming tragedy. "Naturally," they would remark, "the lads form the front line are inclined to be a little morbid about it; one expects that, after all they've been through. Their close contact with the War has diminished their realization of its spiritual aspects." Then they would add something about "the healing of Nations." Such people needed to have their noses rubbed in a few rank physical facts, such as what a company of men smelt like after they'd been in action for a week. . . . (Sassoon 186)

For a veteran like Lewis such poetry was just another hit on a bruise, another impact upon his assumptions; Sassoon's poetry looked bleakly, with no romance or myth, into the abyss of the war. Sassoon and Owen hoped to make their poetry devoid of myth and romance; as Charles Hamilton Sorley warned others,

> When you see millions of the mouthless dead
> Across your dreams in pale battalions go,
> Say not soft things as other men have said, (89)

Yet in *Spirits in Bondage* Lewis also must convey something of the war's realities, and later, in *Dymer*, Lewis himself peers deeply into that abyss in much the same way as did Otto Dix, the German soldier and painter—to rid himself of the war's demons. But Sassoon's work violated what, for Lewis, poetry should accomplish: the conveyance of a romantic ideal, an ideal set quite above the world that is in conflict with it. For Lewis, poetry like Sassoon's described only the world of war and described its brutal realities, and that is something, the bare landscapes of Modernist poetry, that was for Lewis representative of the spirit of the age. One recalls *Pilgrim's Regress*, written after Lewis's conversion and in which he traces his spiritual and mental wanderings after the war up to his conversion. In that work is a passage telling much of how he viewed such poetry and any philosophy bent on describing the material world solely. John, the pilgrim Lewis on his spiritual quest, has been imprisoned by the Spirit of the Age, portrayed as a giant whose gaze made things normally unseen visible, but solely in a material sense (60–61). The personification of Reason comes to free John from the Spirit of the Age, and later tells him that that Spirit has not shown things as they are in actuality, but as they would be if we all had something akin to x-ray vision (70). Reason further explains that should one be able to see inside a person, the person would die, and that is a reality. She explains that in making John believe that all of reality was thus— death being its sum—then the Spirit of the Age convinced him that life itself was the same, grim reality (70).

Those passages in *Pilgrim's Regress* are directly related to Lewis's war and his early poetry, revealing what lies behind the poetry. Lewis, writing them in the early 1930s, had thought much about what he had seen in the war. First, as implied in Lewis's title *Spirits in Bondage* (originally to have been *Spirits in Prison*), his second self, John is imprisoned by a Spirit of the Age that looks only at "Matter"—the Matter of the equation is explained to Arthur Greeves in a letter give earlier: "Matter = Nature = Satan. And on the other side Beauty [. . . .]" (*CL* 371). The war, for Lewis, obliterated dreaming and spirit, obliterated "Beauty," and presented only the worst evils of the material world. Second, beyond Matter's opposition to Beauty, Beauty itself remained the only spiritual factor he observed in this world. Third, the Spirit of the Age worked against pilgrim John's assumptions, making him believe that life was not beautiful, and did so by forcing him to look upon death. Hence in *Dymer* Lewis— beyond the Spirit of the Age's tricks, would record this:

> I saw men's stomachs fall out on their knees;
> And shouting faces, while they shouted, freeze
> Into black, bony masks. (43)

That Lewis preferred older traditions in literature (*CL* 356) even when young evidences the permanence he desired, the lasting, the secure, but foremost the beautiful, the romantic and the ideal. The absence of these traits and the overwhelming presence of the bleak horrors and prevailing dark ironies in

Sassoon's poetry is why Lewis, then, called Sassoon a horrid man (*CL* 403). Sassoon was subscribing to the Spirit of the Age.

In contrast to Sassoon's later style, the poems in *Spirits in Bondage* also parallel Lewis's pre-war paradigm; Lewis's poems are in a style Edward Marsh desired in compiling his *Georgian Poetry* anthologies; Marsh, had he seen them, would have preferred them for their poetic diction. In contrast to Lewis, Edmund Blunden, in his anthology of war poets, would praise Sassoon's book of poetry *Counter-Attack*, appearing in June of 1918, as a "triumph," for Sassoon was "the first man who even described the war fully and exactly" (20). Marsh, however, would reject Sassoon's grim war poetry even after having published some of his earlier work. Instead, Marsh attempted to retain poetry of the type he defended in his first anthology of *Georgian Poetry* (1912): "This volume is issued in the belief that English poetry is now once again putting on a new strength and beauty" (preface). Beauty was Lewis's goddess and security. The war set the toe tag on the corpse of 19th-century assumptions that Marsh hoped to revive; that age had passed, and Sassoon, among others, was communicating that fact. In 1922, Eliot's *Waste Land* appeared, even as Marsh put forth the last volume of his anthologies. In the preface Marsh complained that "Much admired modern work seems to me, in its lack of inspiration and its disregard of form, like gravy imitating lava [. . . .] like tapioca imitating pearls" (preface). He further says, "I have tried to choose no verse but such as in Wordsworth's phrase, 'The high and tender Muses shall accept With gracious smile, deliberately pleased.'" (n.p.) The poems he would select have the same resistance to Modernism and to the spirit of that age that Lewis felt. There was in the central war poets nothing of romantic poetic diction, nothing of myth; there was in Sassoon and Owen and others no focus on anything beyond the mere physical and political aspects of war, nothing transcendent.

To people like Lewis and Marsh, Sassoon's war poetry described a bleak prospect. Yet Sassoon had clearly stated that his purpose in writing was to present to those in command "a few rank physical facts" (186). The focus of Lewis's *Spirits in Bondage* is, in contrast, a young man lamenting the death of his idyllic world—as it stood in his own assumptions—that had once been full of myth and beauty. And if that world is dead, where is one to find solace, an ideal world away from the destruction? Lewis's focus in writing *Spirits* is not to produce "rank physical facts." This is why Lewis wrote to Arthur Greeves in October of 1918 as *Spirits in Bondage* was being prepared for press that "Of course there is none of the fighting element in my book, but I suppose it has some direct bearing on the war" (*CL* 406). But Lewis had also written to Arthur that war poetry, "no worse than the rest of its kind" was "like that great mass of modern poets": "intolerably clumsy and ugly in form" (*CL* 407).

Both the form and content, then, of the new poetry stood in contrast to his own; it moved away from the world he idealized. Otto Dix would describe war just as bleakly:

> The war is something beastly: hunger, lice, mud, insane noises. Just everything is different. Look, before the earlier pictures I have had the feeling that one side of reality was still not represented: the ugly. The war was a hideous thing, but nonetheless overwhelming. In any case, I could not miss that! One had to see man in this chaotic condition in order to know something about him. (McGreevey, *Life*, 20)

If Lewis saw war poetry and modern poetry as ugly, it was because it had been intent on describing the ugly.

Lewis's work instead held a complaint against such war poets as Sassoon, a sentiment expressed by one of Remarque's protagonists:

> a man cannot talk of such things; I would do it willingly, but it is too dangerous for me to put these things into words. I am afraid they might then become gigantic and I be no longer able to master them. What would become of us if everything that happens out there were quite clear to us? (166–167)

Lewis's intent was to preserve his ideal world, for that was his security. It was the world he observed years later in Tolkien's works, the ideal world of hobbits. It is significant that at the end of Tolkien's *Ring* trilogy, the elves withdraw to the west, leaving the world of humankind: the richness of myth had gone. One recalls that Tolkien himself was, like Lewis, in the war; he was at the Somme near Thiepval on 1 July 1916.

Still, in those relatively few moments when Lewis's poems include war's grim realities, the descriptions are embedded within a context that reveals the shattering effects of those realities upon the speaker's expectations and assumptions. The expectations are always that a world of beauty is the norm. The actualities of war shatter the expectation of beauty.

SPIRITS IN BONDAGE

I will not examine each poem in *Spirits in Bondage* but will present exemplary moments typifying the assumptions confronted by realities of war, with dreams of an ideal past and place that stand in opposition to those realities; other moments in the poems contain laments for the shattered the assumptions of a beautiful and benevolent world.

The first poems in the collection establish the issues essential to all the others. The Prologue of *Spirits in Bondage* speaks of a people presumably in league with the poet in his a refusal to accept the "facts" of life on earth—that war and death occur, what Lewis in his letter to Arthur called "Matter." He rebels against an implacable God who taunts the people in supplication before him (xlii). It is the same sense expressed by Ernst Toller:

> Instead of heroes there were only victims; conscripts instead of volunteers . . . . We were all of us cogs in a great machine which sometimes rolled forward, nobody knew where, sometimes backwards, nobody knew why. (qtd. in McGreevy, *Life* 20)

The world he describes stands in contrast to another world assumed to be perpetually beautiful and which has as its focus the spirit, not the physical world of matter. The Prologue establishes an image of a people fleeing the shattered world and its god to reach an ideal land. They seek that land which is far from those things which have shattered their assumptions of a beautiful and secure world, and the assumptions of a benign Lord ruling over it. They persist in "Dreaming of the wondrous islands" (xli), yet that ideal land is a "port that none has seen" (xlii). Nonetheless, as in "Song of the Pilgrims" (47), the people seek that place. In that poem (47) it is cast as a land perhaps following the idea of George MacDonald's story, *At the Back of the North Wind*, and it combines the ideals which Lewis found in Wagner's *Ring*, the "Twilight of the Gods"—his love of the north, with hard, vast expanses in faint light (*SBJ* 73), perhaps akin to the evening skies in Casper David Friedrich's bleak landscapes. These things, the idea of the north especially, he said, caused him to feel an inconsolable passion for the past, the remembrance of having experienced indescribable moments of joy, moments which could not be experienced again although sought after (*SBJ* 73). Just so with these poems: Lewis recounts his lost life of idyllic peace and beauty.

Thus the first poem in Part I, "Satan Speaks," relates directly to changes in Lewis's philosophy while he was in France. He explained to Arthur, that in the trenches he had perceived "spirit continually dodging matter (shells, bullets, animal fears, animal pains)" and that he had created an "equation": "Matter = Nature = Satan. And on the other side Beauty, the only spiritual & not-natural thing I have yet found" (*CL* 371).[1] As in the title of the poem, "Satan Speaks," the equation is presented by the speaker (the personified force (Nature) behind Matter, we may say) in an obscene trinity which imposes its irresistible will upon the material world (ll. 1–2).

It includes all of the things Lewis finds disturbing in his material world at the time: "lust" (l. 4); "battle's filth and strain/[. . .] the widow's empty pain" (ll. 5–6); "the sea to smother" (7) (for sailors, soldiers, nurses, and civilians were dying as ships were attacked by German U-boats); "the bomb" (l. 8). But why does Lewis include "flower and the dewdrop" (l. 3) as one of the shattering elements? It is precisely because of the pain such things bring, the same pain that T. S. Eliot would express in the opening of *The Waste Land*:

April is the cruelest month [. . .]
Winter kept us warm, covering
Earth in forgetful snow [. . . .] (29, ll. 1–6)

Therefore Lewis describes "the fact and the crushing reason/to thwart your fantasy of newborn treason" (ll. 10–11)—that is, one's fantasy of escaping what the world has become, in words that echo Tennyson's description of "Nature red in tooth and claw" (*In Memoriam* LVI). Another instance that echoes Tennyson, associated here with rebellion, is heard in "Victory," which describes the "yearning, high, rebellious spirit of man/That never rested yet since life began/From striving with red Nature and her ways" (7, ll.14–16). Such aspiration, however, within the confines of a world at war will not succeed (ll. 17–18).

The collection is laden with the conflict between myth, heroism and dream set on one side against reality. In "De Profundis," the millennia of human endeavor and aspiration the God of this world has brought to nothing (20). In the same poem, if but one part of human endeavor has not been futile, yet the speaker must admit that the God in the poem can "shatter all things of worth" (21) should any be attained. The shattering of a beautiful world is, of course, the collection's persistent lament. The ancient ways, the ancient songs of legend, all the heroes and heroines of myth and lore are gone. In sum, "the good is dead" (14).

Some vestiges of beauty yet exist as a haven amidst the destruction of all things of worth. The good that remains are dreams of an ideal place, as expressed, for instance, in "Night" (55), with its druid garden peopled with faeries dancing beneath the moon, and in an earlier poem of the same title, (16), there the speaker pleads with the Night, personified, to grant dreams of one's love and "After the fret and failure of this day [. . . .] With tenderest love [. . .] The bruised and wary heart/In slumber blind" (16–17). "Sonnet" is another of these poems in which such rest can remove all such effects of toil and hardship (33). Such sleep with idyllic dreams is a motif in the collection and is always an escape from the realities of the material world. There are also memories of a time before war, as in the poem "Milton Read Again (in Surrey)" (32), which certainly recalls what was for Lewis an ideal time at Kirkpatrick's, and the poem "Oxford" combines memory, desire, and the ideal in its praising of "palaces of peace/And discipline and dreaming and desire," for without them we may "forget our heritage and cease/The Spirit's work—to hunger and aspire" (57). As with other poems in which an ideal place is longed for if not praised, Oxford is contrasted with the realities of the moment. Humans, spiritual creatures, have forgotten themselves in the midst of the blood of war, their carnal desires, in their agonies, in their commercial pursuits; yet there is still a part that is spiritual and above the material world (57).

Oxford in this poem, is as it was for the young Lewis, "The Spirit's stronghold—barred against despair" (57). And one sees that such poems, presenting nothing of barbed wire and bombs, directly deal with escaping the trauma of war and retaining one's assumptions even as they are being shattered by the war.

If the world is as Lewis described it—and if one can only recall what seemed an ideal world beyond the war—then there is little choice left as to what humans can do. They may only lament, and that in vain: "Now cry for all your torment: now curse your hour of birth" for "Nature will not pity, nor the red God lend an ear" (13–14). The poem "In Prison" is the most dire lament of the collection, perhaps:

> I cried out for the pain of man,
> I cried out for my bitter wrath
> Against the hopeless life that ran
> For ever in a circling path
> From death to death since all began (19)

Above are the stars, indifferent, and below the are the dead who feel nothing, and given that this is all, the emptiness compounds in the fact that there is neither memory of nor concern for this world (19).

In bitter wrath, mentioned above, Lewis echoes (20) Lot's wife's advice, that Job should curse God and die. To rebel against the forces that have allowed such a world to exist is, for Lewis, imperative: it shows his defiant tenacity in holding to a vision of beauty beyond the realities confronting him in the trenches; it is his way of surviving. It seems to me a healthy reaction albeit many of the poems are mere escapism: the word "fancy"recurs in the collection. At this time in his life, Lewis remarked that he was preoccupied with these issues: "How could [nature] be so beautiful and also so cruel, wasteful, and futile?" he wonders, and comes very near this conclusion: "All that is good is imaginary; all that is real is evil" (*SBJ* 170–171). Indeed, Lewis *was* saying it all along in this collection of poems.

The reason for his bitterness is not so much the absence of God or the indifference of Nature, but his knowledge that human fancy has adhered to a fantasy that good exists (15). That is, humankind has assumed a beautiful and beneficent world; that assumption was being shattered. There remains only the futility of both the dream and aspiration to escape to another, ideal country (15).

Yet even as the speaker of the poems realizes humankind's predicament—that all humans are trapped within a de-mythologized and un-beautified world by an un-caring God, exasperating dreams of escape and unexpected visions of beauty continue to occur, dreams that only produce angst and self-loathing for continuing in the dreams (4). The speaker perceives that although a spark remains of their spiritual nature, men have been essentially reduced to beasts (57). Or, put this way: "I am a wolf [among] fellow-brutes that once were men/Our throats can bark for slaughter" (4). It was expressed in a similar way by one French solider:

> Not only did the war make us dead, impotent or blind. In the midst of beautiful actions, of sacrifice and self-abnegation, it also awoke within us, sometimes to the point of parox-ysm, ancient instincts of cruelty and barbarity. At times, I . . . who have never punched anyone, who loathes disorder and brutality, took pleasure in killing. (Audoin-Rouzeau and Becker 41).

Finding that one can brutalize another person is something that war effected in individuals and which shattered the most basic assumptions about self and other. It brought, as we have seen earlier, the guilt associated with killing. It also instilled a grave sense of having "sinned"—and *Spirits in Bondage* contains that motif as well. As will be shown in the next chapter, *Dymer* is a poem gnawed more intensely by this same sense of sin and guilt.

Beyond recording Lewis's reactions to the shattering of his ideals, other unexpected remnants of the war exist in the collection where one might not expect to find them. "In Praise of Solid People" evokes those whom Lewis described in his unit, men from the working class (*SBJ* 193). These are among the people he praised in the poem, those whom Tolstoy might admire for their less complicated lives and concerns (*SIB* 43).

Another unexpected relation to the war comes in the collection's treatment of lust, which Lewis includes as one of the elements (57) that take away the pain of war. In *Surprised by Joy*, however, he wrote that his ideal of Joy was not merely lust: if so, giving all young men lovers would put an end to aspiration for higher things (*SBJ* 169).

It relates to his relationship with Mrs. Moore; he had learned this only by having had his mistress and continuing to long for an ideal world. And this awareness is the substance behind his comment in his autobiography,

> before I say anything of my life [after war service] I must warn the reader that one huge and complex episode will be omitted. I have no choice about this reticence. All I can or need say is that my earlier hostility to the emotions was very fully and variously avenged. (*SBJ* 198)

The relationship with Mrs. Moore was a significant part of the collective wartime experiences, significant to the shattering of Lewis's view of himself, and is inextricably linked to Lewis's trauma. As will be seen, *Dymer* also treats this experience: Dymer's chase of a mysterious lover is directly related to Lewis's relationship with Mrs. Moore.

Another poem should not be unexpected among the collection but is somewhat surprising to us because place names along the Front are rare in the collection. "French Nocturne (Monchy-le-Preux)" provides a glimpse of Lewis while writing in the trenches. It was presumably written not long after he had entered the trenches and gives an indication of where he was in the line. He wrote of the sun sinking in the west, behind the piles of rubble the village had become by the time Lewis arrived there. The poem carries a sinister sense of the front lines (4) in which he lives, and the low, broken walls of the houses protrude like the teeth of the wolf in the previous poem ("Satan Speaks"). But beyond these descriptions, this poem like the others records his responses to trauma. The imagery is mythical, high and shining in contrast to Nature and the inconsistant nature of that world's god which sways between indifference and cruelty.

The last poem in the collection is Lewis's first-ever publication, having appeared in *Reveille*, "Death in Battle." Human defenses in the poem exist in the ability to retain images of an ideal country, to retain dreams of "the peaceful castle, rosy in the West" (74). That place is only found in death. Going West was for the soldiers the term for being killed. By ending the poem and the collection thus, Lewis is nevertheless saying the soft things Soreley warned against ("say not soft things that other men have said").

Throughout the collection is the longing for a world before war, which was "But a moment agone" (74). He cannot bring himself to abandon a lingering hope that he may again find that world. Many soldiers felt the same, as Edmund Blunden pointed out: the memory of or hope for a future world of peace and beauty served to recall "healing presences of the world you had known" (26). Guy Chapman, while serving in France, records his longing: "There was a country called England somewhere. It had once possessed beauties, perhaps more beautiful in dreams than in reality" (260). Lewis's *Spirits in Bondage* is a record of the hope Lewis bore against reality and the hope that his romantic ideal would survive the war. But the collection also records how the war's realities shattered that hope.

NOTE

1. In his preface to *SIB* Hooper records the statement as "[. . .] Beauty, the only spiritual & *non*-natural thing [. . .]" (xxxii, emphasis mine).

WORKS CITED

Audoin-Rouzeau, Stephane, and Annette Becker. *14–18: Understanding the Great War*. Trans. Catherine Temerson. New York: Hill and Wang, 2002.

Blunden, Edmund. *War Poets 1914–1918*. London: Longmans, 1958.

Chapman, Guy. *A Passionate Prodigality: Fragments of Autobiography*. Shedfield, England: Ashford, 1993.

Eliot, T. S. *The Waste Land. The Waste Land and Other Poems*. New York: Harcourt, 1962. 27–46.

Fussell, Paul. *The Great War and Modern Memory*. Oxford: Oxford UP, 1975.

Hooper, Walter. Preface. *Spirits in Bondage* by C. S. Lewis. San Diego: Harcourt, 1984. ix-xl.

Kermode, Frank. Introduction. *Decline and Fall* by Evelyn Waugh. New York: Knopf, 1993. v–xix.

King, Don W. "C. S. Lewis's *Spirits in Bondage*: World War I Poet as Frustrated Dualist." *Christian Scholar's Review*. XXVII:4. 454–474.

———. *C. S. Lewis: Poet*. Kent, Ohio: Kent State UP, 2001.

Lewis, C. S. *Pilgrim's Regress*. Grand Rapids: Eerdmans, 1979.

———. *Poems*. New York: Harcourt, 1964.

———. Preface. *Dymer. Narrative Poems*. New York: Harcourt, 1979. 3–6.

Mallarmé, Stéphane. *The Afternoon of a Faun*. Trans. Roger Fry. 26 July 2003. http://www.angel fire.com/art/doit/mallarme.html

McGreevy, Linda F. *Bitter Witness: Otto Dix and the Great War*. New York: Peter Lang, 2001.

———. *The Life and Works of Otto Dix: German Critical Realist*. Ann Arbor: UMI, 1981.

Remarque, Erich Maria. *All Quiet on the Western Front*. Boston: Little, Brown, 1929.

Sassoon, Siegfried. *Memoirs of an Infantry Officer*. London: Faber, 1965.

Sorley, Charles Hamilton. "When you see millions of the mouthless dead." *Penguin Book of First World War Poetry*. Ed. John Silkin. London: Penguin, 1996.

Waugh, Evelyn. *Put Out More Flags*. London: Penguin, 1943.

Winter, J. M. *The Experience of World War I*. New York: Oxford UP, 1995.

CHAPTER *14*

A Morning After War

LEWIS'S NARRATIVE POEM *DYMER* MOVES BEYOND *Spirits in Bondage* in reveal-ing his responses to war's trauma. In a preface to the poem's 1950 edition, Lewis wrote about the likelihood that "Everyone may allegorise it or psycho-analyse it as he pleases," but also recognized that "if I did so myself my inter-pretations would have no more authority than anyone else's" (3). I believe this is a swerve away from the issues that for Lewis are central to it; let others spec-ulate on it, he is saying but do not ask me to discuss it. At the poem's center I find his long-formed mode of defense. Lewis remarked in the preface to the poem that from an early age he felt the intense longing he called Joy, which was something well beyond mere fancy although it could produce "systems of imagery" (*D* Preface 4).

His romantic retreat from reality, whether by means of Christina Dreams[1] or by other means, was something that Lewis had begun to see through by the time he came to write the poem. He writes that "My hero [Dymer] was to be a man escaping from illusion. He begins by egregiously supposing the universe to be his friend and seems for a time to find confirmation of his belief" (*D* Preface 5). The correlations between Dymer's and Lewis's assumptions about life and the world are obvious. The conflict appears as "he tries, as we all try, to repeat his moment of youthful rapture. It cannot be done; [. . . .] Hunger and the shock of real danger bring him to his senses and he at last accepts reality" (*D* Preface 6). In these words Lewis is describing the violation of his pre-war assumptions as well as being forced to adjust his paradigm in order to integrate the traumatic events he has endured.

I see the poem as a record of how Lewis faces the trauma of his war as he attempts to rebuild or adjust his paradigm to contend with the realities met in war, just as Janoff-Bulman described as occurring in trauma cases. In the midst of motifs running through *Dymer* that are usually treated in Lewis scholarship—for instance in both George Sayer's and Don King's work—the insufficiency of the old paradigm is the underlying concern of the poem, but more: the poem is a lament for the romance that Lewis has abandoned only in the face of war's realities. He comes to see lust as the panacea, but it is a deception, diverting one from real desire and aspiration. That lust is a creation, however, of our own making, a monster that needs slaying.

The poem is balanced oddly between romance on the one hand and the shattering realities of the war on the other. In the midst of recording the memories of war as they violently reassert themselves into Lewis's romantic assumptions about life and the cosmos, the poem then becomes Lewis's attempt to adjust his paradigm after war.

Dymer, the protagonist of the poem, is the youthful Lewis just before he entered the war and during its early days—but also Lewis as he recalls those days from the distance of 1921. Like Lewis, Dymer understands the old assumptions and their errors, and those events which destroyed the prewar world are revisited with an aim towards, albeit with halting steps onto, a final paradigmatic resolution.

The poem recalls and describes the events of his war with the same stark vision Sassoon used in his poetry. Sassoon spent "exactly half his life" in "plowing and re-plowing the earlier half, motivated by what [. . .] he calls 'my queer craving to revisit the past and give the modern world the slip'" (Fussell 92). Such a life after war shows how the war, as in Woolf's *Mrs. Dalloway*, as in Remarque's *The Road Back*, was never quite over but continued "to be fought within the psyche" (qtd. in Fussell 113). Sassoon's prose work after the war, like his poetry, contains frank and detailed examination of the war's worst moments. *Spirits in Bondage* does not contain such detailed recollections of the war; at the time of writing that collection, I believe Lewis was still in a state which would not allow him to look plainly at the events of his war. However, removed a few years from the traumatizing events, Lewis like other veterans remained bothered by intrusive thoughts and nightmares. But in recalling them with the detail found in *Dymer*, he faced his demons of war instead of repressing them just as other soldiers eased their trauma by recalling the events in detail but doing so with an adjusted viewpoints. Lewis was not alone in easing his trauma through his art, although that is not a purpose for art that he would articulate to himself or to anyone else. The German veteran of the war and painter Otto Dix is similar to Lewis in working through his respective war experiences.

Dix was a soldier in the German army who did not enlist but waited, like Lewis, until he was compelled to fight. He became a machine gunner in various places along the Western and on the Eastern Front, being wounded a number of times (McGreevy, *Life*, 19). Between attacks, Dix could be found sketching the most horrible scenes of death in the trenches around him: "When asked why he took the trouble to draw during lulls in the battles [. . .], Dix's ironic reply was, 'It's fun to draw in this tedious slaughter'" (McGreevy, *Life*, 19). After the war, "Dix would continue to attempt to come to terms with his war experiences for several years, and from memories of this period would come some of his greatest works" (McGreevy, *Life*, 21). One might say that the same is observed in the most famous war writers—Remarque and Sassoon, for instance. As to Dix, however, it seems remarkable to us that after the war—in wishing to recall the grim actualities of war for later paintings—he visited morgues to study corpses and dismembered limbs. He did so in order to recall what that perpetual presence of the dead had been to him. Whatever changes occurred in Dix's style under the influences of Cubism and Dada, no matter if (quite unlike Lewis) Dix "absolutely had to experience" and "wanted to" experience the war at its worst (McGreevy, *Bitter Witness*, 274), he was nevertheless like Lewis in seeing his art as "an effort to produce order; order in yourself. There is much chaos in me, much chaos in our time" (McGreevy, *Bitter Witness*, 201). And Dix is like Lewis in this experience:

> As a young person, you don't even notice that it has been weighing on you inside. Because for years, at least ten years, I kept having these dreams where I would have to crawl through the ruins of houses, through corridors hardly wide enough for me to get through. The ruins were always in my dreams. Not that painting was a release for me. (McGreevy, *Bitter Witness*, 233)

Dix might say in one moment it was no release, and Lewis would likely state the same regarding his own works: that it was not a psychological exercise. Yet in another moment Dix said, "I painted [war] in order to banish war" (McGreevy, *Bitter Witness*, 234). Not merely to banish the prospect of war from society, "He painted, he said, 'to rid himself of the demons of war'" (O'Brien-Twohig). It was an exorcism of war's ghosts, war's nightmare visions, war's guilt—the guilt both of killing and of surviving. But for Lewis, there was one other thing: the guilt of his relationship with Mrs. Moore.

DYMER

The narrative runs thus. Dymer, the youthful protagonist, rebels against what he believes are the antiquated laws of his native city. In an impetuous moment, Dymer strikes and kills his lecturer before the other students of his class and then flees. Freed, he thinks, from the confines of his society, which (to use William Blake's words) were "binding with briars my joys and desires," he comes into a luxurious wood, and during a night in what is essentially Spenser's (or perhaps Mallarmé's faun's) bower of bliss,

> He opened wide
> His arms. The breathing body of a girl
> Slid onto them. From the world's end, with the stride
> Of seven-leagued boots came passion to his side.
> Then, meeting mouths, soft-falling hair, a cry,
> Heart-shaken flank, sudden cool-folded thigh [. . . .] (24–25)

She disappears without Dymer knowing in the least who she was. It is a reversal of roles, essentially, of Cupid and Psyche, and Dymer's quest is not only to persist in his new freedom, but within that freedom to seek the ecstasy he experienced with his mysterious lover. His quest is to pursue not only her, but as in *Spirits in Bondage*, a dwelling in an ideal place, in this case a place where laws cannot inhibit desire. Late in the poem Dymer discovers the identity of his lover and that their offspring is a monster let loose upon the earth. The begetting of a monster is a Frankensteinian event, but here it is set within the narcissistic afternoon (here a night) of Mallarmé's faun, interpreted by Nijinsky's dance in Debussy's ballet:

> Was it a dream I loved?
> My doubt, a heap of ancient night, is finishing
> In many a subtle branch, which, left the true
> Wood itself, proves, alas! that all alone I gave
> Myself for triumph the ideal sin of roses. (Fry)

Yet unlike Nijinsky's faun who makes love to a silken scarf, Dymer's object is eventually realized to be a romantic idealization of his own lust which appears as a horrific reality; it is not love of a real human, of another being, sovereign in her own right. To use Shakespeare's words, Dymer finds lust to be "an expense of spirit in a waste of shame," "before a joy proposed, behind a dream." In this case, lust has become a nightmare. Dymer describes it, however, as "chewing the cud of lusts which are despair" (*D* 85).

    But Dymer can only articulate this later, after he has seen the reality of what he has begotten and understood its origin. However, during his quest to find his mysterious lover, Dymer finds a magician who promises to show him the way to her. For him, the dream is everything. "His secret lust, his soul's dark citadel" (*D* 66) stands against shattering forces of the world he has fled. The access to the romantic dream world that the magician promises to Dymer is the parallel to the blue flower of Novalis's novel *Heinrich Von Ofterdingen*, symbol of German romanticism, and Lewis himself was just such "a votary of the blue flower." In their desire for romantic ecstasy, Dymer, like Lewis, is similar to Lucy Honeychurch in Forster's *Room with a View*. She stands in the profusion of that symbol of romance: "the violets ran down in rivulets and streams [. . .] the well-head, the primal source whence beauty gushed out to water the earth" (Forster 78); however, like the contrasting image of Charlotte Bartlett in that novel, I believe that the reality of Mrs. Moore's character broke the "silence of life" and, like Charlotte, she "stood brown against the view" (Forster 78). The societal laws of Dymer's world were similar to those which Charlotte represented in Forster, those standing against the romantic vision of life: "the brown network of the bushes shattered [the view] into countless pieces" (Forster 77). During the war, Lewis had written in despair that the life he once knew with Arthur, the vision they shared, could never be regained (*CL* 355).

I believe that between the time this letter was written and the time, years later, when he was writing *Dymer*, Lewis had become aware of a very different Mrs. Moore: it was the one Warnie described in harsh terms, one quite distinct from the mysterious lover in the night, one that had been hidden not by night but by Lewis's own romantic assumptions about love and the world. He had a vision of Janie Moore that was a product of his own romantic vision; he found instead he had begotten a monster, their sexual relationship. By the time Dymer discovers that he has merely pursued a "reflection of self" (70), the narrative has almost wholly been taken up with his quest to find a "woods beyond the West" (71) and his mysterious lover. Nevertheless, his desire for love and an ideal place has been very real for these things (not merely fanciful lust or the romantic notions he is swayed by). His error was in thinking that lust, full of promise, could deliver the objects of his desire. The dangers that Dymer encounters awaken him from his romantic notions.

The dream world Dymer has created has a narrowly defined source, as the poem indicates in a moment of weakness for Dymer: "he staggered to the bookcase to renew/Yet once again the taint he had taken from it" (66). It came from his books; the tales often fuelled his romantic rebellion against the realities of life. So far has he come that he can see this use of literature as a "taint."

Akin to Dymer's rebellion against the lecturer who proclaims society's laws, Lewis's relationship with Moore also is partly the embodiment of his rebellion against his father. Albert did not know what to make of the relationship, and his language in this description of it to Warnie reveals his suspicions:

I do confess I do not know what to do about Jack's affair. It worries and depresses me greatly. All I know about the lady is that she is old enough to be his mother, and that she is in poor circumstances. I also know that Jacks has frequently drawn cheques in her favour running up to £10—for what I don't know. If Jacks were not an impetuous kindhearted creature who could be cajoled by any woman who had been through the mill, I should not be so uneasy. (*CL* 451)

The relationship has something of Dymer's rebellion against the old laws, and it transpires directly from his deeply romantic assumptions about the world and about love. Albert must have known well this propensity in his son. War and death, Lewis found, were quite apart from the heroic elevation of them in much of literature, not least like something found in Homer. Lewis also discovered that Mrs. Moore's nature was very much other than what he, dizzied with romantic notions, had assumed her to be. Like Dymer, Lewis found literature had provided the "taint" of his romantic vision.

Lewis took care of Mrs. Moore for the rest of her life. That decision was based on at least two things: the promise of the two young officers and Lewis's gratitude for having survived the war. The decision might also be underpinned with the guilt of surviving. That Mrs. Moore and Jack shared moments of sexual love I do not doubt; that it continued through the decades after the war I doubt very much, for *Dymer* is a poem showing not only Lewis looking back at the war and its trauma, similar to Otto Dix re-visiting death at a postwar morgue, but it shows Lewis looking back at his blind infatuation for Mrs. Moore as well as the consummation of its "lust" with his dream lover. In a discussion with Owen Barfield, Lewis "condemned" Christina Dreams—the love dream made a man incapable of real love, the hero dream made him a coward" (*AMR* 39). Lewis is looking at himself in Dymer, looking at both his earlier love, his earlier, romantic assumptions about life, and at his war; these are inseparably linked in his experience.

At the beginning of the narrative, however, when Dymer first pursues his dream lover, he is impeded by an old hag; she is much like Ezra Pound's description of the best men in the nation dying for post-Victorian England: For an old bitch gone in the teeth,/For a botched civilization [. . . .]

Others have seen in her figure a plethora of mythical sources (King Poet 119). Whatever her sources, she stands in Victorian silence, stolid and cold: Dymer attempts to push by her "That I might be the breaker of bad laws" (33), for "We'll taste/Whatever is" and follow "the wild gods in the heart?" (42).

Her effect on Dymer is that of cold water on enamored dogs. Cold realities
squelch lost like a numbing punch (35), from which Dymer can only stagger
on "past knowledge of his misery" (35). That is also precisely the effect of war
upon Lewis. As he said in his preface to the poem, only two things (real desire
and danger), awake Dymer to reality, but such realities are a shattering force
upon his earlier romantic assumptions; they traumatize. He becomes like
Woolf's Septimus Warren Smith who, as we have seen, "could not feel" in the
face of the realities.

The imagery Lewis uses in describing the dangers and realities Dymer faces
are those derived from Lewis's experiences in battle. After Dymer flees his city,
other citizens follow his example of rebellion, and under the movement's
leader, Bran, violence erupts and many are killed. After a battle Dymer encounters a wounded man and through him comes to realize that his own initial
rebellion is responsible for the horrible events that have transpired. The man
tells his tale of battle, and I believe the tale is in large part Lewis recalling his
own experiences in combat.

The poem becomes full of the ear-piercing thunder and the fire that sur-
rounds one on the battlefield (37). The poem evokes the shells that shatter the
trees "even where he stood! And there—ah, that came near!" (37). With reference to the apocalyptic nature of WWI, Lewis writes,

> —Oh, then came the worst hour for flesh and blood,
>
> It was the waking world that will not end
> Because hearts break [. . .] (38)

The lines describe the shattering force the war had upon all the world, but that
force emerges only in the death it brings to individuals. Dymer comes upon
the wounded man:

> —"I'm hit. I'm finished. Let me be."
> —"Put out your hand, then. Reach me. No, the other."
> —"Don't touch. Fool! Damn you! Leave me."—"I can't see.
> Where are you?" Then more groans. "They've done for me.
> I've no hands. Don't come near me. No, but stay,
> Don't leave me . . . O may God! Is it near day?" (39)

Dymer fears doing anything to help (39) as the two men await the morning
light. During those hours the wounded man begins his tale. For me, this narrator is the man in one of Otto Dix's etchings ("Verwunderter", Baupaume,
March 1916).

Figure 18. "Wounded Man" by Otto Dix, Fall 1916; reproduced through The Los Angeles Country Museum of Art).

The picture seems to have evoked for Dix particular horrors as does the wounded narrator for Dymer. Men, dead or dying, are not merely a ghastly image in themselves; their horror extends in their ability to articulate our own relations to war. That is the horror that Dymer's wounded narrator communicates.

The narrator had joined the rebellion led by Bran; Dymer's name becomes the catchword of their cause as the group commences its attack. The description is that of advancing over the top of a trench and meeting the enemy: it carries an important change from past to present tense at the word "freeze"—a change which indicates traumatic immediacy in the narrator recalling these events:

> The wave where I was swallowed swelled and broke,
> After long surge, into the open square.
> And here there was more light: new clamour woke.
> Here first I heard the bullets sting the air
> [. . . .]
> Then charge and cheer and bubbling sobs of death,
> We hovered on their front. Like swarming bees
> Their spraying bullets came—no time for breath.
> I saw men's stomachs fall out on their knees;
> And shouting faces, while they shouted, freeze

Into black, bony masks. Before we knew
We're into them . . ."Swine!"—"Die, then!"—That's for you!" (43)

Memories of killing and associated guilt are implicit in these lines from
Dymer. It was the same for others, as one soldier recalled of looking into a
bombed dug out: "One man—an elderly fellow—[was] sitting up with his back
to a bit of earth with his hands half raised. He was smiling a little, though he'd
been stabbed through the belly . . ." (McGreevy 72). The wounded man in
Dymer recalls

> [. . .] I saw an old, old man
> Lying before my feet with shattered skull,
> And both my arms dripped red. (44)

We do not know if Lewis killed men in war. If Lewis is recalling his own experiences in such passages as these in which the speaker is cast as participant, then
such lines would convince one that he had killed and suffered beneath the lingering memories of those moments where a soldier looks upon his work. It is
to be marked that when Lewis was wounded, he becomes aware of co-exist-
ing but only loosely linked selves within himself; here the wounded narrator,
telling of his deeds in killing, is a distanced self from Dymer. Both may be Lewis.
Killing enemies and surviving friends: in these aspects war creates a confusion
of the soul. The sum of such deeds is, as Audoin-Rouzeau and Becker have put
it, the weight of the dead upon the living.

Dymer's wounded narrator continues to relate how events transpired,
that behind Bran those in the rebellion become mere killers, seeming to forget their cause (43), and the narrator explains how he suddenly awoke to what
was happening as atrocities were being committed: they "flay men and spit
women on the pike,/Bidding them dance" (44). Audoin-Rouzeau and Becker
have confirmed the occurrences, the nature, and the purposes behind atrocities in the First World War. Lewis may well have seen the results of such events
in the village of Riez near Bernenchon as the Germans were driven back, for
the civilians had not fled before the attack.

Such scenes bring Dymer's wounded man to understand that,

> "God! . . . Once the lying spirit of a cause
> With maddening words dethrones the mind of men,
> They're past the reach of prayer. (44)

The lines evoke Wilfred Owen's rejection of "the old lie" that it is sweet and
fitting to die for one's fatherland. The man who narrates his tale to Dymer
retains, as did Lewis, "Faces of men in torture" (44) that will not leave his
thoughts.

Parallel to Lewis's experience at Riez, the wounded man relates that "Day found us on the border of this wood,/Blear-eyed and pale" (44). At Riez the attack began the previous evening; troops advanced during the night and stood against the Germans in Riez and Bois de Pacaut. The wounded man in Dymer, however, was the third to be singled out as a lingerer (a man who secretly held to the old laws of the city), and for this his old friends "cut away my two hands and feet" (45).

Dymer realizes that he is responsible for all the misery that has been narrated to him by this suffering being, and he feels both awe and guilt (46) at the wounded man's story as well as numbness (46).

Dymer sleeps in his misery, only to awaken to the "present horror, screaming," for

all at once it filled with night alarms
And rapping guns: and men with splintered faces,
—No eyes, no nose, all red—were running races
With worms along the floor. (47)

It is that moment Lewis is recalling in which he saw men still moving like smashed bugs (*SBJ* 196). But beyond these ghastly memories, he is coming to understand the comprehensive efficacy of war's shattering nature: Dymer ponders how brief and transitory his joy had been (48). Its result has been all this death.

Attempting to discover the depth of his responsibility, he repeatedly asks, "What have I done?" (49). It is the cry of a victim of trauma: what did I do to deserve this? How have I contributed to the suffering and deaths of others? Dymer can only see that he has pursued his lust, and that was the trap he fell into (49). His romantic pursuits did not protect him; his assumptions failed. This awareness for Dymer is as shattering as the awareness that he caused the violence that transpired. A moment of realization like this is critical in those who show symptoms of PTSD. That Lewis articulates such a moment reveals that he has most assuredly recognized the fallacy of—if still not having moved beyond the lingering feeling of—his own responsibility for death of the men around him and his own survival. For just as Lewis lost his close friends— Johnson, Ayers, Somerville, Sutton, Davey, and Moore, Dymer observes "I have lost my brothers and my love and all./Nothing is left but me" and asks God to "take back your world. I will have none of all your glittering gauds but death alone" (50). I believe the point Dymer reached is that which Lewis looks back upon: the time when he was writing the poem "Death in Battle" from *Spirits in Bondage*. There the speaker pleads for the gates of death to open for him, for he has been oppressed by war

And driven and hurt beyond bearing this summer day,
[. . . .]
But a moment agone,
Among men cursing in fight and toiling, blinded I fought,
[. . . .]
And now—alone! (*SIB* 74)

But that point was not before Lewis was himself wounded.

One response to trauma is the abandonment of old assumptions if they are perceived as being a delusion: thus, he says "This, this was best,/This giving up of all. He need not strive" (52). Echoing the World War I song, "Pack up Your Troubles," Dymer steps out against "coward fancy," and says to himself, "Pack up the dreams and let the life begin" (55). Danger had forced Dymer's thoughts towards new assumptions; hunger also drives him—this time to a magician who tempts Dymer into entering once more into his life of romantic reverie, "Dream again/And deeper" (61), and realize that "your wrong and right/Are also dreams" (62). His dreaming is induced by a drug, and in a single moment Dymer discovers the true nature of his mysterious lover: that she is a mirror of his own lust and that the magician's works are deceptions (67). At this epiphane, he is released from his delusions (71).

In the next passage Dymer is wounded, and in writing the passages Lewis was without doubt recalling the moment he was wounded. He stood near Riez, in the back yards of houses at the south-east of the village. Gardens are in those yards today as no doubt they were in 1918. When the shell landed, similar to Dymer's being shot, Lewis would have heard an explosion, followed by

the splash of light
Vanished as soon as seen. Cool garden clay
Slid from his feet. He had fallen and he lay
Face downward among leaves—then up and on
Through branch and leaf till sense and breath were gone. (74)

He next finds he is somewhere away from house, garden, and trees (75). As explained about the attack on Riez, Lewis's unit passed along the Rue de Passerelle, the footbridge road which was little more than a lane. After being wounded, Lewis crawled away from the spot and back from the line of battle and was picked up by medics. Dymer's condition reflects both the physical wounds of Lewis and their incessant, gnawing pain (75). This juxtaposition, an event like being wounded set against a backdrop of the beauty one finds at Mount Bernenchon, is just what many soldiers remark about the war, how a sunny and still day lingers while bodies are torn beneath the beauty of the sky. It seems to compound the horror, to emphasize the illogical nature of the event.

Once Dymer is wounded, the narration takes on the puzzled state of a man moving in and out of consciousness. He perceives dimly his bleeding body, but then sees a woman by him, their eyes meeting (76). Was this the nurse whom Lewis said reminded him of a goddess (*SBJ* 197)? This woman, for Dymer, is not the embodiment of his love but is one who directs him in understanding the true object of his love. In a Platonic sense, he had loved the shadows, not anything true and lasting, a theme that would eventually become important in not only Lewis's autobiography but also in works like *The Great Divorce*. Dymer realizes he had pursued lusts, not Beauty as he believed, and the woman does not so much lead him to this awareness as lead him into a Socratic dialog. Aware that he has "used/The embreathing spirit amiss" (79), he moves closer to final resolution. Yet racked with the torment of his wounds, he moves beyond concern for his own life and the impotent guilt he feels about his deeds. A "new life breathed in unmoved and vast" as he empathizes: "'It was like this,'he thought—'like this, or worse,/For him that I found bleeding in the wood . . .'" (80). Certainly Lewis is in the process of articulating his paradigmatic resolution, forming new assumptions after coming to terms with war's horrors and comprehending a proper disinterestedness towards his own life (80–81). Lewis takes up the same view of himself in writing his autobiography, the same disinterested (indeed, a third-person) look at himself when he described the moment, exploring, philosophizing about this person who might be ceasing to exist (197–198).

Dymer is a poem of progression but much more than Dymer's progress from a self-full life to a more selfless existence (he attempts reparation for all he has done by killing the monster offspring of his own lust, an event culminating in Dymer's death). But the poem is much more than the simple, moral narrative that some have seen in it. It is, like the paintings of Otto Dix, centered on the war and its shattering force. It is a phenomenon, a struggle to leave war behind and regain some ideal that existed in one's mind before war. Perhaps it is described best by Remarque:

> We have clamoured and searched; we have steeled ourselves and yet have surrendered; we tried to elude it, yet it sprang upon us; we lost our way, yet we still ran on further— but ever we felt the shadow at our heels and tried to escape it. We thought it was pursuing us. We did not know we were dragging it with us; that there where we were, it was also, silently standing—not behind us, but within us—in us ourselves. (292)

And, as in Remarque, Lewis's relationship with Mrs. Moore began, I believe, as a means of escaping war; as often happens, it was a relationship from which too much was expected:

and when he returned he had nothing; his repressed youth, his gagged desires, his hunger for home and affection then cast him blindly upon this one human being whom he supposed that he loved. And when that was all shattered [. . . .] (Remarque 293)

As for many soldiers, when everything was shattered, nothing remained but destruction of self and destruction of others. But not for Lewis. *Dymer* is the moment when Lewis gathers his courage, like Septimus Warren Smith heading towards the window, and plunges into the depths of his trauma. He continued to have nightmares through the years; he continued to carry shell fragments in his chest for decades after the war. And he continued to posture on the topic of his war until his death. In that morning, when Lewis wept uncontrollably and then sat down to write *Dymer*, he confronted his war, moved toward survival, and toward the possibilities that lay in his future:

> What now my friends? You get no more from me
> Of Dymer. He goes from us. What he felt
> Or saw from henceforth no man know but he
> Who has himself gone through the jungle belt
> Of dying, into peace. (90)

NOTE

1. In the preface to *Dymer*, Lewis explained that "Christina Dreams" was the name by which Lewis and others at the time of his return to Oxford identified their early Romantic wishfulness and is an epithet associated with Samuel Butler's character Christina Pontifex in *The Way of All Flesh*. In that novel Butler described his own disillusion with and rebellion against the traditional religious values of his family and society. Lewis indicated that his hero Dymer was deluded not by religious assumptions but by the romantic aspirations he eventually saw through as being a cruel deception and which he battled to overcome. In his preface to *Dymer*, Lewis's references to Christina Dreams and other wishful aspirations reveals his preoccupation with the destruction of his pre-war assumptions about life, the world, and himself; *Dymer* is, then, a narrative identifying the vulnerability of those earlier assumptions, their destruction, but most importantly the point where Lewis begins to reconstruct his shattered assumptions."

WORKS CITED

Audoin-Rouzeau, Stephane, and Annette Becker. *14–18: Understanding the Great War*. Trans. Catherine Temerson. New York: Hill and Wang, 2002.
Eliot, T. S. *The Waste Land. The Waste Land and Other Poems*. New York: Harcourt, 1962. 27–46.
Fussell, Paul. *The Great War and Modern Memory*. Oxford: Oxford UP, 1975.

Hooper, Walter. Preface. *Spirits in Bondage* by C. S. Lewis. San Diego: Harcourt, 1984. ix-xl.

Kermode, Frank. Introduction. *Decline and Fall* by Evelyn Waugh. New York: Knopf, 1993. v–xix.

King, Don W. "C. S. Lewis's *Spirits in Bondage*: World War I Poet as Frustrated Dualist." *Christian Scholar's Review*. XXVII:4. 454–474.

———. *C. S. Lewis: Poet*. Kent, Ohio: Kent State UP, 2001.

Lewis, C. S. *Pilgrim's Regress*. Grand Rapids: Eerdmans, 1979.

———. *Poems*. New York: Harcourt, 1964.

———. Preface. *Dymer. Narrative Poems*. New York: Harcourt, 1979. 3–6.

Mallarmé, Stephané. *The Afternoon of a Faun*. Trans. Roger Fry. 26 July 2003. http://www.angel fire.com/art/doit/mallarme.html

McGreevy, Linda F. *Bitter Witness: Otto Dix and the Great War*. New York: Peter Lang, 2001.

———. *The Life and Works of Otto Dix: German Critical Realist*. Ann Arbor: UMI, 1981.

O'Brien-Twohig, Sarah. *The Great War*. Video tape. PBS, episode II.

Remarque, Erich Maria. *All Quiet on the Western Front*. Boston: Little, Brown, 1929.

———. *The Road Back*. New York: Fawcett, 1958.

Sassoon, Siegfried. *Memoirs of an Infantry Officer*. London: Faber, 1965.

Sorley, Charles Hamilton. "When you see millions of the mouthless dead." *Penguin Book of First World War Poetry*. Ed. John Silkin. London: Penguin, 1996.

Winter, J. M. *The Experience of World War I*. New York: Oxford UP, 1995.

Afterword

THE LAST IMAGE WE HAVE OF DYMER is his dead body upon the field of battle: he has fought the monster he conceived in a dark night of confusion and has been killed in the process. It may be taken as an image of the maturing Lewis at the end of a quest to trace and put to death his romantic young self, which he must have believed had begotten a more monstrous trauma than he otherwise might have faced in war. Lewis invested much in the formulation of his early assumptions—stretching from the time of his mother's death. Nevertheless, we must recognize how important those assumptions were to his mental survival in war. And yet, in slaying those assumptions, it may have seemed to Lewis that the monster had won, that the romantic part of him died in the ensuing battle.

Lewis converted to Christianity in later life and would, in his last years, contend with the assumptions he had formed around his Christian faith. When his wife, Joy Gresham, died (the film *Shadowlands* is a narrative based on their marriage), Lewis kept a journal of the trauma that inevitably accompanies such loss. Once again his assumptions about life and now about a benevolent God, were shattered. He said that if the assumptions of his faith were a house of cards, set as a citadel against loss and grief, then it deserved to be knocked down "as often as proves necessary. Unless I have to be finally given up as hopeless, and left building pasteboard palaces in Hell forever; 'free among the dead'" (*Grief*

53). Clearly he came to think that our assumptions about life were not to become our living idols, that if we beget such monsters they deserve to be slain. It is not an irony that as late in his life as his wife's death—a few years before his own—Lewis looks briefly again to the war:

> Grief is like a bomber circling round and dropping its bombs each time the circle brings it overhead; physical pain is like the steady barrage on a trench in World War One, hours of it with no let-up for a moment. (*Grief* 34)

The ideal England of Mr. Britling was forever changed from its pre-war vestige—and even that vestige as many have argued was itself idealized if not also *idolized*. After the war, Warren Lewis, it will be recalled, wrote to his father that "the whole state of the world now is enough to make any sane man dispair [sic]. Everything which is worth living for is disappearing or has disappeared" (*LP* VI.93); he wished the world before the war had survived beyond him. His words evoke assumptions about the pre-war world that must have echoed over the West even as Warren wrote them. Jack Lewis ended his journal, *A Grief Observed*, with a rebuilding of assumptions about his relation to God and the world. It was a similar exercise to what Lewis undertook in *Dymer*: the main character undertakes to right the wrongs he had precipitated from a romantic set of assumptions. In both works, those assumptions are shattered. Both works record trauma and recovery.

I wrote this book for two reasons. First, but not foremost, I felt that the image of Lewis sustained by his adulators was like Lewis's house of cards: not solid—he is too often perceived as a plaster saint, or no, a paper prince, fun to make dance, but not rounded, not believable, not human. I have worked to provide a greater human context for Lewis as well as to fill gaps within his biography and to correct errors that exist concerning his war service. As Lewis himself affirmed, "all reality is iconoclastic" (*Grief* 52), and "looked at steadily, is unbearable" (*Grief* 25)—at least such are the realities of this world's traumatic events. And as T. S. Eliot, like Lewis a convert to Christianity, wrote in *Burnt Norton*, "Human kind cannot bear very much reality."

Some of what Lewis faced in France was, indeed, unbearable; if he could not emerge unscathed from war and its dire effects, no apology need be made. Who could do so?

Rather, the things Lewis met in France and the fragments—metal or metaphorical—that he carried within him from that place gave him a knowledge of grief, of loss, of the atrocities that humankind is capable of producing, of relationships awry and relationships lost, of the wanderings of youth— knowledge that after his conversion continued to inform his views of life, the cosmos, and his faith beyond a point where many people can follow. Dark knowledge it may be; nevertheless, what Lewis experienced in this time became a foundation to much of his writing and thinking in later years.

Second, but foremost in importance, I wrote because of a photo of young men in the Oxford Officer Training Corps in 1917. Lewis sits behind Paddy Moore, looking over his friend's shoulder. Beneath my print of it is written Hamlet's last words, spoken to his friend Horatio:

> If thou didst ever hold me in thy heart,
> Absent thee from felicity a while
> And in this harsh world draw thy breath in pain
> To tell my story. (V.2.288–291)

Lewis never told Paddy's tale nor his own. Perhaps no more fitting an end exists for the story of such men as appear in the photo than the quotation inscribed on Laurence Johnson's grave stone: "The rest is silence."

Figure 19. Oxford Officer Training Corps men in the Wytham Hills, September 1917. Lewis is third from the right, looking over Paddy Moore's shoulder. None of the other men have been identified. (The Marion E. Wade Center)

WORK CITED

Lewis, C. S. *A Grief Observed*. London: Faber, 1983.

Index